John Owen

The True Nature of a Gospel Church and it's Government

John Owen

The True Nature of a Gospel Church and it's Government

ISBN/EAN: 9783742814258

Manufactured in Europe, USA, Canada, Australia, Japa

Cover: Foto ©Lupo / pixelio.de

Manufactured and distributed by brebook publishing software (www.brebook.com)

John Owen

The True Nature of a Gospel Church and it's Government

THE TRUE NATURE OF A Gospel Church AND ITS GOVERNMENT:

WHEREIN

These following particulars are distinctly handled:

I. The *subject Matter of the Church.*
II. The *formal Cause of a particular Church.*
III. *Of the Polity, Rule or Discipline of the Church in general.*
IV. The *Officers of the Church.*
V. The *Duty of Pastors of Churches.*
VI. The *Office of Teachers in the Church.*
VII. *Of the Rule of the Church, or of Ruling Elders.*
VIII. The *nature of Church Polity or Rule, with the Duty of Elders.*
IX. *Of Deacons.*
X. *Of Excommunication.*
XI. *Of the Communion of Churches.*

The Publishing whereof was mentioned by the Author in his *Answer to the Unreasonableness of Separation.*

By the late Pious and Learned Minister of the Gospel, *JOHN OWEN,* D. D.

LICENSED, *June* 10. 1688.

LONDON, Printed for William Marshall, at the *Bible* in *Newgate-street,* MDCLXXXIX.

THE PREFACE TO THE READER.

THE *Church of Chrift, according as it is reprefented unto us, or defcribed by the holy Spirit of God, in the* Old *and* New Teftament, *hath but a twofold Confideration, as* Catholick *and* Myftical; *or as* Vifible *and* Organized *in particular Congregations*. The Catholick Church *is the whole Myftical Body of Chrift, confifting of all the Elect which are purchafed and redeemed by his Blood, whether already called or uncalled,* Militant *or* Triumphant; *and this is the Church that God gave him to be head unto, which is his Body and his Fullneſs, and by union with him* Chrift Myftical, Ephef. 1. 22, 23. *and this is that* πανήγυρις *(the only word moft fully expreffing the* Catholick Church, *ufed in Scripture) the Church of the Firft-born, whofe Names are written in Heaven,* Heb. 12. 23. *i. e. in the Lamb's Book of Life, and fhall all appear one Day gathered together to their Head, in the perfection and fullneſs of the* New Jerufalem-ftate;

where

The PREFACE

where they will make a glorious Church, not having Spot or Wrincle or any such thing; but Holy and without Blemish. The day of Grace which the Saints have passed in the respective Ages of the Church was but the days of its Espousals, wherein the Bride hath made her self ready; but then will be her full married state unto Christ, then will be the perfection not only of every particular Member of Christ, but of the whole Body of Christ, called a perfect Man, and the measure of the Stature of the Fullness of Christ, to which we are called Edifying and building up, by the Ministry and Ordinances of Christ, whilst we are in Via, in our passage unto this Country, a City with a more durable fixed Foundation which we seek.

In order therefore unto the compleating this great and mystical Body, Christ hath his particular Visible Churches and Assemblies in this World, wherein he hath ordained Ordinances, and appointed Officers for the glorious forementioned Ends and Purposes.

There is no other sort of Visible Church of Christ Organized, the subject of the aforesaid Institutions spoken of, but a particular Church or Congregation (either in the Old or New Testament) where all the Members thereof do ordinarily meet together in one place to hold Communion one with another, in some one or more great Ordinances of Christ. The first Churches were Oeconomick when the Worship of God was solemnly performed in the large Families of the Antidiluvian and Postdiluvian Patriarchs, where, no doubt, all frequently assembled to the Sacrifices as then offered, and other parts of Worship then in use.

After the descent of a numerous Progeny from Abraham's Loins,

to the READER.

Loins, God takes them to himself in one Visible Body, a National but Congregational Church, *to which he forms them Four hundred and thirty Years after the Promise in the Wilderness; and although all* Abraham's *Natural Posterity, according to the External part of the Promise made to him, were taken into visible Church-Fellowship, so that it became a National Church; yet it was such a National Church always, in the* Wilderness, *and in the* Holy Land, *as was* Congregational; *for it was but one Congregation during the Tabernacle, or Temple-state, first or second; they were always bound to assemble to the Tabernacle, or Temple, thrice at least every Year; hence the Tabernacle was still called the* Tabernacle of the Congregation. *They were to have but one Altar for Burnt-Offerings and Sacrifices; what others were at any time elsewhere called High-Places, were condemned by God as Sin.*

Lastly, when Christ had Divorced this People, Abolished their Mosaical Constitution, by breaking their Staff of Beauty *and their Staff of* Bonds, *he erects his Gospel Church, calls in Disciples by his Ministry, forms them into a Body, furnisheth them with Officers and Ordinances; and after he had suffered, rose again, and continued here Forty days; in which time he frequently appeared to them, and acquainted them with his Will, ascends unto his Father, sends his Spirit in a plentiful manner at* Pentecost, *whereby most of them were furnished with all necessary miraculous Gifts, to the promoting the Glory and Interest of Christ among* Jews *and* Gentiles.

Hence the whole Evangelical Ministry was first placed in the Church of Jerusalem *(so far as extraordinary, or such a part*

The PREFACE

part of it as was to descend to Churches of after Ages) neither were they placed as abiding or standing Officers in any other Church as we find. In this Church they acted as the Elders thereof, and from this Church they were, it's very likely, solemnly sent by Fasting and Prayer to the Exercise of their Apostolick Function, in Preaching, Healing and working Miracles, gathering Churches, and setling Officers in them; even so as Barnabas and Paul were sent forth by the Church of Antioch.

Their distinguishing Apostolick Office and Charge (from which the Evangelist differed but little) was to take care of all the Churches, not to sit down as standing Pastors to all, or any particular Congregation, but at the first planting, to gather, to direct, and confirm them, in practice of their Doctrine, Fellowship, breaking Bread, and in Prayer. Wherefore, this Apostolick Care committed to them proves nothing either of the Catholick Authority, claimed by an Oecumenick Pastor; or that charge of many Congregations, claimed by Diocesan Bishops.

Whence it's most evident, That all Church Officers, so far as they had any Pastoral or Episcopal Office, was given to a particular Congregation, as the πρῶτον δεκτικόν. We read of no Pastors of many Congregations, nor of no Church made up of many Congregations, to which Officers were annexed, nor of any representative Church, as some would have.

That Apostolick Power did descend to Successors we utterly deny, it being not derivable; for none after them could say, They had been Eye Witnesses of our Lord, before or after his Resurrection; none since so qualified by an extraordinary

to the READER.

dinary measure of the Spirit for Preaching and working Miracles; and none but the Pope challenges such an extensive Care for, and Power over all Churches. That which descends from them to the ordinary Ministry, is a Commission to Preach and Baptize; and why not to Head, it being always in the Commission that Christ gave, a Pastoral Relation, or Presbytership which was included in their Apostleship, and Exercised toward the Church of Jerusalem. *Such Presbyter-ship* John *and* Peter *both had. Hence there remains no other Successors*jure *to the Apostles, but ordinary Pastors and Teachers.*

These are relative Officers, and are always in, and to some particular Congregations; we know of no Catholick visible Church that any Pastors are ordained to. 1. *The Scripture speaks of no Church as Catholick visible.* 2. *The thing it self is but a Chimæra of some Men's Brains; it's not* in rerum naturâ; *for if a Catholick visible Church be all the Churches that I see at a time, I am not capable of seeing much more than what can Assemble in one place. And if it be meant of all the Churches actually in being, how are they visible to me? where can they be seen in one place? I may as well call all the Cities and Corporations in the World the Catholick visible City or Corporation; which all rational Men would call Nonsence. Besides, if all Organized Churches could be got together, it's not Catholick in respect of Saints Militant, much less of Triumphant; for many are no Church Members that are Christs Members, and many visible Members are no true Members of Christ Jesus. Where is any such Church capable of Communion in all Ordinances in one place? and*

the

The PREFACE

the Scripture speaks of no other Organized visible Church.

Again, to a Catholick visible Church constituted, should be a Catholick visible Pastor or Pastors; for as the Church is, such is the Pastor and Officers; to the Mystical Church Christ is the mystical Head and Pastor; he is called the chief Pastor and Shepherd of our Souls, 1 Pet. 2. 25. hence the uncalled are his Sheep, as John 10. 16. but to all visible Churches Christ hath appointed a visible Pastor or Pastors; and where is the Pastor of the Catholick visible Church? he is not to be found, unless it suffice us to take him from Rome. To say that all individual Pastors are Pastors to the Catholick Church, is either to say that they are invested with as much Pastoral Power and Charge in one Church as in another, and then they are indefinite Pastors; and therefore all Pastors have mutual Power in each others Churches; and so John may come into Thomas his Church and exercise all parts of Jurisdiction there, and Thomas into John's; or a Minister to the Catholick Church hath an universal Catholick Power over the Catholick Church; if so, the Power and Charge which every ordinary Pastor hath, is Apostolick. Or, lastly, he is invested with an Arbitrary Power, at least, as to the taking up a particular Charge where he pleaseth, with a non obstante to the Suffrages of the People; for if he hath an Office whereby he is equally related to all Churches, it's at his liberty, by virtue of this Office, to take where he pleaseth.

But every Church-Officer, under Christ, is a visible relate, and the correlate must be such, whence the Church must be visible to which he is an Officer. It's absurd to say a Man is

a vi-

to the READER.

a visible Husband to an invisible Wife, the relate and correlate must be ejusdem naturæ. It's true, Christ is related to the Church as mystical Head, but it's in respect of the Church in its mystical Nature, for Christ hath substituted no mystical Officers in his Church.

There is a great deal of difference between the mystical and external visible Church, though the latter is founded upon it, and for the sake of it. It's founded upon it as taking its true spiritual Original from it, deriving vital Spirits from it by a mystical Union to, and Communion with Christ and his Members; and it's for the Sake of it, all external visible Assemblies, Ministers, Ordinances are for the sake of the mystical Body of Christ, for calling in the Elect, and the Edifying of them to that full measure of Stature they are designed unto.

But the different consideration lies in these Things,

1. That the mystical Church doth never fail, neither is diminished by any Shocks of Temptation or Suffering, that in their visible Profession any of them undergo, whereas visible Churches are often broken, scattered, yea unchurched, and many Members fail of the Grace of God by final Apostasy. Likewise Christ's mystical Church is many times preserved in that State only, or mostly, when Christ hath not a visible organized Church according to Institution to be found on the Face of the Earth, so it was with his Church often under the Old Testament-*Dispensation,* as in Ægypt, *in the* Days of the Judges *when the* Ark *was carried away by the* Philistins, *in the* Days *of* Manasseh, *and other wicked Kings, and especially in* Babylon. *In such times the Faithful Ones were preserved with-*

The PREFACE

out the true *Sacrifices*, the teaching *Priest*, and the *Law*. So hath it been in the days of the New Testament, *in divers places; under the* Draconick *Heathen Persecutions, and afterward in the Wilderneß-state of the Church, under the Anti-Christian Usurpations, and false Worship. Which mystical State is the place prepared of God to hide the Seed of the Woman in, from the Dragons Rage, for the space of One thousand two hundred and sixty Days.*

Again, Unto this Mystical Church is only essentially necessary, a mystical Union unto the Lord Jesus Christ, by the Gift of the Father, Acceptation, and Covenant-undertaking of the Son, the powerful and efficacious Work of the Spirit of the Father, and the Son, working true saving Faith in the Lord Jesus Christ, and sincere Love to him and all his True Members. Whereby as they have a firm and unshaken Union, so they have a spiritual Communion, though without those desirable Enjoyments of external Church Privileges, and means of Grace, which they are providentially often hindred from. Visible Churches being but Christ's Tents and Tabernacles, which he sometimes setteth up, and sometimes takes down and removes at his Pleasure, as he sees best for his Glory in the World.

But of these he hath a special regard as to their Foundation, Matter, Constitution and Order, he gives forth an exact pattern from Mount Zion, *as of that Typical Tabernacle from* Mount Sinai *of Old.*

The Foundation part of a visible Church is the credible Profession of Faith and Holineß, wherein the Lord Jesus Christ is the Corner Stone, Eph.ij.20. Matth.xvi.18. *This Profession is the Foundation, but not the Church it self. It's*

not

to the READER.

not Articles of Faith, or Profession of them in particular individual Persons that make an organized visible Church. We are the Houshold of Faith built upon the Foundation, &c. 2. *It's Men and Women, not Doctrine, that are the Matter of a Church; and these professing the Faith, and practising Holiness.* The Members of Churches are always called in the New Testament, *Saints, Faithful, Believers:* They was such that were added to the Churches; neither is every Believer so as such, but as a professing Believer, for a Man must appear to be fit Matter of a visible Church before he can challenge Church Privileges, or they can be allowed him. 3. *It's not many professing Believers that make a particular Church.* For though they are fit Matter for a Church, yet they have not the Form of a Church, without a mutual Agreement and Combination (explicite, or, at least, implicite) whereby they become, by vertue of Christs Charter, a spiritual Corporation, and are called a *City, Houshold, House,* being united together by *Joints and Bands,* not only by internal Bonds of the Spirit, but external; the Bonds of Union must be visible as the House is, by profession.

This is a Society that Christ hath given Power to, to choose a *Pastor,* and other Officers of Christ's Institution, and enjoy all Ordinances: The *Word, Sacrament,* and *Prayer,* as Christ hath appointed.

Hence a visible Church must needs be a separate Congregation; Separation is a proper and inseparable adjunct thereof; the Apostle speaks of Church Membership, 2 Cor. vi. 14. *Be not unequally yoked together* [ἑτεροζυγοῦντες, *yoked with those of another kind, the Plowing with an Ox and Ass together, being forbidden under the Law*] *with Unbelievers,*

a 2

The PREFACE

believers, ἀπίστοις, *i. e. Visible Unbelievers of any sort or kind; for what participation,* μετοχὴ, *hath Righteousness with Unrighteousness? what* κοινωνία, *Communion or Fellowship hath Light with Darkness?* Verf. 13. τίς δὲ συμφώνησις, *what harmony hath* Chrift *with* Belial, *Men of corrupt Lives and Converfation, or what part,* μερὶς πιστῷ μετὰ ἀπίστου, *hath a Believer, i. e. a vifible Believer with an Unbeliever?* it ought not to be rendred *Infidel*; but it was done by our Tranflaters, to put a blind upon this place, *as to its true intention, and to countenance Parifh Communion;* for why did they not here, Verf. 14. and every where elfe render, ἄπιστος, an Infidel? Verf. 16. τίς δὲ συγκατάθεσις ναῷ Θεοῦ μετὰ εἰδώλων, *what confiftency hath the Temple of God* (i. e. *the Gofpel Church*) *with Idols?* &c. I take this place to be a full Proof of what is before fpoken, *That a Gofpel Church is a Company of Faithful profeffing People, walking together by mutual Confent, or Confederation to the Lord Jefus Chrift and one to another, in Subjection to and Practice of all his Gofpel-Precepts and Commands, whereby they are feparate from all Perfons and Things manifeftly contrary or difagreeing thereunto.*

Hence as it's feparate from all fuch impurities that are without, fo Chrift hath furnifhed it with fufficient Power and means to keep it felf Pure; and therefore hath provided Ordinances and Minifters for that end and purpofe; for the great end of Church-Edification cannot be obtained without Purity be alfo maintained in Doctrine and Fellowfhip.

Purity cannot be maintained without Order; a diforderly Society will corrupt within it felf; for by Diforder

it's

to the READER.

it's divided, by divisions the joints and bands are broken, not only of Love and Affection, but of visible Conjunction; so that roots of bitterness, and sensual Separation arising, many are defiled.

It's true, there may be a kind of Peace and Agreement in a Society that is a stranger to Gospel-Order, when Men agree together, to walk according to a false Rule, or in a supine and negligent Observation of the True Rule. There may be a common Connivance at each one to walk as he list, but this is not Order but Disorder by Consent: Besides a Church may, for the most part, walk in Order, when there is Breaches and Divisions. Some do agree to walk according to the Rule, when others will deviate from it. It's orderly to endeavour to reduce those that walk not orderly; though such just Undertakings seem sometimes grounds of Disturbance, and causes of Convulsion in the whole Body, threatning even its breaking in pieces; but yet this must be done to preserve the whole.

The Word Translated Order, Colos. ij. 5. τάξις, is a Military Word; it's the Order of Souldiers in a Band, keeping Rank and File, where every one keeps his place, follows his Leader, observes the Word of Command, and his Right-hand Man. Hence the Apostle joys to see their close Order, and Stedfastness in the Faith, their Firmness, Valour, and Resolution in fighting the good Fight of Faith, and the Order in so doing; not only in watching as single Professors, but in Marching Orderly together as an Army with Banners. There is nothing more comly than a Church walking in Order when every one keeps his place, knows and practiseth his Duty according to the Rule,

each

The PREFACE

each submitting to the other in the performance of Duty. When the Elders know their places, and the People theirs. Christ hath been more Faithful than Moses *, and therefore hath not left his Churches without sufficient Rules to walk by.*

That Order may be in a Church of Christ, the Rules of the Gospel must be known, and that by Officers and People. They that are altogether Ignorant of the Rule, or negligent in attending it, or doubtful, and therefore always contending about it, will never walk according to it. Hence it's the great Duty of Ministers to study Order well, and acquaint the People with it. It's greatly to be bewailed, that so few Divines bend their Studies that way. They content themselves only with Studying and Preaching the Truths that concern Faith in the Lord Jesus, and the meer Moral part of Holiness; but as to Gospel-Churches or Instituted Worship, they generally in their Doctrine and Practice let it alone, and administer Sacraments as indefinitely as they Preach; care not to stand related to one People more than another, any further than Maintained by them. Likewise many good People are as great Strangers to Gospel Churches and Order, and (as their Ministers) have a great Averseness to both, and look upon it as Schism and Faction; and this is the great reason of the readiness of both to comply with Rules of Men for making Churches, (Canons established by humane Laws,(being carried away (if they would speak the Truth) by corrupt Erastian *Principles, That Christ hath left the Church to be altogether Guided and Governed by Laws of Magistratick Sanction. Reformation from the gross Idolatrous part of Antichristianism was engaged in with some Heroick Courage*

to the READER.

rage and Resolution, but the coldness and indifference of Protestants to any further progress, almost ever since is not a little to be lamented. Many think it enough that the Foundation of the House is laid in Purity of Doctrine, (and it's well if that were not rather written in the Books than preached in Pulpits at this Day) but how little do they care to set their Hands to Building the House. Sure a great matter is from that Spiritual Sloathfulness that many are fallen under, as likewise being ready to sink under the great Discouragements laid before them by the Adversaries of Judah, *when they find the Children of the Spiritual Captivity are about to Build a Gospel Church unto the Lord. And how long hath this great Work ceased? And will the Lord's Ministers and People yet say, The Time is not come, the Time that the Lord's House should be Built? Is it time to Build our own Houses, and not the House of the Lord? Surely it's time to Build, for we understand by Books the number of Years whereof the Word of the Lord came to* Daniel *the Prophet, and to* John *the beloved Disciple, and* New Testament Prophet; *that he would accomplish* 1260. *Years in the Desolation of our* Jerusalem, *and the Court which is without the Temple, viz. The generality of Visible Professors, and the external part of Worship, which hath been so long trod down by* Gentilism. *Wherefore consider your Ways, Go up to the Mountain, and bring Wood, build the House, saith the Lord, and I will take pleasure in it, (* Hag. i. 8. *) and I will be glorified. Men, it may be, have thought they have got, or, at least, saved by not troubling themselves with the Care, Charge, and Trouble of gathering Churches, and walking*

The PREFACE

in Gospel Order; but God saith, Ye looked for much and lo it came to little, and when ye brought it Home I did blow upon it. Why, saith the Lord, because of my House that is waste, and ye run every Man to his own House. I doubt not but the time is nigh at Hand that the Gospel-Temple must be built with greater Splendor and Glory than ever Soloman's or Zerubbabel's was; and though it seems to be a great Mountain of Difficulties, yet it shall become a Plain before him that is exalted far above all Principalities and Powers, and as he hath laid the Foundation thereof in the Oppressed state of his People, so his Hands shall finish it, and bring forth the Head-stone thereof with shouting in the New Jerusalem-State, crying, now Grace, Grace, but then Glory, Glory to it.

This hastening Glory we should endeavour to meet, and fetch in by earnest Prayers and faithful Endeavours, to promote the great Work of our Day. The Pattern is of late Years given forth with much clearness, by Models, such as God hath set up in this latter Age in the Wilderness, and sheltered by Cloud and Smoke by Day, and the shining of a flaming Fire by Night; for upon all its Glory hath been a Defence, yea, and it hath been a Tabernacle for a Shadow in the Day time from the Heat, and for a place of Refuge and Covert from the Storm and from the Rain. Neither have we been left to Act by the Examples or Traditions of Men, we have had a full Manifestation of the revealed Mind and Will of Christ, with the greatest Evidence and Conviction; God having in these latter Times raised up many most Eminent Instruments for Direction and Encouragement unto his People, which he furnished accordingly with

great

to the READER.

great Qualifications to this End and Purpose, That the true Original, Nature, Institution and Order of Evangelical Churches might be known, distinguished, prized and adhered to, by all that know the Name of Christ, and would be followers of him as his Disciples, in Obedience to all his revealed Mind and Will. Amongst which faithful and renowned Servants of Christ, the late Author of this most useful and practical Treatise, hath approved himself to be one of the chief. I need say nothing of his stedfast Piety, universal Learning, indefatigable Labours in incessant Vindication of the Doctrines of the Gospel (of greatest weight) against all Opposition made thereto, by Men of corrupt Minds. His surviving Works will always be bespeaking his honourable Remembrance, amongst all impartial Lovers of the Truth. They that were acquainted with him, knew how much the state and standing of the Churches of Christ, under the late Sufferings and Strugglings for Reformation, was laid to heart by him. And therefore how he put forth his utmost strength to Assist, Aid, Comfort and Support the sinking Spirits of the poor Saints and People of God, even wearied out with long and repeated Persecutions. It is to be observed, That this ensuing Treatise was occasioned by one of the last and most vigorous Assaults made upon Separate and Congregational-Churches, by a Pen dipt in the Gall of that persecuting Spirit, under which God's People groaned throughout this Land. He then wrote an elaborate account of Evangelical Churches, their Original, Institution, &c. with a Vindication of them from the Charges laid in against them, by the Author of The Unreasonableness of Separation. This he lived to Print, and promised

The PREFACE

promised to handle the Subject more particularly, which is here performed. He lived to finish it under his great bodily Infirmities; whereby he saw himself hastening to the end of his Race; yet so great was his Love to Christ, that whilst he had Life and Breath he drew not back his Hand from his Service. This Work he finished (with others) through the gracious support and assistance of Divine Power, and Corrected the Copy before his departure. So that, Reader, thou maist be assured, That what thou hast here, was his, (Errata's of the Press only excepted) and likewise that it ought to be esteemed as his Legacy to the Church of Christ, being a great part of his dying Labours; and therefore it's most uncharitable to suppose, That the things here wrote, were penned with any other Design, than to advance the Glory and Interest of Christ in the World; and that they were not matters of great weight on his own Spirit. And upon the perusal that I have had of these Papers, I cannot but recommend them to all diligent Enquirers after the true Nature, Way, Order and Practice of Evangelical Churches, as a true and faithful Account, according to what Understanding the Professors thereof, for the most part have had and practised. Who ever is otherwise Minded, he hath the liberty of his own Light and Conscience. Lastly, whereas many serious Professors of the Faith of the Lord Jesus (it may be) well grounded in the main saving Truths of the Gospel, are yet much to seek of these necessary Truths, for want of good Information therein, and therefore walk not up to all the revealed Mind of Christ, as they sincerely desire. Let such, with unprejudiced

to the READER.

judiced Minds, Read, and Consider what is here offered to them, and receive nothing upon humane Authority; follow no Man in Judgment or Practice any further than he is a follower of Christ. And this is all the Request of him that is a lover of all them that Love the Lord Jesus Christ.

J. C.

THere is lately Published, by the same Author, *A Treatise of the Dominion of Sin and Grace.* Wherein Sin's Reign is discovered, in whom it is, and in whom it is not: how the Law supports it, and how Grace delivers from it, by setting up its Dominion in the Heart. *Price bound* 1 s.

The Author also ushered into the World, by his Preface, another very useful Book, Entituled, *The best Treasure: or, the way to be truly Rich.* Being a Discourse on *Ephes.* iij. 8. wherein is opened and commended to Saints and Sinners, the personal and purchased Riches of Christ, as the best Treasure to be preserved and ensured by all that would be Happy here and hereafter. By *Bartholomew Ashwood*, late Minister of the Gospel. *Price bound* 2s. 6d.

Another Book of the same Authors, Entituled, *The heavenly Trade; or the best Merchandize,* the only way to live well in impoverishing Times. A Discourse occasioned from the decay of Earthly Trades, and visible waste of practical Piety, in the Day we live in. Offering Arguments and Counsels to all, towards a speedy revival of dying Godliness; and timely prevention of the dangerous issues thereof hanging over us. Very necessary for all Families. *Price* 2s. 6d.

Some

Some other Books Printed for and Sold by William Marshal.

Caryl's Expofition on the whole Book of *Job*. In Two Volumes in Folio.
Pool's Synopfis Criticorum. In V. Volumes. *Latin*.
——'s *Synopfis* on the *New Teftament*. In Two large Volumes, in Latin, with the *Index*, are to be fold very cheap. In Quires both Volumes for 20s, and both Vol. well bound for 30s.
Pool's Annotations in *Englifh*. Two Volumes.
Index's to the *Old* and *New Teftament* to be fold alone. Price 5s.
Dr. *Owen* on the *Hebrews*. In Four Volumes.
Owen on the Spirit.
Clark's Martyrology.

Mellificium Chirurgiæ, or the Marrow of Chirurgery. An Anatomical Treatife. Inftitutions of Phyfick, with *Hippocrates*'s Aphorifms largely Commented upon. The *Marrow of Phyfick*, fhewing the Caufes, Signs and Cures of moft Difeafes incident to humane Bodies. Choice experienced *Receipts* for the Cure of feveral Diftempers. The Fourth Edition, enlarged with many Additions, and purged from many Faults that efcaped in the former Impreffions. Illuftrated with Twelve Copper Cuts. By *James Cooke* of *Warwick*, Practitioner in Phyfick and Chirurgery.

There is alfo a very ufeful Book of the fame Authors, for thofe That are defirous of being their own Phyficians, Entituled, *Select Obfervations of Englifh Bodies*, *of Eminent Perfons*, *in defperate Difeafes*. To which is now added an Hundred rich Counfels and Advices for feveral honourable Perfons. With all the feveral Medicines and Methods by which the feveral Cures were effected. With Directions about Drinking the *Bath* Water. Price bound 2s. 6d.

Clarkfon's Primitive Epifcopacy. *Octavo*. Price bound, 1s. 6d.
Owen of Juftification.
——'s Brief and Impartial Account of the Nature of the Proteftant Religion.

THE

THE TRUE NATURE
OF A
Gospel Church
AND ITS
GOVERNMENT.

CHAP. I.

The Subject Matter of the Church.

THE Church may be considered either as unto its *Essence*, Constitution and Being; or as unto its *Power* and *Order*, when it is *Organized*. As unto its *Essence* and Being, its constituent parts are its *Matter* and *Form*. These we must enquire into.

By the *Matter* of the Church, we understand the persons whereof the Church doth consist, with their Qualifications: And by its *Form*, the reason, cause and way of that kind of Relation among them, which gives them the Being of a Church, and therewithal an Interest in all that belongs unto a Church, either privilege, or power, as such.

The Subject Matter of the Church.

Our first Enquiry being concerning *what sort of Persons* our Lord Jesus Christ requireth and admitteth to be the *visible Subjects* of his Kingdom, we are to be regulated in our Determination by respect unto his Honour, Glory, and the Holiness of his Rule. To reckon such persons to be Subjects of Christ, Members of his Body, such as he requires and owns, (for others are not so) who would not be tolerated, at least not approved, in a well Governed *Kingdom* or *Commonwealth* of the World, is highly dishonourable unto him. But it is so come to pass; that let Men be never so notoriously and flagitiously wicked; until they become pests of the earth, yet are they esteemed to belong to the Church of Christ. And not only so, but it is thought little less than *Schism* to forbid them the Communion of the Church in all its sacred Privileges. Howbeit, the Scripture doth in general represent the Kingdom or Church of Christ, to consist of persons *called Saints*, separated from the World, with many other things of an alike nature, as we shall see immediately. And if the *Honour of Christ* were of such weight with us as it ought to be; if we understood aright the nature and ends of his Kingdom, and that the peculiar Glory of it, above all the Kingdoms in the World, consists in the *Holiness of its Subjects*, such an Holiness as the World in its wisdom knoweth not, we would duly consider whom we avow to belong thereunto. Those who know ought of these things, will not profess that persons openly profane, vicious, sensual, wicked and ignorant, are approved and owned of Christ as the Subjects of his Kingdom, or that it is his will that we should receive them into the Communion of the Church. But an old *opinion* of the unlawfulness of separation from a Church, on the account of the *mixture of wicked men* in it, is made a scare-crow to frighten men from attempting the Reformation of the greatest Evils, and a covert for the composing Churches of such Members only.

*Psal.*15.1, 2,3, 4, 5.
Psal. 24. 3, 4.
Psal. 93.5.
2 *Cor.* 8. 23.
Ephes. 5. 27.

2 *Tim.*3.1, 2, 3, 4, 5.

Some things therefore are to be premised unto what shall be offered unto the right stating of this Enquiry: As,

1. That if there be no more required of any as unto *Personal Qualifications* in a visible uncontroulable profession, to constitute them

them Subjects of Chrifts Kingdom, and Members of his Church, but what is required by the moſt righteous and ſevere Laws *of Men* to conſtitute a *good Subject* or *Citizen*, the diſtinction between his viſible Kingdom and the Kingdoms of the World, as unto the principal cauſes of it, is utterly loſt. Now all negative Qualifications, as that Men are not Oppreſſors, Drunkards, Revilers, Swearers, Adulterers, &c. are required hereunto. But yet it is ſo fallen out, that generally more is required to conſtitute ſuch a *Citizen* as ſhall repreſent the righteous Laws he liveth under, than to conſtitute a Member of the Church of Chriſt. *Ezek.* 22. 26.

2. That whereas *Regeneration* is expreſly required in the Goſpel, to give a Right and Privilege unto an entrance into the Church or Kingdom of Chriſt, whereby that Kingdom of his is diſtinguiſhed from all other Kingdoms in and of the World, unto an Intereſt wherein never any ſuch thing was required; it muſt of neceſſity be ſomething *better*, more *excellent* and *ſublime* than any thing the Laws and Polities of Men pretend unto or preſcribe. Wherefore it cannot conſiſt in any outward *Rites*, eaſie to be obſerved by the worſt and vileſt of Men; beſides the Scripture gives us a deſcription of it, in oppoſition unto its conſiſting in any ſuch *Rite*, 1 *Pet.* 3. 21. And many things required unto good Citizens, are far better than the meer obſervation of ſuch a *Rite*. *Joh.* 3. 3. *Tit.* 3. 3, 4, 5.

Of this Regeneration *Baptiſm* is the *Symbol*, the Sign, Expreſſion and Repreſentation. Wherefore unto thoſe who are in a due manner partakers of it, it giveth all the external Rights and Privileges which belong unto them that are *Regenerate*, until they come unto ſuch Seaſons, wherein the *perſonal* performance of thoſe Duties whereon the continuation of the eſtate of viſible Regeneration doth depend, is required of them. Herein if they fail, they loſe all privilege and benefit by their Baptiſm. *Joh.* 3. 5. *Act.* 2. 38. 1 *Pet.* 3. 21.

So ſpeaks the Apoſtle in the caſe of Circumciſion under the Law, *Rom.* 2. 25. *For Circumciſion verily profiteth, if thou keep the Law; but if thou be a breaker of the Law, thy Circumciſion is made uncircumciſion.* It is ſo in the caſe of *Baptiſm*: Verily it profiteth,

4 *The Subject Matter of the Church.*

profiteth, if a Man stand unto the Terms of the Covenant which is tendered therein between God and his Soul; for it will give him Right unto all the outward Privileges of a *Regenerate State*; but if he do not, as in the sight of God his *Baptism* is no *Baptism*, as unto the real communication of Grace and acceptance with him; so in the sight of the Church, it is *no Baptism*, as unto a participation of the external Rights and Privileges of a *Regenerate State*.

Phil. 3. 18, 19. *Tit.* 1. 15, 16.

4. God alone is judge concerning this *Regeneration*, as unto its *internal, real principle and state in the Souls of Men*, whereon the participation of all the spiritual advantages of the Covenant of Grace doth depend: The Church is judge of its *evidences* and *fruits* in their external Demonstration, as unto a participation of the *outward Privileges* of a *Regenerate State*, and no farther. And we shall hereon briefly declare what belongs unto the forming of a right judgment herein, and who are to be esteemed fit Members of any Gospel Church State, or have a Right so to be.

Act. 15. 8. *Revel.* 2. 23.

Act. 8. 13.

1. Such as from whom we are obliged to *withdraw* or *withhold Communion*, can be no part of the matter *constituent* of a Church, or are not meet Members for the first constitution of it. But such are all *Habitual Sinners*; those who having prevalent habits and inclinations unto Sins of any kind unmortified, do walk according unto them. Such are profane Swearers, Drunkards, Fornicators, Covetous, Oppressors, and the like, *who shall not inherit the Kingdom of God*. 1 *Cor*. 6. 9, 10, 11. *Phil*. 3. 18, 19. 2 *Thess*. 3. 6. 2 *Tim*. 3. 5. as a Man living and dying in *any known Sin*, that is *habitually*, without Repentance cannot be saved; so a Man known to live in Sin, cannot regularly be received into any Church. To compose Churches of *Habitual Sinners*, and that either as unto Sins of Commission, or Sins of Omission, is not to erect Temples to Christ, but Chapels unto the Devil.

1 *Cor.* 6. 9, 10, 11. *Phil.* 3. 18, 19. 2 *Thes.* 3. 6. 2 *Tim.* 3. 5. *Rom.* 9. 6, 7. *Tit.* 1. 16.

2. Such as being in the fellowship of the Church, are to be *admonished of any scandalous Sin*, which if they repent not of, they are to be *cast out of the Church*, are not meet Members for the *Original Constitution* of a Church. This is the state of them

Mat. 18. 16, 17, 18.

them who abide *Obstinate in any known Sin*, whereby they have given *offence* unto others, without a professed Repentance thereof, although they have not lived in it *habitually*. 1 Cor. 5. 11.

3. They are to be such as *visibly answer* the Description given of Gospel Churches in the Scripture, so as the *Titles* assigned therein unto the Members of such Churches, may on good grounds be appropriated unto them. To compose Churches of such persons as do not visibly answer the character given of what they were of old, and what they were always to be by virtue of the Law of Christ or Gospel-constitution, is not Church *Edification* but *Destruction*. And those who look on the things spoken of all Church Members of old, as that they were *Saints by calling*, *lively stones* in the house of God, *justified* and *sanctified, separate from the World*, &c. as those which were in them, and did indeed belong unto them, but even deride the necessity of the same things in present Church Members, or the Application of them unto those who are so, are themselves no small part of that woful *Degeneracy* which Christian Religion is fallen under. Let it then be considered what is spoken of the Church of the *Jews* in their Dedication unto God, as unto their *Typical Holiness*, with the Application of it unto Christian Churches in *real Holiness*, 1 Pet. 2. 5, 9. with the Description given of them constantly in the Scripture, as *Faithful, Holy, Believing*, as the *House of God*, as his *Temple* wherein he dwells by his Spirit, as the *Body of Christ* united and compacted by the communication of the Spirit unto them; as also what is said concerning their ways, walkings and duties; and it will be uncontrolably evident of what sort our *Church Members* ought to be; nor are those of any other sort able to discharge the *Duties* which are incumbent on all Church Members, nor to use the *Privileges* they are intrusted withal. Wherefore, I say, to suppose Churches regularly to consist of such persons for the greater part of them, as no way answer the *Description given of Church Members* in their Original Institution, nor capable to discharge the Duties prescribed unto them, but giving evidence of Habits and actions inconsistent therewithal, is not only to disturb all Church Order, but utterly to *overthrow* the Ends and

and Being of Churches. Nor is there any thing more scandalous unto Christian Religion, than what *Bellarmine* affirms to be the judgment of the *Papists* in opposition unto all others; namely, that *no internal Vertue or Grace is required unto the Constitution of a Church in its Members.* Lib. 3. de *Ecclef. cap.* 2.

<small>*Rom.* 10. 10. 2 *Cor.* 8.5. Chap. 9. 13. *Matth.* 10. 32, 33. *Luke* 9.16. 2 *Tim.* 2. 12. *Rom.* 15.9. *Joh.*12.42. 1 *Joh.*4. 2, 3, 15.</small>
4. They must be such as do *make an open profession of the subjection of their Souls and Consciences unto the Authority of Christ in the Gospel, and their readiness to yield Obedience unto all his Commands.* This I suppose will not be denied; for not only doth the Scripture make this *Profession* necessary unto the participation of any benefit or privilege of the Gospel; but the nature of the things themselves requires indispensably that so it should be. For nothing can be more unreasonable than, that Men should be taken into the privileges attending *Obedience* unto the Laws and Commands of Christ, without avowing or professing that *Obedience.* Wherefore, our Enquiry is only what is required unto *such a Profession*, as may render Men meet to be Members of a Church, and give them a Right thereunto. For to suppose such a confession of Christian Religion to be compliant with the Gospel, which is made by many who openly *live in Sin,* being *disobedient, and unto every good work reprobate,* is to renounce the Gospel it self. Christ is not the High-Priest of such a *Profession.* I shall therefore declare briefly what is necessary unto this *Profession,* that all may know what it is which is required unto the Entrance of any into our Churches, wherein our *Practice* hath been sufficiently traduced.

1. There is required unto it a *competent knowledge* of the Doctrines and Mystery of the Gospel, especially concerning the *Person and Offices of Christ.* The Confession hereof, was the ground whereon he granted the *Keys of the Kingdom of Heaven,* or all Church Power unto Believers, *Matth.* 16. 17, 18, 19. The first Instruction which he gave unto his Apostles, was, That they should *teach Men* by the Preaching of the Gospel, in the knowledge of the Truth revealed by him. The knowledge required in the Members of the *Judaical Church,* that they might be Translated into the *Christian,* was principally, if not solely, that of his *Person,* and the acknowledgment of him to be

be the true *Messiah*, the Son of God. For as on their unbelief thereof their Eternal ruine did depend, as he told them, *if you believe not that I am he, you shall die in your sins*; so the confession of him was sufficient on their part unto their Admission into the Gospel Church State. And the Reasons of it are apparent. With others, an Instruction in all the Mysteries of Religion, especially in those that are *fundamental*, is necessary unto the Profession we enquire after. So *Justin Martyr* tells us what pains they took in those Primitive Times, to instruct those in the Mysteries of Religion, who upon a *general Conviction of its Truth*, were willing to adhere unto the Profession of it. And what was their judgment herein, is sufficiently known, from the keeping a multitude in the state of *Catechumens*, before they would admit them into the Fellowship of the Church. They are not therefore to be blamed, they do but discharge their Duty, who refuse to receive into Church-Communion such as are *ignorant* of the fundamental Doctrines and Mysteries of the Gospel; or if they have learned any thing of them from a form of words, yet really *understand nothing* of them. The promiscuous driving of all sorts of persons who have been Baptized in their Infancy, unto a participation of all Church privileges, is a *profanation* of the holy Institutions of Christ. This knowledge therefore belonging unto profession is it self to be professed.

2. There is required unto it *a professed subjection of Soul and Conscience unto the Authority of Christ in the Church*. This in general is performed by all that are *Baptized* when they are *Adult*, as being by their own actual consent *Baptized in the Name of Christ*. And it is required of all them who are Baptized in their Infancy, when they are able with Faith and Understanding to profess their consent unto, and abiding in that Covenant whereinto they were initiated. *Matth.* 28. 18, 19, 20. 2 *Cor.* 8. 5.

3. An Instruction in, and consent unto the *Doctrine of Self-denial and bearing of the Cross*, in a particular manner: For this is made indispensably necessary by our Saviour himself, unto all that will be his Disciples. And it hath been a great disadvantage unto the Glory of Christian Religion, that Men have *Matth.* 10. 37, 38, 39. *Mar.* 8. 34, 38. *Luke* 9. 23.

Phil. 3.18.
Act. 4. 10,
11; 20.
Act. 24. 14.

have not been more and better instructed therein. It is commonly thought, that who ever will, may be a Christian at an *easie rate,* it will cost him nothing. But the Gospel gives us another account of these things. For it not only warns us, that Reproaches, Hatred, Sufferings of all sorts, oft-times to Death it self, are the common lot of all its Professors, *who will live Godly in Christ Jesus;* but also requires, that at our initiation into the Profession of it, we consider aright the dread of them all, and engage cheerfully to undergo them. Hence, in the *Primitive Times,* whilst all sorts of miseries were continually presented unto them who Embraced the Christian Religion, their willing engagement to undergo them, who were Converted, was a firm Evidence of the sincerity of their Faith, as it ought to be unto us also in times of Difficulty and Persecution. Some may suppose that the Faith and Confession of this Doctrine of *Self-denial* and *readiness for the Cross,* is of use only in time of *Persecution,* and so doth not belong unto them who have continually the countenance and favour of publick Authority. I say, it is, at least as they judge, well for them; with others it is not so, whose outward state makes the publick avowing of this Duty indispensably necessary unto them: And I may add it as my own thoughts, (though they are not my own alone) That notwithstanding all the Countenance that is given unto any Church by the *publick Magistracy,* yet whilst we are in this World, those who will faithfully discharge their Duty, as Ministers of the Gospel especially, shall have need to be prepared for sufferings. To escape sufferings, and enjoy worldly advantages by sinful compliances, or bearing with Men in their Sins, is no Gospel Direction.

4. *Conviction and Confession of Sin, with the way of deliverance by Jesus Christ, is that answer of a good Conscience,* that is required in the Baptism of them that are Adult. 1 *Pet.* 3.

Matth. 28. 19, 20.

5. Unto this Profession is required the *constant performance of all known Duties* of Religion, both of *Piety* in the publick and private Worship of God, as also of *Charity* with respect unto others. *Shew me thy Faith by thy Works.*

6. A

The Subject Matter of the Church.

6. A careful *Abstinence from all known Sins*, giving scandal or offence, either unto the World, or unto the Church of God. And the Gospel requires, that this Confession be made (*with the Mouth Confession is made unto Salvation*) against (1.) *Fear*, (2.) *Shame*, (3.) The *Course of the World*, (4.) The *Opposition* of all Enemies whatever.

1 Cor. 10. 32.
Phil 1. 10.

Hence it appears, that there are none excluded from an Entrance into the Church State, but such as are either, (1.) *grosly Ignorant*, or, (2.) *Persecutors*, or reproachers of those that are Good, or of the ways of God wherein they walk; or, (3.) *Idolaters*; or, (4.) Men *scandalous in their Lives* in the Commission of Sins, or Omission of Duties, through vitious Habits or Inclinations; or, (5.) such as would partake of Gospel-Priviledges and Ordinances, yet openly avow that they *will not submit unto the Law and Commands of Christ in the Gospel*, concerning whom, and the like, the Scripture Rule is peremptory; *From such turn away*.

And herein we are remote from exceeding the example and care of the Primitive Churches. Yea, there are but few, if any, that arrive unto it. Their endeavour was to Preach unto all they could, and rejoiced in the *multitudes that came to hear the Word*. But if any did essay to join themselves unto the Church, their diligence in their Examination and Instruction, their severe Enquiries into their Conversation, their disposing of them for a long time into a state of *Expectation* for their Trial, before their Admittance, were remarkable. And some of the Ancients complain, that their *promiscuous Admittance* of all sorts of persons that would profess the Christian Religion, into Church Membership, which took place afterwards, ruined all the Beauty, Order and Discipline of the Church.

The things ascribed unto those who are to be esteemed the proper *Subject Matter of a Visible Church*, are such as in the *judgment of Charity* entitle them unto all the Appellations of *Saints; Called, Sanctified*, that is *Visibly* and by *Profession*, which are given unto the Members of all the Churches in the New Testament, and which must be answered in those who are

are admitted into that Privilege, if we do not wholly neglect our only Patterns. By these things, although they should any of them not be *real living Members* of the Mystical Body of Christ, unto whom he is an Head of spiritual and vital influence; yet are they meet Members of that Body of Christ unto which he is an *Head of Rule and Government*; as also meet to be esteemed Subjects of his Kingdom. And none are excluded but such, as concerning whom Rules are given, either to withdraw from them, or to cast them out of Church Society, or are expresly excluded by God himself from any share in the *Privileges of his Covenant*, Psal. 50. 16, 17.

Divines, of all sorts, do dispute from the Scripture and the Testimonies of the *Ancients*, that *Hypocrites*, and persons *unregenerate* may be true Members of Visible Churches. And it is a matter very easie to be proved; nor do I know any by whom it is denied. But the only Question is, That whereas undoubtedly, *Profession* is necessary unto all Church Communion; whether, if Men do *profess themselves Hypocrites in State*, and Unregenerate in Mind, that Profession do sufficiently qualify them for Church Communion. And whereas there is a double Profession, one by *Words*, the other by *Works*, as the Apostle declares, *Tit.* 1. 16. Whether the latter be not as *interpretative* of the Mind and state of Men as the former; other contest we have with none, in this matter.

Belarmine de Eccles. lib. 3. cap. 2. gives an account out of *Augustine*, and that truly, from *Brevec. Collat. Col.* 3. of the state of the Church. "It doth, *saith he*, consist of a Soul and "Body. The Soul is the internal Graces of the Spirit: The "Body is the Profession of them, with the Sacraments. All "true Believers making Profession, belong to the Soul and "Body of the Church. Some, (as believing *Catechumens*) "belong to the Soul, but not to the Body: Others are of the "Body, but not of the Soul; namely, such as have no internal "Grace or true Faith; and they are like the Hair or the Nails, "or evil Humours in the Body. And thereunto adds, That his *Definition* of the Church comprizeth this *last sort only*; which is all one, as if we should define a Man to be a *Thing constituted and*

and made up of Hair, Nails, and ill Humours; and let others take heed that they have not such Churches.

There is nothing more certain in matter of Fact, than that *Evangelical Churches* at their first constitution, were made up, and did consist of such Members as we have described, and no other. Nor is there one Word in the whole Scripture intimating any *Concession* or *Permission* of Christ, to receive into his Church those who are not so Qualified. Others have nothing to plead for themselves but *Possession*; which being *malæ fidei*, ill obtained, and ill continued, will afford them no real advantage, when the time of trial shall come. Wherefore, it is certain that *such they ought to be*. No Man, as I suppose, is come unto that profligate sense of Spiritual things, as to deny, That the *Members of the Church* ought to be *visibly Holy*. For if so, they may affirm, that all the promises and privileges made and granted to the Church, do belong unto them who *visibly live and die in their Sins*; which is to overthrow the Gospel. And if they *ought so to be*, and were so at first, when they are not so, *openly and visibly*, there is a declension from the Original Constitution of Churches, and a Sinful Deviation in them from the Rule of Christ.

This Original Constitution of Churches, with respect unto their *Members*, was for the substance of it, as we observed, preferred in the Primitive Times, whilst *Persecution* from without, was continued, and Discipline preserved within. I have in part declared before, what great care and circumspection the Church then used in the *Admission* of any into their Fellowship and Order, and what trial they were to undergo, before they were received; and it is known also, with what *severe Discipline* they watched over the Faith, walking, conversation and manners of all their Members. Indeed, such was their care and diligence herein, that there is scarce left in some Churches, at present, the least *Resemblance* or Appearance of what was their State and manner of Rule. Wherefore, some think it meet to Ascend no higher in the imitation of the Primitive Churches, than the times of the *Christian Emperours*, when all things began

began to rush into the fatal Apostasie, which I shall here speak a little farther unto: For,

Upon the *Roman Emperours* Embracing Christian Religion, whereby not only outward Peace and Tranquility was secured unto the Church, but the Profession of Christian Religion was countenanced, encouraged, honoured and rewarded; the *Rule*, *Care* and *Diligence* of the Churches about the *Admission* of Members, were in a great measure relinquished and forsaken. The *Rulers of the Church* began to think, that the Glory of it consisted in its *numbers*; finding both their own Power, Veneration and Revenue encreased thereby. In a short time, the Inhabitants of whole Cities and Provinces, upon a bare outward Profession, were admitted into Churches. And then began the *outward Court*, that is, all that which belongs unto the outward Worship and Order of the Church, *to be trampled on by the Gentiles*, not kept any more to the *measure* of Scripture Rule, which thenceforth was applied only to the *Temple of God* and them that Worshipped therein: For this corruption of the Church, as to the *matter* of it, was the occasion and means of introducing all that corruption in *Doctrine*, *Worship*, *Order* and *Rule* which ensued, and ended in the great Apostacy. For whatever belonged unto any of these things, especially these that consist in practice, were accommodated unto the state of the *Members* of the *Churches*: And such they were as stood in need of *superstitious Rites* to be mixed with their Worship, as not understanding the Power and Glory of that which is Spiritual; such as no interest in *Church Order* could be committed unto, seeing they were not qualified to bear any share in it; such as stood in need of a *Rule over them*, with *Grandeur* and *Power*, like unto that among the *Gentiles*. Wherefore, the Accommodation of all Church concerns, unto the state and condition of such corrupt Members as Churches were filled with, and at length made up of, proved the Ruine of the Church in all its Order and Beauty.

But so it fell out, that in the *Protestant Reformation* of the Church, very little regard was had thereunto. Those great and

and worthy Persons who were called unto that Work, did set themselves principally, yea, *solely* for the most part, against the *false Doctrine* and *Idolatrous Worship* of the *Church of Rome*; as judging, that if they were removed and taken away, the people by the Efficacy of Truth and Order of Worship, would be retrived from the evil of their ways, and Primitive Holiness be again reduced among them. For they thought it was the *Doctrine* and *Worship* of that Church, which had filled the people with Darkness and corrupted their Conversations. Nor did they absolutely judge amiss therein: For although they were themselves at first introduced in compliance with the ignorance and wickedness of the people, yet they were suited to *promote* them, as well as to *countenance* them; which they did effectually. Hence it came to pass, that the Reformation of the Church as unto the *matter* of it, or the Purity and Holiness of its Members, was not in the least attempted, until *Calvin* set up his *Discipline* at *Geneva*, which hath filled the World with clamours against him from that day to this. In most other places, Churches, in the matter of them, continued the same as they were in the *Papacy*, and in many places as bad in their Lives as when they were *Papists*.

But this *Method* was designed in the Holy, Wise Providence of God, for the good and advantage of the Church, in a *progressive Reformation*, as it had made a gradual Progress into its decay. For had the *Reformers* in the first place, set themselves to remove out of the Church such as were *unmeet for its Communion*, or to have gathered out of them such as were meer Members of the Church according to its Original Institution; it would through the *paucity of the number* of those who could have complied with the Design, have greatly obstructed, if not utterly defeated their endeavour for the *Reformation of Doctrine and Worship*. This was that in the Preaching of the Gospel and the Profession of it, which God hath since made effectual, in these Nations especially, and in other places, to turn Multitudes from *Darkness to Light, and from the Power of Satan unto Himself, translating them into the Kingdom of His dear Son*. Hereby way is made for a necessary addition unto the work of

Reformation,

Reformation, if not to the closing of it, which could not at first be attained unto, nor well attempted; namely the Reduction of Churches, as unto their *matter*, or the Members of them unto their Primitive Institution.

The sum of what is designed in this Discourse, is this only. We desire no more to constitute *Church Members*, and we can desire no less, than what in judgment of Charity may comply with the *Union* that is between Christ the Head and the Church; 1 *Cor.* 12. 27. *Eph.* 2. 22. 1 *Cor.* 3. 16, 17. 2 *Cor.* 11. 1, 18. 1 *Thess.* 1. 1, 2, &c. that may in the same judgment answer the way of the beginning and increase of the Church according unto the Will of God, who adds unto the Church such as shall be saved, *Act.* 2. 47. the Rule of our receiving of them, being *because he hath received them*, *Rom.* 14. 1, 2. that may answer that Profession of Faith which was the Foundation of the Church, which was not what *flesh and blood*, but *what God himself revealed*, *Matth.* 16. 16. and not such as have a form of Godliness but deny the Power thereof, 2 *Tim.* 3. 5. We acknowledge that many Church Members are not what they ought to be, but that many *Hypocrites* may be among them; that the judgment which is passed on the Confession and Profession of them that are to be Admitted into Churches, is *charitative*, proceeding on evidence of moral Probability, not determining the reality of the things themselves; that there are sundry *measures* of Light, Knowledge, Experience, and Abilities and Readiness of Mind in those that are to be Admitted, all whose Circumstances are duly to be considered, with indulgence unto their weaknesses: And if the Scripture will allow us any further Latitude, we are ready to embrace it.

Our present Enquiry yet remaining on these considerations, is, What is our Duty *in point of Communion with such Churches* as are made up or composed of Members *visibly unholy*; or such as comply not with the Qualifications that are by the Rules of the Gospel indispensably required, to give unto any a Regular entrance into the Church, with a participation of its Privileges. For it is in vain to expect, that *such Churches will*

Reform

The Subject Matter of the Church.

Reform themselves, by any Act, Duty or Power of their own; seeing the generality of them are justly supposed averse from, and enemies unto any such Work. I answer therefore,

1. It must be remembred, that *Communion with particular Churches* is to be regulated absolutely by *Edification*. No Man is or can be obliged to abide in or confine himself unto the Communion of any particular Church, any longer, than it is for his *Edification*. And this liberty is allowed unto all persons by the *Church of England*. For, allow a Man to be born in such a *Parish,* to be *baptized* in it, and there educated; yet, if at any time he judge that the *Ministry of the Parish* is not useful unto his Edification, he may withdraw from all Communion in that *Parish,* by the removal of his Habitation, it may be to the next door. Wherefore,

2. If the corruption of a Church, as to the *matter of it,* be such as that,

 1. It is *inconsistent* with, and overthroweth *all that Communion* that ought to be among the Members of the same Church, in *love without dissimulation,* whereof we shall treat afterwards.

 2. If the *scandals* and *offences* which must of necessity abound in such Churches, be really obstructive of Edification.

 3. If the *ways and walking* of the generality of their Members, be dishonourable unto the Gospel, and the Profession of it, giving no Representation of the holiness of Christ or his Doctrine.

 4. If such Churches *do not, can not, will not* Reform themselves: Then,

It is the Duty of every Man who takes care of his own present Edification, and the future salvation of his Soul, *peaceably to withdraw from the Communion of such Churches,* and to join in such others, where all the ends of Church Societies may in some measure be obtained. Men may not only do so, because all obligation unto the use of means for the attaining of such an end, doth cease, when the means are not suited thereunto, but obstructive of its attainment; but also the giving of a *Testimony* hereby against the Declension from the Rule of Christ in the Institution of Churches, and the dishonour that by this means is reflected on the Gospel, is necessary unto all that desire to acquit themselves as *Loyal Subjects* unto their Lord and King. And it cannot be questioned by any, who understand the nature, use and end of *Evangelical Churches*, but that a relinquishment of the Rule of the Gospel in any of them, as unto the practice of Holiness, is as just a cause of withdrawing Communion from them, as their forsaking the same Rule in Doctrine and Worship.

It may be some will judge that sundry *inconveniences* will ensue on this Assertion, when any have a mind to practise according unto it. But when the matter of Fact supposed, is such as is capable of an uncontrollable evidence, no *inconvenience* can ensue on the practice directed unto, any way to be compared unto the *mischief* of obliging Believers to abide always in such Societies, to the ruine of their Souls.

Two things may be yet enquired into, that relate unto this part of the state of *Evangelical Churches*: As,

1. Whether a Church may not, ought not, to *take under its Conduct*, Inspection and Rule, such as are not yet meet to be received into full Communion; such as are the *Children* and *Servants* of *those* who are compleat Members of the Church. *Answ.* No doubt the Church in its Officers, may and ought so to do; and it is a great evil when it is neglected. For, (1.) They are to take care of *Parents* and *Masters* as such, and as unto the discharge of their Duty in their Families; which, without an inspection into the condition of their *Children* and *Servants*, they cannot do. (2.) *Housholds* were constantly reckoned unto the Church, when the Heads of the Families were entred into Covenant, *Luk.* 19. 9. *Act.* 16. 15. *Rom.* 16. 10, 11. 1 *Cor.* 1. 16. 2 *Tim.* 4. 19. (3.) *Children* to belong unto, and have an Interest in their *Parents Covenant*; not only in the promise of it, which gives them Right unto *Baptism*; but in the Profession of it in the *Church Covenant*, which gives them a Right unto all the Privileges of the Church, whereof they are capable, until they voluntarily relinquish their claim unto them. (4.) *Baptizing the Children of Church Members*, giving
them

them thereby an Admission into the visible *Catholick* Church, puts an Obligation on the Officers of the Church, to take care, what in them lieth, that they may be kept and preserved *meet Members* of it, by a due watch over them, and instruction of them. (5.) Though neither the Church nor its Privileges be continued and preserved as of old, by *carnal generation* ; yet, because of the nature of the Dispensation of Gods Covenant, wherein he hath promised to be a *God unto Believers and their Seed* ; the advantage of the means of a gracious Education in such Families, and of conversion and edification in the Ministry of the Church, *ordinarily* the continuation of the Church, is to depend on the addition of Members out of the Families already incorporated in it. The Church is not to be like the Kingdom of the *Mamalukes*, wherein there was no regard unto natural Successors ; but it was continually made up of *Strangers* and *Foreigners* incorporated into it : Nor like the beginning of the *Roman Common-weal*, which consisting of *Men* only, was like to have been the matter of *one Age* alone.

The Duty of the Church towards this sort of persons, consists, (1.) In *Prayer* for them. (2.) *Catechetical Instruction* of them, according unto their Capacities. (3.) *Advice* to their Parents concerning them. (4.) *Visiting* of them in the Families whereunto they do belong. (5.) *Encouragement* of them, or *Admonition* according as there is occasion. (6.) *Direction* for a due preparation unto the joining themselves unto the Church, in full Communion. (7.) *Exclusion* of them from a claim unto the participation of the especial Privileges of the Church, where they render themselves visibly unmeet for them, and unworthy of them.

The neglect of this Duty brings unconceivable prejudice unto Churches, and if continued in, will prove their Ruine. For they are not to be preserved, propagated and continued, at the easie rate of a constant supply by the *carnal baptized posterity* of those who do at any time justly or unjustly belong unto them : But they are to prepare a *meet supply of Members*, by all the spiritual means whose administration they are intrusted

trusted withal. And besides, one end of Churches, is, to *preserve the Covenant of God* in the Families once graciously taken thereinto. The neglect therefore herein, is carefully to be watched against. And it doth arise, (1.) From an *ignorance of the Duty*, in most that are concerned in it. (2.) From the *paucity of Officers* in most Churches, both Teaching and Ruling, who are to attend unto it. (3.) The *want of a Teacher or Catechist* in every Church, who should attend only unto the instruction of this sort of persons. (4.) *Want of a sense of their Duty* in Parents and Masters. (1.) In not valuing aright the *great privilege* of having their Children and Servants under the inspection, care and blessing of the Church. (2.) In not *instilling* into them a sense of it, with the Duties that are expected from them, on the account of their Relation unto the Church. (3.) In not *bringing them* duly unto the Church Assemblies. (4.) In not *preparing* and disposing them unto an actual entrance into full Communion with the Church. (5.) In not *advising* with the Elders of the Church about them. And, (6.) Especially by an *indulgence* unto that loose and careless kind of *Education* in Conformity unto the World, which generally prevails. Hence it is, that most of them on various accounts and occasions, drop off here and there from the Communion of the Church, and all Relation thereunto, without the least respect unto them, or enquiry after them; Churches being supplied by such as are occasionally Converted in them.

Where *Churches* are compleat in the *kind* and *number* of their Officers, sufficient to attend unto all the Duties and occasions of them; where whole *Families*, in the conjunction of the Heads of them unto the Church, are Dedicated unto God, according unto the several capacities of those whereof they do consist; where the *Design* of the Church is to provide for its own *successive continuation* in the preservation of the Interest of Gods Covenant in the Families taken thereinto; where *Parents* esteem themselves accountable unto God and the Church, as unto the Relation of their Children thereunto, there is provision for Church Order, Usefulness and Beauty, beyond what is usually to be observed.

The Subject Matter of the Church. 19

2. The especial Duty of the Church in *Admission of Members* in the time of great Persecution, may be a little enquired into. And, (1.) It is evident, that in the *Apostolical and Primitive Times*, the Churches were exceeding careful not to admit into their society, such as by whom they might be *betrayed* unto the rage of their Persecuting Adversaries. Yet, notwithstanding all their care, they could seldom avoid it; but that when Persecution grew severe, some or other would fall from them, either out of fear, with the power of Temptation, or by a discovery of their latent *hypocrisie* and unbelief, unto their great trial and distress. However, they were not *so scrupulous* herein, with respect unto their own safety, as to exclude such as gave *a tolerable account* of their sincerity; but in the discharge of their Duty, committed themselves unto the care of Jesus Christ. And this is the Rule whereby we ought to walk on such occasions. Wherefore, (2.) On supposition of the *establishment of Idolatry*, and *Persecution*, there or in any place, as it was of old, under, first the *Pagan*, and afterwards the *Antichristian* Tyranny; the Church is obliged to receive into its Care and Communion all such as, (1.) *Flee from Idols*, and are ready to confirm their Testimony against them with suffering. (2.) Make *profession of the truth* of the Gospel of the Doctrine of Christ, especially as unto his Person and Offices; are, (3.) Free from *scandalous Sins*; and, (4.) Are *willing to give up themselves* unto the Rule of Christ in the Church, and a subjection unto all his Ordinances and Institutions therein. For in such a season, these things are so full an indication of *sincerity*, as that in the judgment of Charity, they render Men meet to be Members of the visible Church. And if any of this sort of persons, through the severity of the Church in their *non Admission* of them, should be cast on a conjunction in Superstitious and Idolatrous Worship, or be otherwise exposed unto Temptations and Discouragements prejudicial unto their Souls, I know not how such a Church can answer the refusal of them unto the great and universal Pastor of the whole Flock.

D 2 CHAP.

CHAP. II.

Of the Formal Cause of a Particular Church.

THE way or means whereby such persons as are described in the foregoing *Chapter*, may become a Church, or enter into a Church-State, is by *mutual confederation*, or solemn Agreement for the performance of all the Duties which the Lord Christ hath prescribed unto his Disciples in such Churches, and in order to the exercise of the power wherewith they are intrusted, according unto the Rule of the Word.

FOR the most part, the Churches that are in the World at present, know not *how they came so to be*, continuing only in that state which they have received by Tradition from their Fathers. Few there are, who think that any *Act or Duty of their own*, is required to enstate them in Church Order and Relation. And it is acknowledged, that there is a difference between the *continuation* of a Church, and its *first Erection*. Yet, that that *continuation* may be regular, it is required that its first Congregating (for the Church is a Congregation) was so; as also, that the force and efficacy of it be still continued. Wherefore, the causes of that *first gathering*, must be enquired into.

THE Churches mentioned in the New Testament, planted or gathered by the Apostles, were *Particular Churches*, as hath been proved. These Churches did consist each of them of many Members, who were *so Members* of one of them, as that they were *not Members* of another. The *Saints of the Church of Corinth*, were not Members of the *Church at Philippi*. And the Enquiry is, How those Believers in one place and the other became to be a Church, and that distinct from all others? The Scripture affirms in general, that *they gave up themselves unto the Lord and unto the Apostles*, who guided them in these Affairs, *by the will of God*, 2 Cor. 8. 5. and that other *Believers were added unto the Church*, Act. 2.

THAT it is the Will and Command of our Lord Jesus Christ, that all his Disciples should be joined in such Societies, for the Duties,

Of the Formal Cause of a Particular Church.

Duties and Ends of them prescribed and limited by himself, hath been proved sufficiently before. All that are *Discipled by the Word*, are to be *taught to do and observe all his Commands, Matth.* 28. 20.

THIS could *originally* be no otherwise done, but by their own *actual, express, voluntary consent*. There are sundry things which concurr as remote causes, or *prerequisite conditions* unto this conjunction of Believers in a *Particular Church*, and without which it cannot be. Such are *Baptism, Profession of the Christian Faith, convenient Cohabitation*, resorting to the *Preaching of the Word* in the same place. But neither any of these distinctly or separately, nor all of them in *Conjunction*, are or can be the *constitutive Form* of a *Particular Church*. For it is evident that they may all be, and yet no such Church State ensue. They cannot altogether engage unto those Duties, nor communicate those Powers, which appertain unto this State.

WERE there no other *Order* in *Particular Churches*, no other *Discipline* to be exercised in them, nor *Rule* over them, no other *Duties*, no other *Ends* assigned unto them, but what are generally owned and practised in *Parochial Assemblies*, the Preaching of the Word within such a precinct of Cohabitation, determined by Civil Authority, might constitute a Church. But if a Church be such a Society as is *intrusted* in it self with *sundry Powers and Privileges* depending on *sundry Duties* prescribed unto it, if it constitute *new Relations* between Persons, that neither naturally nor morally were before so related, as Marriage doth between Husband and Wife; if it require new *mutual Duties*, and give new *mutual Rights* among themselves, not required of them either as unto their matter, or as unto their manner before; it is vain to imagine that this State can arise from, or have any other *Formal Cause*, but the joint consent and virtual confederation of those concerned, unto these ends: For there is none of them can have any other Foundation; they are all of them resolved into the *Wills of Men*, bringing themselves under an obligation unto them by their voluntary consent. I say unto the *Wills of Men*, as their *Formal Cause*; the supreme efficient cause of them all being

Of the Formal Cause of a Particular Church.

ing the Will, Law and Constitution of our Lord Jesus Christ.

THUS it is in all *Societies*, in all *Relations* that are not meerly *natural*, (such as between Parents and Children, wherein the necessity of Powers and mutual Duties, is predetermined by a Superiour Law, even that of Nature) wherein, Powers, Privileges and mutual Duties are established, as belonging unto that Society. Nor after its first institution, can any one be *incorporated* into it, but by his own consent, and engagement to observe the Laws of it. Nor, if the Nature and Duties of Churches were acknowledged, could there be any contest in this matter; for the things ensuing are clear and evident.

1. THE Lord Christ, by his Authority, hath appointed and *instituted this Church State*, as that there should be such Churches, as we have proved before.

2. THAT by his Word or Law he hath *granted Powers and Privileges* unto this Church, and prescribed *Duties* unto all belonging unto it, wherein, they can have no concernment who are not incorporated into such a Church.

3. THAT therefore, he doth *Require and Command* all his Disciples to join themselves in such Church Relations, as we have proved; warranting them so to do, by his Word and Command: Wherefore,

4. THIS *joining of themselves*, whereon depends all their interest in Church Powers and Privileges, all their obligation unto Church Duties, is a *voluntary Act* of the obedience of Faith, unto the Authority of Christ, nor can it be any thing else.

5. HEREIN do they give *themselves unto the Lord*, and *to one another*, by their Officers, in a peculiar manner, according to the *Will of God*, 2 Cor. 8. 5.

6. TO *give our selves unto the Lord*, that is unto the Lord Jesus Christ, is expresly to engage to do and observe all that he hath appointed and commanded in the Church; as that *Phrase* every where signifieth in the Scripture, as also *joining our selves unto God*, which is the same.

7. THIS

Of the Formal Cause of a Particular Church. 23

7. THIS Resignation of our selves unto the Will, Power and Authority of Christ, with an express ingagement made unto him of doing and observing all his Commands, hath the *nature of a Covenant on our part*; and it hath so on his, by virtue of the promise of his especial presence annexed unto this engagement on our part, *Matth.* 28. 18, 19, 20.

8. FOR, whereas there are three things required unto a *Covenant* between God and Man. (1.) That it be *of Gods appointment and institution*. (2.) That upon a *prescription of Duties* there be a *solemn engagement* unto their performance on the part of Men. (3.) That there be *especial promises of God* annexed thereunto, in which consists the matter of *Confederation*, whereof mutual express *Restipulation* is the form; they all concurr herein.

9. THIS Covenant which we intend, is not the *Covenant of Grace* absolutely considered; nor are all the Duties belonging unto that Covenant prescribed in it; but the principal of them, as *Faith, Repentance,* and the like, are presupposed unto it; nor hath annexed unto it all the promises and privileges of the New Covenant *absolutely* considered; but it is that which is prescribed as a *Gospel Duty in the Covenant of Grace*, whereunto do belong all the Duties of Evangelical Worship, all the powers and privileges of the Church, by virtue of the *especial promise* of the peculiar presence of Christ in such a Church.

10. WHEREAS therefore in the constitution of a Church, Believers do *give up themselves unto the Lord*, and are bound solemnly to engage themselves to *do and observe all the things which Christ hath commanded* to be done and observed in that state, whereon he hath promised to be *present* with them and among them in an especial manner, which presence of his, doth interest them in all the Rights, Powers and Privileges of the Church; their so doing, hath the *nature of a Divine Covenant* included in it, which is the *Formal Cause* of their Church Sate and Being.

11. BESIDES, as we have proved before, there are many *mutual Duties* required of all which join in Church Societies, and *Powers* to be exercised and submitted unto, whereunto none

can

can be obliged without their own consent. They must *give up themselves unto one another by the will of God.* That is, they must agree, consent and engage among themselves to observe all those mutual Duties, to use all those Privileges, and to exercise all those Powers, which the Lord Christ hath prescribed and granted unto his Church. See *Jerem.* 50. 4, 5.

12. THIS compleats the *confederation intended*, which is the *Formal Cause* of the Church; and without which, either expresly or virtually performed, there can be no Church State.

13. INDEED herein most Men deceive themselves, and think they do not that, nor that it ought to be done, and dispute against it as unlawful or unnecessary, which for the substance of it *they do themselves,* and would condemn themselves in their own Consciences, if they did it not. For unto what end do they join themselves unto *Parochial Churches* and Assemblies? To what end do they require all Professors of the *Protestant Religion* so to do, declaring it to be their Duty by penalties annexed unto its neglect? Is it not, that they might yield obedience unto Christ in their so doing? Is it not to profess that they will do and observe all whatsoever he commands them? Is it not to do it in *that Society,* in those Assemblies whereunto they do belong? Is there not therein virtually a *mutual Agreement and Engagement* among them unto all those ends? It must be so with them, who do not in all things in Religion *fight uncertainly as Men beating the Air.*

14. NOW, whereas these things are in themselves, and for the substance of them, *known Gospel Duties,* which all Believers are indispensably obliged unto; the more *express* our engagement is concerning them, the more do we glorify Christ in our Profession, and the greater sense of our Duty will abide on our Consciences, and greater encouragement be given unto the performance of mutual Duties; as also the more evident will the warranty be, for the exercise of Church Power. Yet do I not deny the *Being of Churches* unto those Societies, wherein these things are *virtually* only observed; especially in Churches of some continuance, wherein there is at least an *implicit consent* unto the first Covenant-Constitution.

15. THE

Of the Formal Cause of a Particular Church.

15. THE Lord Christ having instituted and appointed Officers, Rulers or Leaders in his Church, (as we shall see in the next place) to look unto the discharge of all Church Duties among the Members of it, to administer and dispense all its Privileges, and to exercise all its Authority, the *consent and engagement* insisted on, is expresly required unto the constitution of this Order and the preservation of it. For without this, no Believer can be brought into that Relation unto another as his *Pastor, Guide, Over-seer, Ruler* unto the ends mentioned, wherein he must be subject unto him, partake of all Ordinances of Divine Worship administred by him with Authority, in obedience unto the will of Christ; *They gave their own selves to us* (saith the Apostle) *by the will of God.*

16. WHEREFORE, the *Formal Cause of a Church* consisteth in an *Obediential Act of Believers, in such numbers as may be useful unto the ends of Church Edification, jointly giving up themselves unto the Lord Jesus Christ, to do and observe all his Commands, resting on the promise of his especial presence thereon; giving and communicating by his Law, all the Rights, Powers and Privileges of his Church unto them; and in a mutual Agreement among themselves, jointly to perform all the Duties required of them in that State, with an especial subjection unto the Spiritual Authority of Rules and Rulers appointed by Christ in that State.*

17. THERE is nothing herein, which any Man who hath a conscientious sense of his Duty in a *professed subjection unto the Gospel*, can question for the substance of it, whether it be according to the mind of Christ or no. And whereas the nature and essential properties of a Divine Covenant are contained in them, as such it is a Foundation of any Church State.

18. THUS under the Old Testament, when God would take the *posterity of Abraham* into a *new peculiar Church State*, he did it by a *Solemn Covenant*. Herein, as he prescribed all the Duties of his Worship to them, and made them many blessed promises of his presence, with powers and privileges innumerable; so the people *solemnly Covenanted* and engaged with him, that *they would do and observe all that he had Commanded them*; whereby they coalesced into that Church State, which abode

E   unto

unto the *time of Reformation*. This Covenant is at large declared *Exod.* 24. For the Covenant which God made there with the people, and they with him, was not the *Covenant of Grace* under a legal difpenfation; for that was eftablifhed unto the Seed of *Abraham* Four Hundred years before in the Promife, with the Seal of Circumcifion; nor was it the *Covenant of Works* under a Gofpel difpenfation; for God never renewed that Covenant under any confideration whatever: But it was a *peculiar Covenant* which God then *made with them, and had not made it with their Fathers*, Deut. 5. 2, 3. whereby they were raifed and erected into a *Church State*, wherein they were intrufted with all the Privileges, and enjoined all the Duties which God had annexed thereunto. This Covenant was the fole *Formal Caufe* of their Church State, which they are charged fo often to have *broken*, and which they fo often *folemnly renewed* unto God.

19. THIS was that *Covenant* which was to be *abolifhed*, whereon the Church State that was built thereon, was utterly taken away. For hereon the *Hebrews* ceafed to be the peculiar Church of God, becaufe the *Covenant* whereby they were made fo, was abolifhed and taken away, as the Apoftle difputes at large, *Heb.* 7, 8, 9. The *Covenant of Grace* in the promife, will ftill continue unto the *true Seed of Abraham, Act.* 2. 38, 39. But the *Church Covenant* was utterly taken away.

20. UPON the removal therefore of this *Covenant*, and the Church State founded thereon, all Duties of Worfhip and Church Privileges were alfo taken away; (the things fubftituted in their room being totally of another kind. But the *Covenant of Grace*, as made with *Abraham*, being continued and transferred unto the Gofpel Worfhippers, the *fign or token of it* given unto him is changed; but another fubftituted in the room thereof. But whereas the Privileges of this Church Covenant were in themfelves *carnal* only, and no way *fpiritual*, but as they were *Typical*; and the Duties prefcribed in it were *burdenfome*, yea, a *yoke intolerable*; the Apoftle declares in the fame place, that the *New Church State*, whereinto we are called by the Gofpel, hath no Duties belonging unto it, but fuch as are *fpiritual* and *eafie*; but withal, hath fuch *holy and eminent*

nent Privileges as the Church could no way enjoy by virtue of the *first Church Covenant*; nor · could be Believers made partakers of them, before that Covenant was abolished: Wherefore,

21. THE *same way* for the Erection of a Church State for the participation of the more excellent Privileges of the Gospel, and performance of the Duties of it, for the *substance* of it must still be continued. For the constitution of such a Society as a Church is, entrusted with Powers and Privileges, by a *Covenant* or mutual consent, with an ingagement unto the performance of the Duties belonging unto it, hath its foundation in the Light of Nature, so far as it hath any thing in common with other voluntary Relations and Societies; was instituted by God himself, as the way and means of erecting the *Church State* of the Old Testament; and consisteth in the performance of such Duties as are expresly required of all Believers.

CHAP. III.

Of the Polity, Rule, or Discipline of the Church in General.

1. THE things last treated of concern the Essence of the Church, or the *Essential Constituent* Parts of it, according unto the appointment of Christ. It remains in the next place, that we should treat of it as it is *Organical*, or a Body Corporate; a spiritually *Political* Society, for the exercise of the Powers wherewith it is intrusted by Christ, and the due performance of the Duties which he requires. Now, whereas it is brought into this estate, by the setting, fixing or placing *Officers* in it, Method would require that we should first treat of them, their *Nature, Names, Power,* and the ways of coming unto their *Offices.* But, whereas all things concerning them are founded in the *grant*

of *Power* unto the Church it felf, and the Inftitution of *Polity and Rule* therein by Jefus Chrift, I fhall firft treat fomewhat thereof in general.

THAT which we intend on various confiderations and in divers refpects, is called the *Power* or *Authority*, the *Polity*, the *Rule*, the *Government* and the *Difcipline* of the Church. The *Formal Nature* of it, is its Authority or Power. Its *Polity*, is skill and wifdom to act that Power unto its proper ends. Its *Rule*, is the actual exercife of that Power, according unto that *skill* and wifdom. Its *Government* is the Exercife and Application of that Authority according unto that skill, towards thofe that are its proper Objects. And it is called its *Difcipline*, principally with refpect unto its end. Yet is it not *material* whether thefe things are thus accurately diftinguifhed; the fame thing is intended in them all, which I fhall call the *Rule of the Church*.

2. THE *Rule of the Church* is in general *The exercife of the Power or Authority of Jefus Chrift, given unto it according unto the Laws and Directions prefcribed by himfelf unto its Edification*. This Power in *Actu Primo*, or *fundamentally*, is in the Church it felf; in *Actu Secundo*, or its exercife, in them that are efpecially called thereunto. Whether that which is now called the *Rule of the Church* by fome, being a plain *Secular Dominion*, have any Affinity hereunto, is juftly doubted. That it is in it felf the *acting of the Authority of Chrift*, wherein the power of Men is *Minifterial* only, is evident. For, (1.) All this *Authority* in and over the Church is vefted in him alone. (2.) It is over the Souls and Confciences of Men only, which no Authority can reach but his, and that as it is his; whereof we fhall treat more afterwards.

THE *fole end* of the *Minifterial* Exercife of this Power and Rule, by virtue thereof unto the Church, is the *Edification of it felf*, Rom. 15. 1, 2, 3. 2 Cor. 10. 8. Chap. 13. 10. Ephef. 4. 14, 15.

3. THIS is the efpecial nature and efpecial end of *all Power* granted by Jefus Chrift unto the Church; namely, a *Miniftry unto Edification*, in oppofition unto all the ends whereunto it hath

of the Church in General.

hath been abused. For it hath been so unto the Usurpation of a Dominion over the Persons and Consciences of the Disciples of Christ, accompanied with Secular Grandeur, Wealth and Power. The Lord Christ never made a grant of any Authority, for any such ends; yea, they are expresly forbidden by him, *Luk.* 22. 25. *Matth.* 20. 26, 27, 28. *Jesus called his Disciples unto him, and said, Ye know that the Princes of the Gentiles exercise Dominion over them, and they that are Great exercise Authority upon them: But it shall not be so among you; but whosoever will be great among you, let him be your Minister; and whosoever will be chief among you, let him be your Servant; even as the Son of Man came not to be ministred unto, but to minister.*

ALL the Pleas of the *Romanists* are utterly insufficient to secure their *Papal Domination* from this Sword of the Mouth of the Lord Jesus. For, whereas their utmost pretence and defence consists in this, That it is not Dominion and Power *absolutely* that is forbidden, but the *Unlawful, Tyrannical, Oppressive* Exercise of Power, such as was in use among the Princes of the *Gentiles*; never was there any Dominion in the World, no not among the *Gentiles*, more Cruel, Oppressive and Bloody, than that of the *Pope's* hath been. But it is evident, that our Lord Jesus Christ doth not in the least reflect on the Rule or Government of the *Kings and Princes of the Gentiles*, which was Good and Righteous: yea, he speaks of *them* in an especial manner, whom their Subjects for their moderate and equal Rule, with their usefulness unto their Countries, called Ευεργέται or *Benefactors*. Their Rule, as unto the Kind and Administration of it in the Kingdoms of the World, he approves of. And such a Power or Preheminence it was, namely good and just in it self, not Tyrannical and Oppressive, that the *Two Disciples desired in his Kingdom*, which gave occasion unto this declaration of the Nature of his Kingdom, and the Rule thereof. For in this Power or Dominion two things may be considered. (1.) The *Exercise* of it over the Persons, Goods and Lives of Men, by Courts, Coercive Jurisdictions, Processes of Law, and External Force in Punishments. (2.) The *State*, Grandeur, Preheminence,

Preheminence, Wealth, Exaltation above others, which are neceſſary unto the maintenance of their Authority and Power. Both theſe in the leaſt Participation of them, in the leaſt Degree whatever, are forbidden by our Saviour to be admitted in his Kingdom, or to have any place therein, on what pretence ſoever. He will have nothing of Lordſhip, Domination, Preheminence in Lordly Power in his Church. No *Courts*, no *Coercive Juriſdictions*, no Exerciſe of any Humane Authority doth he allow therein; for by theſe means do the *Princes of the Gentiles*, thoſe that are the *Benefactors* of their Countries, rule among them. And this is moſt evident from what in oppoſition hereunto he preſcribes unto his own Diſciples, the greateſt, the beſt in Office, Grace and Gifts; namely a *Miniſtery* only, to be diſcharged in the way of Service. How well this great Command and Direction of our Lord Jeſus Chriſt hath been and is complied withal, by thoſe who have taken on them to be Rulers in the Church, is ſufficiently known.

WHEREFORE there is *no Rule* of the Church, but what is *Miniſterial*, conſiſting in an *Authoritative Declaration* and Application of the Commands and Will of Chriſt unto the Souls of Men, wherein, thoſe who exerciſe it are *Servants unto the Church for its Edification, for Jeſus ſake*, 2 Cor. 4. 5.

IT hence follows, that the introduction of *Humane Authority* into the Rule of the Church of Chriſt in any kind, *deſtroyeth the nature of it*, and makes his Kingdom to be of this World, and ſome of his Diſciples to be in their meaſure like the *Princes of the Gentiles*; nor is it oft-times from themſelves, that they are not more like them than they are. The Church is the *Houſe* of *Chriſt*, his *Family*, his *Kingdom*. To act any power in its Rule, which is not his, which derives not from him, which is not communicated by his legal grant; or to act any Power, by Ways, Proceſſes, Rules and Laws not of his appointment, is an invaſion of his Right and Dominion. It can no otherwiſe be, if the Church be his *Family*, his *Houſe*, his *Kingdom*. For what Father would endure that any Power ſhould be exerciſed in his *Family* as to the diſpoſal of his Children and Eſtate, but his own? What *Earthly Prince* will

bear

bear with such an intrusion into his Rights and Dominion? *Foreign Papal Power* is severely excluded here in *England*, because it entrenches on the *Rights of the Crown*, by the exercise of an Authority and Jurisdiction not derived from the King according unto the Law of the Land. And we should do well to take care that at the same time we do not encroach upon the *Dominion of Christ*, by the exercise of an Authority not derived from him, or by Laws and Rules not Enacted by him, but more Foreign unto his Kingdom, than the *Canon Law* or the *Popes* Rule is unto the Laws of this Nation, left we fall under the *Statute of Præmunire*, Matth. 10. 26, 27, 28. The power of Rule in the Church, then, is nothing but a *Right to yield Obedience* unto the Commands of Christ, in such a way, by such Rules, and for such ends, as wherein and whereby his Authority is to be acted.

THE *persons* concerned in this Rule of the Church, both those that Rule and those that are to be Ruled, as unto all their *Civil* and *Political* concerns in this World, are subject unto the *Civil Government* of the Kingdoms and Places wherein they inhabit. And there are sundry things which concern the *outward state and condition of the Church* that are at the disposal of the Governours of this World: But, whereas the Power to be exercised in the Church is meerly *Spiritual* as unto its *objects*, which are the Consciences of Men; and as unto its *ends*, which are the tendency of their Souls unto God, their spiritual obedience in Christ and Eternal Life, it is a *Phrensy* to dream of any other Power or Authority in this Rule, but that of Christ alone.

TO sum up this Discourse; If the Rulers of the Church, the greatest of them, have only a *Ministerial Power* committed unto them, and are precisely limited thereunto; if in the exercise thereof they are *Servants of the Church* unto its Edification; if all *Lordly Domination* in an exaltation above the Church or the Members of it, in Dignity and Authority of this World, and the exercise of Power by external Coercive Jurisdiction be *forbidden* unto them; if the whole Power and Rule of the Church be *Spiritual* and *not Carnal*, mighty through God
and

and not through the Laws of Men; and be to be exercised by *spiritual means* for spiritual ends only; it is apparent how it hath been lost in, or cast out of the World, for the introduction of a Lordly Domination, a Secular Coercive Jurisdiction, with Laws and Powers no way derived from Christ, in the room thereof. Neither is it possible for any Man alive to reconcile the present Government of some Churches, either as unto the *Officers* who have the Administration of that Rule, or the *Rules* and Laws whereby they act and proceed, or *Powers* which they exercise, or the *Jurisdiction* which they claim, or the *manner* of their proceeding in its Administration, unto any tolerable consistency with the Principles, Rules and Laws of the Government of the Church given by Christ himself. And this alone is a sufficient Reason why those who endeavour to preserve their *Loyalty* entire unto Jesus Christ, should in their own practice seek after the Reduction of the Rule of the Church, unto his Commands and Appointments; in the publick disposals of Nations we have no concernment.

4. WHEREAS therefore there is a Power and Authority for its Rule unto Edification, given and committed by the Lord Christ unto his Church, I shall proceed to enquire *how this Power is Communicated, what it is,* and *to whom it is granted,* which shall be declared in the ensuing Observations.

1. THERE was an *extraordinary Church Power* committed by the Lord Jesus Christ unto his *Apostles,* who in their own persons were the *first* and *only* subject of it. It was not *granted unto the Church,* by it to be communicated unto them according unto any Rules prescribed thereunto. For their office as it was *Apostolical,* was *Antecedent* unto the existence of any Gospel Church State properly so called; neither had any Church the least concurrence or influence into their call or mission. Howbeit, when there was a Church State, the Churches being called and gathered by their Ministry, they were given unto the Church, and placed in the Church for the exercise of all Office, with Power unto their Edification according to the Rules and Laws of their constitution, *Act.* 1. 14, 15. Chap. 6. 1, 2, 3, 4. 1 *Cor.* 3. 22. Chap. 12. 28. *Ephes.* 4. 11, 12, 13, 14.

2. THIS

2. THIS Power is *ceased in the Church.* It is so, not by virtue of any Law or constitution of Christ; but by a *cessation* of those actings whence it did flow, and whereon it did depend. For unto this *Apostolical* Office and Power there was required, (1.) An immediate *personal call* from Christ himself. (2.) A *Commission equally extensive unto all Nations* for their Conversion, and unto all Churches equally for their Edification. (3.) An *Authority* in all Churches, comprehensive of all that power which is in the ordinary constitution of them, distributed among many. (4.) A *Collation of extraordinary Gifts*; as of infallibility in Teaching, of working Miracles, speaking with Tongues, and the like. Whereas therefore all these things do cease, and the Lord Christ doth not act in the same manner towards any, this Office and Power doth absolutely cease. For any to pretend themselves to be *Successors* unto these Apostles, as some with a strange confidence and impertinency have done, is to plead that they are personally and immediately called by Christ unto their Office, that they have Authority with respect unto all Nations and all Churches, and are indued with a spirit of Infallibility, and a power of working Miracles, whereof outward pomp and ostentation are no sufficient evidences. And certainly, when some of them consider one another, and talk of being the Apostles Successors, it is but *Aruspex Aruspicens.*

3. LEAST of all in the ordinary state of the Church, and the continuation thereof hath the Lord Christ appointed a *Vicar,* or rather as is pretended a *Successor,* with a plenitude of all Church Power, to be by him parcelled out unto others. This is that which hath overthrown all Church Rule and Order, introducing *Luciferian* Pride and Antichristian Tyranny in their room. And whereas the only way of Christs acting his Authority over the Churches, and of communicating Authority unto them, to be acted by them in his Name, is by his Word and Spirit, which he hath given to continue in his Church unto that end unto the consummation of all things, the *Pope of Rome* placing himself in his stead for these ends, doth thereby *sit in the Temple of God,* and *shew himself to be God.* But this is sufficiently

ciently confuted among all sober Christians; and those who embrace it, may be left to contend with the *Mahometans*, who affirm, that *Jesus* left *John* the *Baptist* to be his Successor, as *Haly* succeeded unto *Mahomet*.

5. ALL these, by whom the ordinary Rule of the Church is to be exercised unto its Edification, are as unto their Office and Power *given unto the Church*, set or placed in it, not as *Lords of their Faith*, but as helpers of their joy, 1 Cor. 2. 2. Chap. 3. 21, 22, 23. 2 Cor. 1. 24. *Ephes.* 4. 11, 12, 13, 14. 1 Pet. 5. 1, 2. For the Church is the *Spouse of Christ, the Lambs Wife*; and by virtue of that Relation the enfeoffment into this power is her Due and Dowry; all particular Persons are but her Servants for Chrifts sake. For though some of them be *Stewards*, and set over all their fellow Servants, yet he hath not given them the trust of power to rule his Spouse at their own will, and to grant what they please unto her.

6. BUT as this *whole Church Power* is committed unto the *whole* Church by Christ; so all that are called unto the peculiar exercise of any part of it, by virtue of Office-Authority, do receive that Authority from him by the only way of the communication of it, namely, by his Word and Spirit through the *Ministry of the Church*, whereof we shall treat afterwards.

V. THESE things being thus premised in general concerning Church Power, we must treat yet particularly of the *communication of it from Christ*, and of its distribution as unto its Residence in the Church.

1. EVERY *Individual Believer* hath *Power* or Right given unto him upon his believing to *become the Son of God*, *Joh.* 1. 12. Hereby, as such, he hath a Right and Title radically and originally unto, with an interest in all Church Privileges, to be actually possessed and used according to the Rules by him prescribed. For he that is a *Son of God* hath a right unto all the privileges and advantages of the *Family of God*, as well as he is obliged unto all the Duties of it. Herein lies the foundation of all right unto Church Power, for both it, and all that belongs unto it, is a part of the *purchased Inheritance*, whereunto right is granted by Adoption; wherefore, the first original grant of

all

all Church Power and Privileges is made unto Believers as such. Theirs it is with these Two Limitations; (1.) That *as such only* they cannot exercise any Church Power, but upon their due observation of all Rules and Duties given unto this end; such are *Joint Confession and Confederation*. (2.) That each individual, do actually participate therein, according to the especial Rules of the Church, which peculiarly respects *Women* that do believe.

2. WHERE-ever there are *two or three of these Believers*, (the smallest number) *Right and Power* is granted unto them, actually to *meet together* in the name of Christ, for their mutual Edification, whereunto he hath promised his presence among them, *Matth*. 18. 19, 20. To *meet and to do any thing in the name of Christ*; as to exhort, instruct and admonish one another, or to pray together, as *v*. 19. there is an especial Right or Power required thereunto. This is granted by Jesus Christ unto the least number of *consenting Believers*. And this is a *second preparation* unto the communication of Church Power. Unto the former, *Faith* only is required, unto this, *Profession* with mutual consent unto, and agreement in the Evangelical Duties mentioned, are to be added.

3. WHERE the *number* of Believers is encreased, so as that they are sufficient as unto their *number* to observe and *perform all Church Duties* in the way and manner prescribed for their performance, they *have Right and Power* granted unto them, to make a *joint solemn Confession of their Faith*, especially as unto the Person of Christ and his Mediation, *Matth*. 16. 16, 18. as also to give up themselves unto him and to one another, in an holy Agreement or *Confederation* to do and observe all things whatever that he hath Commanded. Hereon, by virtue of his Laws in his Institutions and Commands, he gives them *power to do all things in their Order* which he grants unto his Church, and enstates them in all the Rights and Privileges thereof. These Believers, I say, thus congregated into a Church State, have immediately by virtue thereof, *power to take care that all things be done among them, as by the Lord Christ they are Commanded to be done, in and by his Church*.

F 2   THIS

Of the Polity, Rule, or Discipline

THIS therefore is the Church *Essential* and *Homogeneal*, unto which the Lord Christ hath granted all that Church Power which we enquire after, made it the Seat of all Ordinances of his Worship, and the Tabernacle wherein he will dwell. Nor since the ceasing of *extraordinary Officers*, is there any other way possible for the congregating of any Church, than what doth virtually include the things we have mentioned.

4. BUT yet this Church State is not compleat; nor are the ends of its institution attainable in this State. For the Lord Christ hath appointed such things in and unto it, which in this State it cannot observe. For he hath given *Authority* unto his Church to be exercised both in its Rule and in the Administration of his solemn Ordinances of Worship. The things before mentioned, are all of them acts of *Right* and *Power*, but not of *Authority*.

5. WHEREFORE the Lord Christ hath ordained *Offices*, and appointed *Officers* to be established in the Church, *Ephes.* 4. 13, 14. Unto these is all *Church Authority* granted. For all *Authority* is an act of Office-Power, which is that which gives unto what is performed by the Officers of the Church, the formal nature of Authority.

6. THEREFORE unto the Church, in the State before described, *Right and Power* is granted by Christ to *call, chuse, appoint and set apart* persons made meet for the work of the Offices appointed by him, in the ways and by the means appointed by him. Nor is there any other way whereby *ordinary Officers* may be fixed in the Church, as we have proved before, and shall farther confirm afterwards.

THAT which hereon we must enquire into, is, How or by what means, or by what acts of his Sovereign Power, the Lord Christ doth communicate *Office-Power*, and therewith the *Office* it self unto any persons whereon their Authority is directly *from him*; and what are the Acts or Duties of the Church in the collation of this Authority.

THE *Acts* of Christ herein may be reduced unto these Heads.

1. HE

1. HE hath inſtituted and appointed the Offices themſelves, and made a *grant* of them unto the Church for its Edification. As alſo, he hath determined and limited the *Powers* and *Duties* of the Officers. It is not in the power of any or of all the Churches in the World, to appoint any *Office* or *Officer* in the Church, that Chriſt hath not appointed. And where there are any ſuch, they can have no Church Authority properly ſo called; for that entirely riſeth from, and is reſolved into the inſtitution of the *Office* by Chriſt himſelf. And hence, in the firſt place all the Authority of *Officers* in the Church proceeds from the Authority of Chriſt in the inſtitution of the *Office* it ſelf; for that which gives *being* unto any thing, gives it alſo its *eſſential properties*.

2. BY virtue of his *Relation* unto the Church as its *Head*, of his *Kingly Power* over it and care of it, whereon the continuation and edification of the Church in this World do depend; where ever he hath a Church called, he furniſheth ſome perſons with ſuch *Gifts*, *Abilities* and *Endowments*, as are neceſſary to the diſcharge of ſuch Offices, in the Powers, Works and Duties of them. For it is moſt unqueſtionably evident, both in the nature of the thing it ſelf, and in his inſtitution, that there are ſome *eſpecial Abilities* and Qualifications required to the diſcharge of every Church Office. Wherefore, where the Lord Chriſt doth not communicate of *theſe Abilities* in ſuch a meaſure as by virtue of them *Church Order may be obſerved*, *Church Power exerciſed*, *and all Church Ordinances adminiſtred according to his mind unto the Edification of the Church*, it is no more in the power of Men to conſtitute Officers, than to erect or create an Office in the Church, *Epheſ*. 4. 11, 12, 13. 1 *Cor*. 12. 4, 5, 6, 7, 8, *&c*. *Rom*. 12. 6.

THIS collation of ſpiritual Gifts and Abilities for *Office* by Jeſus Chriſt unto any; doth not immediately conſtitute all thoſe, or any of them, Officers in the Church, on whom they are collated, without the obſervation of that *Method and Order* which he hath appointed in the Church for the communication of Office-Power; yet is it ſo *prerequiſite* thereunto, that no perſon not made partaker of them in the meaſure before mentioned,

mentioned, can, by virtue of any *outward Rites*, Order or Power, be really vested in the Ministry.

3. THIS *communication of Office-Power* on the part of Christ, consists in his institution and appointment of the *way and means*, whereby persons *gifted and qualified* by himself, ought to be actually admitted into their Offices, so as to administer the Powers, and perform the Duties of them. For the *way of their Call and Ordination*, whereof we shall speak afterwards, is efficacious unto this end of *communicating Office-Power*, meerly from *his institution* and appointment of it. And what is not so, can have no *causal influence* into the communication of this Power. For although sundry things belonging hereunto are directed by the *light of Nature*, as it is, that where one Man is set over others in Power and Authority, which before he had no natural right unto, it should be by their own consent and choice: And some things are of a *moral nature*, as that especial prayer be used in and about affairs that need especial divine assistance and favour; and there may be some *circumstances* of outward actions herein, not to be determined but by the Rule of Reason on the present posture of occasions; yet nothing hath any *causal influence* into the communication of Office-Power, but what is of the institution and appointment of Christ. By virtue hereof, all that are called unto this Office, do derive all their Power and Authority from him alone.

4. HE hath hereon given *Commands* unto the whole Church to *submit themselves* unto the Authority of these Officers in the discharge of their Office, who are so appointed, so prepared or qualified, so called by himself, and to obey them in all things, according unto the limitations which himself also hath given unto the Power and Authority of such Officers. For they who are called unto Rule and Authority in the Church by virtue of their Office, are not thereon admitted unto an *unlimited* Power to be exercised at their pleasure in a Lordly or *Despotical* manner; but their Power is stated, bounded, limited and confined as to the objects of it, its Acts, its manner of Administration, its Ends, and as unto all things wherein it is concerned. The swelling over these Banks by *Ambition*, the breaking up of these bounds

bounds by Pride and love of Domination, by the introduction of a Power over the perfons of Men in their outward concerns, exercifed in a Legal, Coercive, Lordly manner, are fufficient to make a forfeiture of all Church Power in them who are guilty of them. But after that fome Men faw it fit to tranfgrefs the bounds of Power and Authority prefcribed and limited unto them by the Lord Chrift; which was really *exclufive* of Lordfhip, Dominion and all Elation above their Brethren, leaving them *Servants to the Church for Chrifts fake*, they began to prefcribe bounds unto themfelves, fuch as were fuited unto their Intereft, which they called *Rules* or *Canons*, and never left enlarging them at their pleafure, untill they enftated the moft *abfolute Tyranny* in and over the Church, that ever was in the World.

BY thefe ways and means doth the Lord Chrift *communicate Office Power* unto them that are called thereunto, whereon they become not the Officers or Minifters of Men, no, not of the Church, as unto the actings and exercife of their Authority, but only as the good and edification of the Church is the end of it; but the Officers and Minifters of Chrift himfelf.

2. IT is hence evident, that in the communication of Church Power in Office unto any perfons called thereunto, the work and duty of the Church confifts *formally* in *Acts of Obedience* unto the Commands of Chrift. Hence, it doth not give unto fuch Officers a Power or Authority that was *formally* and *actually* in the Body of the Community, by virtue of any Grant or Law of Chrift, fo as that they fhould receive and act the Power of the Church, by virtue of a Delegation from them; but only they defign, chufe, fet apart the individual perfons, who thereon are intrufted with Office-Power by Chrift himfelf, according as was before declared. This is the Power and Right given unto the Church *effentially* confidered with refpect unto their Officers, namely to defign, call, chufe, and fet apart the perfons by the ways of Chrifts appointment unto thofe Offices, whereunto by his Laws he hath annexed Church Power and Authority.

WE

Of the Polity, Rule, or Discipline

WE need not therefore trouble our selves with the disputes about the *first subject* of Church Power, or any part of it. For it is a certain Rule, *That in the performance of all Duties which the Lord Christ requires, either of the whole Church, or of any in the Church, especially of the Officers, they are the first subject of the Power needful unto such Duties*, who are immediately called unto them. Hereby, all things become to be done in the Name and Authority of Christ. For the Power of the Church, is nothing but a right to perform Church Duties in obedience unto the Commands of Christ, and according unto his mind. Wherefore all Church Power is *originally* given unto the Church *essentially* considered, which hath a double exercise; First, in the *call* or choosing of Officers; Secondly, in their *voluntary acting* with them and under them in all Duties of Rule. (1.) All *Authority* in the Church is committed by Christ unto the Officers or Rulers of it, as unto all Acts and Duties whereunto Office-Power is required; and, (2.) Every individual person hath the liberty of his own judgment, as unto his own consent or dissent in what he is himself concerned.

THAT this Power under the name of the *Keys of the Kingdom of Heaven* was originally granted unto the whole professing Church of Believers, and that it is utterly impossible it should reside in any other who is subject unto Death, or if to be renewed upon any *occasional intermission*, is so fully proved by all *Protestant Writers* against the Papists, that it needs not on this occasion be again insisted on.

VI. THESE things have been spoken concerning the *Polity of the Church in General*, as it is taken *objectively* for the constitution of its State, and the laws of its Rule; we are in the next place to consider it *subjectively*, as it is a *power or faculty of the minds of Men, unto whom the Rule of the Church is committed*. And in this sense it is the *wisdom or understanding* of the Officers of the Church, to exercise the Government in it appointed by Jesus Christ, or to rule it according to his Laws and Constitutions: Or,

THIS *Wisdom* is a *Spiritual Gift* (1 Cor. 12. 9.) *whereby the Officers of the Church are enabled to make a due application of all the*

of the Church in General.

the *Rules* and *Laws of Christ*, unto the *Edification* of the Church and all the Members of it.

UNTO the attaining of this *Wisdom*, are required, (1.) *Fervent Prayer* for it, *Jam.* 1. 5. (2.) *Diligent study of the Scripture*, to find out and understand the Rules given by Christ unto this purpose, *Ezra* 7. 6, 7, 9. 1 *Tim.* 2. 14, 15. (3.) *Humble waiting on God* for the Revelation of all that it is to be exercised about, *Ezek.* 43. 11. (4.) A *conscientious exercise* of the skill which they have received. Talents traded with duly will encrease. (5.) A continual *sense of the account* which is to be given of the discharge of this great trust, being called to rule in the House of God, *Heb.* 13. 17.

HOW much *this Wisdom* hath been neglected in Church Government; yea, how much it is despised in the World, is evident unto all. It is skill in the *Canon Law*, in the proceedings of vexatious Courts, with the Learning, Subtilty and Arts which are required thereunto, that is looked on as the *only skill* to be exercised in the Government of the Church. Without this a Man is esteemed no way meet to be employed in any part of the Church Government. And according as any do arrive unto a dexterity in this *Polity*, they are esteemed eminently useful. But these things belong not at all unto the Government of the Church appointed by Christ; nor can any sober Man think in his Conscience that so they do. What is the use of this Art and Trade, as unto political ends, we enquired. Nor is the *true wisdom* required unto this end, with the means of attaining of it, more despised, more neglected by any sort of Men in the World, than by those whose pretences unto *Ecclesiastical Rule* and Authority would make it most necessary unto them.

TWO things follow on the supposition laid down.

1. THAT the *Wisdom* intended is not promised unto *all the Members of the Church in General*; nor are they required to seek for it by the ways and means of attaining it before laid down; but respect is had herein only unto the *Officers* of the Church. Hereon dependeth the equity of the obedience of the people unto their Rulers. For *Wisdom for Rule* is

peculiarly

peculiarly granted unto them, and their Duty it is to seek after it in a peculiar manner. Wherefore, those who on every occasion are ready to advance their own Wisdom and Understanding in the affairs and proceedings of the Church, against the Wisdom of the Officers of it, are proud and disorderly.

I speak not this to give any countenance unto the out-cries of some, that all sorts of Men will suppose themselves *Wiser than their Rulers*, and to know what belongs unto the Government of the Church better than they; whereas, the Government which *they* exercise belongs not at all unto the Rule of the Church, determined and limited in the Scripture, as the meanest Christian can easily discern; nor is it pretended by themselves so to do: For they say that the Lord Christ hath prescribed nothing herein, but left it unto the Will and Wisdom of the Church to order all things as they see necessary, which *Church* they are. Wherefore, if that will please them, it shall be granted, that in *skill* for the management of *Ecclesiastical Affairs* according to the *Canon Law*, with such other Rules of the same kind as they have framed, and in the legal proceedings of *Ecclesiastical Courts*, as they are called, there are none of the people that are equal unto them, or will contend with them.

2. IT hence also follows, that those *who are called unto Rule in the Church of* Christ, should diligently endeavour the attaining of, and encreasing in this *Wisdom*, giving evidence thereof on all occasions, that the Church may safely acquiesce in their Rule. But hereunto so many things do belong, as cannot in this place be meetly treated of; somewhat that appertains to them shall afterwards be considered.

CHAP.

CHAP. IV.

The Officers of the Church.

THE Church is considered either as it is *Essential* with respect unto its Nature and Being; or as it is *Organical* with respect unto its Order.

THE constituent causes and parts of the Church as unto its *Essence* and Being, are its *Institution, Matter* and *Form*; whereof we have treated.

ITS Order as it is *Organical*, is founded in that communication of Power unto it from Christ, which was insisted on in the foregoing Chapter.

THE *Organizing* of a Church, is the placing or implanting in it those *Officers* which the Lord Jesus Christ hath appointed to act and exercise his Authority therein.

FOR the *Rule* and *Government* of the Church, are the exertion of the Authority of Christ in the hands of them unto whom it is committed, that is the *Officers* of it; not that all *Officers* are called to Rule, but that none are called to Rule that are not so.

THE Officers of the Church in General are of two sorts; *Bishops* and *Deacons, Phil.* 1. 1. And their Work is distributed into *Prophecy* and *Ministry, Rom.* 12. 6. 7.

THE *Bishops* or *Elders* are of two sorts; (1.) Such as have *Authority* to *Teach* and Administer the Sacraments, which is commonly called the *power of Order*, and also of *Ruling*, which is called a *Power of Jurisdiction* corruptly: And some have only *Power for Rule*; of which sort, there are some in all the Churches in the World.

THOSE of the first sort are distinguished into *Pastors* and *Teachers*.

THE distinction between the *Elders* themselves, is not like that between *Elders* and *Deacons*, which is as unto the whole kind

kind or nature of the *Office*; but only with respect unto *Work* and Order, whereof we shall treat distinctly.

THE first sort of Officers in the Church are *Bishops* or *Elders*; concerning whom there have been mighty contentions in the *late Ages* of the Church. The Principles we have hitherto proceeded on, discharge us from any especial interest or concernment in this Controversy. For if there be no Church of Divine or Apostolical constitution, none in Being in the Second or Third *Centuries*, but only a particular Congregation, the foundation of that contest which is about *Preheminence and Power in the same Person over many Churches*, falls to the ground.

INDEED, strife about *Power, Superiority, and Jurisdiction* over one another, amongst those who pretend to be Ministers of the Gospel, is full of scandal. It started early in the Church; was *extinguished* by the Lord Christ in his Apostles; *rebuked* by the Apostles in all others; yet through the Pride, Ambition and Avarice of Men, hath grown to be the stain and shame of the Church in most Ages. For neither the sense of the Authority of Christ forbidding such ambitious designings, nor the proposal of his own *example* in this particular case; nor the experience of their own insufficiency for the least part of the work of the Gospel-Ministry, have been able to restrain the minds of Men from coveting after and contending for a prerogative in Church-Power over others. For though this *Ambition*, and all the fruits or rewards of it, are laid under a severe interdict by our Lord Jesus Christ, yet when Men (like *Achan*) saw the *wedge of Gold*, and the *goodly Babylonish Garment*, that they thought to be in Power, Domination and Wealth, they *coveted* them, and took them, to the great disturbance of the Church of God.

Matth. 18. 1, 2, 3, 4. Chap. 23. 7, 8, 9, 10, 11. *Luke* 22. 24, 25, 26, 27. 1 *Pet.* 5. 1, 2, 3, 4, 5. 2 *Joh.* 9. 10.

IF Men would but a little seriously consider, what there is in that care of Souls, even of all them over whom they pretend *Church-Power*, Rule or Jurisdiction; and what it is to give an *Account* concerning them before the Judgment Seat of Christ, it may be it would abate of their earnestness in contending for the enlargement of their *Cures*.

THE

The Officers of the Church.

THE claim of *Episcopacy*, as consisting in a rank of persons distinct from the Office of *Presbyters*, is managed with great variety. It is not agreed whether they are distinct in *Order* above them, or only as unto a certain *degree* among them of the *same* Order. It is not determined, what doth constitute that pretended *distinct Order*, nor wherein that *degree* of preheminence in the same Order, doth consist, nor what *Basis* it stands upon. It is not agreed whether this Order of *Bishops*, hath any Church-Power appropriated unto it, so as to be acted singly by themselves alone, without the concurrence of the *Presbyters*; or how far that concurrence is necessary in all Acts of Church-Order or Power. There are no Bounds or Limits of the *Dioceses* which they claim the Rule in and over, as Churches whereunto they are peculiarly related, derived either from Divine *Institution*, or *Tradition*, or general Rules of Reason respecting both or either of them; or from the consideration of Gifts and Abilities, or any thing else wherein Church-Order or Edification is concerned. Those who plead for *Diocesan Episcopacy*, will not proceed any farther, but only that there is and ought to be a *superiority in Bishops over Presbyters* in Order or Degree. But whether this must be over *Presbyters* in *one Church* only, or in many *distinct* Churches; whether it must be such, as not only hinders them utterly from the discharge of any of the Duties of the *Pastoral Office*, towards the most of them whom they esteem their Flocks, and necessitates them unto a Rule by *unscriptural* Church-Officers, Laws and Power, they suppose doth not belong unto their Cause; whereas indeed the weight and moment of it, doth lie in and depend on these things. Innumerable other *uncertainties*, *differences* and variances there are about this *singular Episcopacy*, which we are not at present concern'd to enquire into, nor shall I insist on any of those which have been already mentioned.

BUT yet, because it is necessary unto the clearing of the *Evangelical Pastoral Office*, which is now under consideration; unto what hath been pleaded before about the *non institution* of any Churches beyond *particular Congregations*, which is utterly exclusive of all pretences of the *present Episcopacy*,

I shall

I shall briefly, as in a diversion, add the Arguments which undeniably prove, That in the whole *New Testament*, *Bishops* and *Presbyters*, or *Elders*, are every way the same Persons, in the same Office, have the same Function, without distinction in Order or Degree; which also, as unto the Scripture, the most learned Advocates of Prelacy begin to grant.

1. THE Apostle describing what ought to be the Qualifications of *Presbyters* or *Elders*, gives this Reason of it, *because a Bishop must be so*, Tit. 1. 5, 6, 7. *Ordain Elders in every City, if any be blameless*, &c. *for a Bishop must be blameless*. He that would prove of what sort a *Presbyter* that is to be Ordained so, ought to be, gives this Reason for it, That *such a Bishop ought to be*, intends the same Person and Office by *Presbyter* and *Bishop*, or there is no congruity of Speech, or consequence of Reason in what he asserts. To suppose that the Apostle doth not intend the *same Persons*, and the *same Office* by *Presbyters* and *Bishops* in the same place, is to destroy his Argument, and render the context of his discourse unintelligible. He that will say, that if you make a *Justice of Peace* or a *Constable*, he must be magnanimous, liberal, full of clemency and courage, for so a *King* ought to be, will not be thought to argue very wisely. Yet such is the Argument here, if by *Elders* and *Bishops*, distinct Orders and Offices are intended.

2. THERE were *many Bishops* in one City in one particular Church, Phil. 1. 1. *To all the Saints that are at Philippi, with the Bishops and Deacons.* That the Church then at *Philippi* was one particular Church or Congregation was proved before. But to have *many Bishops* in the same Church, whereas the nature of the *Episcopacy* pleaded for, consists in the Superiority of *one over the Presbyters* of many Churches, is absolutely inconsistent. Such *Bishops*, whereof there may be many in the same Church, of the same Order, equal in Power and Dignity with respect unto Office, will easily be granted; but then they are *Presbyters* as well as *Bishops*. There will, I fear, be no end of this contest, because of the prejudices and interests of some; but that the identity of *Bishops* and *Presbyters* should be more plainly expressed, can neither be expected nor desired.

3. THE

The Officers of the Church. 47

3. THE Apostle being at *Miletus*, sent to *Ephesus* for the Elders of the Church to come unto him, that is the Elders of the *Church* at *Ephesus*, as hath been elsewhere undeniably demonstrated, *Act.* 20. 17, 18. unto these Elders he says, *Take heed unto your selves, and to all the Flock, over which the Holy Ghost hath made you Bishops, to feed the Church of God*, ver. 28. If *Elders* and *Bishops* be not the same Persons, having the same Office, the same Function and the same Duties, and the same Names, it is impossible, so far as I understand, how it should be expressed. For these *Elders* are they whom the Holy Ghost made *Bishops*; they were *many* of them in the same Church; their Duty it was to *attend* unto the Flock; and to *feed* the Church, which comprize all the Duties, the whole Function of *Elders* and *Bishops*, which must therefore be the same. This plain Testimony can no way be evaded by pretences and conjectures unwritten and uncertain; the only answer unto it, is, It was indeed so then, but it was otherwise afterwards; which some now betake themselves unto. But these *Elders* were either *Elders only* and *not Bishops*; or *Bishops only* and *not Elders*; or the same Persons were Elders and Bishops, as is plainly affirmed in the words. The latter is that which we plead. If the first be asserted, then was there no *Bishop* then at *Ephesus*; for these *Elders* had the whole oversight of the Flock: If the Second, then were there no *Elders* at all, which is no good exposition of those words, *that Paul called unto him the Elders of the Church*.

4. THE Apostle *Peter* writes unto the *Elders of the Churches*, that they should feed the Flock, ἐπισκοποῦντες; taking the oversight, or exercising the *Office and Function of Bishops* over them, and that not as *Lords* but as *ensamples* (of Humility, Obedience and Holiness) to the whole Flock, 1 *Pet.* 5. 1, 2, 3. Those on whom it is incumbent to *feed the Flock*, and to superintend over it, as those who in the first place are accountable unto Jesus Christ, are Bishops; and such as have no *other Bishop* over them, unto whom this charge should be principally committed. But such, according unto this Apostle, are the *Elders* of the Church. Wherefore, those Elders and Bishops are the same.

And

And such were the ἡγούμενοι, the *Guides* of the Church at *Jerusalem*, whom the members of it were *bound to obey*, as those that did *watch for*, and were to give an account of their Souls. Heb. 13. 17.

5. THE substance of these and all other Instances or Testimonies of the same kind, is this; *Those whose names are the same equally common and applicable unto them all, whose Function is the same, whose Qualifications and Characters are the same, whose Duties, Account and Reward are the same, concerning whom there is in no one place of Scripture the least mention of inequality, disparity or preference in Office among them, they are essentially and every way the same.* That thus it is with the *Elders* and *Bishops* in the Scripture cannot modestly be denied.

I do acknowledge that where a Church is greatly encreased, so as that there is a necessity of *many Elders* in it for its Instruction and Rule, that *Decency* and *Order* do require, that one of them do in the management of all Church Affairs *preside*, to guide and direct the way and manner thereof. So the *Presbyters* at *Alexandria* did choose one from among themselves that should have the preheminence of a President among them. Whether the Person that is so to preside, be directed unto by being first *Converted* or first *Ordained*, or on the account of *Age*, or of *Gifts* and Abilities, whether he continue for a *Season* only, and then another be deputed unto the same Work, or *for his Life*, are things in themselves indifferent, to be determined according unto the General Rules of Reason and Order, with respect unto the Edification of the Church.

I shall never oppose this *Order*, but rather desire to see it in practice; namely, that particular Churches were of such an extent, as necessarily to require *many Elders* both Teaching and Ruling for their Instruction and Government; for the better observation of Order and Decency in the publick Assemblies; the fuller Representation of the Authority committed by Jesus Christ unto the Officers of his Church; the occasional instruction of the Members in *lesser Assemblies*, which as unto some ends may be stated also, with the due attendance unto all other means of *Edification* and Watching, Inspecting, Warning, Admonishing, Exhorting

Exhorting, and the like; and that *among these Elders* one should be chosen by themselves, with the consent of the Church, not into a New *Order*, not into a *degree of Authority* above his Brethren, but only unto his part of the common work in a peculiar manner, which requires some kind of *Precedency*. Hereby no New Officer, no New Order of Officers, no New *degree* of Power or Authority is constituted in the Church; only the Work and Duty of it is cast into such an *Order*, as the very light of nature doth require.

BUT there is not any intimation in the Scripture of the least imparity or inequality, in Order, Degree or Authority, among Officers of the same sort, whether extraordinary or ordinary. The *Apostles* were all *equal*; so were the *Evangelists*, so were *Elders* or *Bishops*, and so were *Deacons* also. The Scripture knows no more of an *Arch-Bishop*, such as all *Diocesan Bishops* are, nor an *Arch-Deacon*, than of an *Arch-Apostle*, or of an *Arch-Evangelist*, or an *Arch-Prophet*. Howbeit, it is evident, that in all their Assemblies, they had *one* who did preside in the manner before described, which seems among the Apostles to have been the prerogative of *Peter*.

THE *Brethren* also of the Church may be so *multiplied*, as that the constant meeting of them all in *one place* may not be absolutely best for their Edification. Howbeit, that on all the solemn occasions of the Church whereunto their *consent* is necessary, they did of old and ought still, to meet in *the same place* for advise, consultation and consent, as was proved before. This is so fully expressed and exemplified in the two great Churches of *Jerusalem* and *Antioch*, *Act.* 15. that it cannot be gain-said. When *Paul* and *Barnabas*, sent by the Brethren or Church at *Antioch* (*v.* 1, 3.) were come to *Jerusalem*, they were received by the *Church*, as the *Brethren* are called in distinction from the *Apostles* and *Elders*, v. 4. So when the *Apostles* and *Elders* assembled to consider of the case proposed unto them, the whole *multitude* of the Church, that is the *Brethren* assembled with them, *v.* 6, 12. neither were they *mute Persons*, meer Auditors and Spectators in the Assembly, but they concurred both in the debate and determination of the Question; inso-
much

much as they are expresly joined with the *Apostles and Elders* in the advice given, *ver.* 22, 23. And when *Paul* and *Barnabas* returned unto *Antioch*, the *multitude* unto whom the Letter of the Church at *Jerusalem* was directed, came together about it, *ver.* 23. 30. Unless this be observed the *Primitive-Church-State* is overthrown: But I shall return from this Digression.

THE first Officer or Elder of the Church is the *Pastor*. A *Pastor*, is the Elder that *Feeds and Rules the Flock*, 1 Pet. 5. 2. that is, who is its *Teacher* and its *Bishop*; ποιμαίνατε, ἐπισκοποῦντες, Feed, taking the oversight.

IT is not my present design nor work to give a full account of the *Qualifications* required in Persons to be *called* unto this Office; nor of their *Duty* and *Work*, with the Qualities or Vertues to be exercised therein. It would require a large Discourse to handle them practically, and it hath been done by others. It were to be wished, that what is of this kind expressed in the Rule, and which the nature of the Office doth indispensably require, were more exemplified in practice than it is. But some things relating unto this *Officer* and his *Office* that are needful to be well stated, I shall treat concerning.

THE *name* of a *Pastor* or *Shepherd* is *Metaphorical*. It is a Denomination suited unto his Work, denoting the same Office and Person with a *Bishop* or *Elder*, spoken of absolutely without limitation unto either *Teaching* or *Ruling*. And it seems to be used or applied unto this Office, because it is more comprehensive of, and instructive in all the Duties that belong unto it, than any other Name whatever; nay, than all of them put together. The Grounds and Reasons of this *Metaphor*, or whence the Church is called a *Flock*, and whence God termeth himself the *Shepherd of the Flock*; whence the *Sheep* of this Flock are committed unto Christ, whereon he becomes the *good Shepherd that lays down his Life for the Sheep*, and the *Prince of Shepherds*; what is the interest of Men in a *participation* of this Office, and what their Duty thereon, are things well worth the consideration of them who are called unto it. *Hirelings*, yea, *Wolves* and *dumb Dogs*, do in many places take on themselves to be *Shepherds* of the Flock, by whom it is devoured and destroyed.

Act. 20.18, 29.
1 *Pet.* 5. 2, 3.
Cant. 1. 7.
Jerem. 13. 17.
Chap. 23. 2.
Ezek. 34. 3.
Gen. 49. 24.
Psal. 23.1.
Psal. 80. 1.
Joh. 10. 11, 14, 16.
Heb. 13. 20.
1 *Pet* 2.25.
Chap. 5. 4.

WHEREAS

The Officers of the Church.

WHEREAS therefore this *Name* or Appellation is taken from, and includes in it *Love, Care, Tenderness, Watchfulness* in all the Duties of *going before, preserving, feeding, defending* the Flock, the Sheep and the Lambs, the Strong, the Weak and Diseased, with accountableness as Servants unto the *chief Shepherd*, it was generally disused in the Church; and those of *Bishops* or *Overseers, Guides, Presidents, Elders* which seem to include more of Honour and Authority, were retained in common use; that though one of them, at last, namely that of *Bishops*, with some elating compositions and adjuncts of power, obtained the preheminence. Out of the Corruption of these Compositions and Additions in *Arch-Bishops, Metropolitans, Patriarchs*, and the like, brake forth the *Cockatrice* of the Church, that is the *Pope*.

BUT this name is by the Holy Ghost appropriated unto the *principal Ministers* of Christ in his Church, *Ephes.* 4. 11. And under that name they were promised unto the Church of old, *Jerem.* 3. 15. And the Work of these Pastors, is to *feed* the Flock committed to their charge as it is constantly required of them, *Act.* 20. 29. 1 *Pet.* 5. 2.

OF *Pastoral Feeding* there are two parts. (1.) *Teaching* or Instruction. (2.) *Rule* or Discipline. Unto these two Heads may all the Acts and Duties of a *Shepherd* toward his Flock be reduced. And both are intended in the term of *feeding*, 1 *Chron.* 11. 2. Chap. 17. 6. *Jer.* 23. 2. *Mic.* 5. 4. Chap. 7. 14. *Zech.* 11. 7. *Act.* 20. 28. *Joh.* 21. 14. 1 *Pet.* 5. 2, *&c.* wherefore he who is the *Pastor*, is the *Bishop*, the *Elder*, the *Teacher* of the Church.

THESE Works of *Teaching* and *Ruling* may be distinct in several Officers, namely of *Teachers* and *Rulers*; but to divide them in the same Office of Pastors, that some Pastors should *feed by Teaching only*, but have no right to Rule by Virtue of their Office; and some should attend in exercise unto *Rule only*, not esteeming themselves obliged to labour continually in *feeding the Flock*, is almost to overthrow this Office of Christs Designation, and to set up *two* in the room of it, of Mens own projection.

H 2 OF

The Officers of the Church.

OF the *call* of Men unto this Office, so many things have been spoken and written by others at large, that I shall only insist, and that very briefly, on some things which are either of the most *important consideration*, or have been *omitted* by others: As,

1. UNTO the *call* of any person unto this Office of a *Pastor* in the Church, there are certain *Qualifications* previously required in him, disposing and making him fit for that Office. The *outward call* is an act of the Church, as we shall shew immediately. But therein is required an obediential acting of him also who is called. Neither of these can be Regular, neither can the Church act according to Rule and Order, nor the person called act in such a due Obedience, unless there are in him some *previous Indications* of the mind of God, designing the person to be called by such Qualifications, as may render him meet and able for the discharge of his Office and Work. For *ordinary vocation* is not a *collation* of Gracious *Spiritual Abilities* suiting and making Men meet for the Pastoral Office: But it is the communication of *Right* and *Power* for the regular use and exercise of Gifts and Abilities received antecedently unto that call, unto the Edification of the Church, wherein the Office it self doth consist. And if we would know what these Qualifications and Endowments are for the substance of them, we may learn them in their *great example* and pattern, our Lord Jesus Christ himself. Our Lord Jesus Christ being the *good Shepherd*, whose the Sheep are, the *Shepherd* and *Bishop* of our Souls; the *chief Shepherd*, did design in the undertaking and exercise of his *Pastoral Office*, to give a *Type* and *Example* unto all those who are to be called unto the same Office under him. And if there be not a *conformity* unto him herein, no Man can assure his own Conscience or the Church of God, that he is or can be *lawfully called* unto this Office.

THE Qualifications of Christ unto, and the gracious Qualities of his Mind and Soul in the discharge of his *Pastoral Office*, may be referred unto Four Heads.

1. THAT *furniture with spiritual Gifts and Abilities* by the communication of the Holy Ghost unto him, in an unmeasurable fulness, whereby he was fitted for the discharge of his

The Officers of the Church.

his Office. This is expressed with respect unto his undertaking of it, *Isa.* 11. 2, 3. Chap. 61. 1, 2, 3. *Luk.* 4. 14. Herein was he *anointed with the oyl of gladness above his fellows*, Heb. 1. 9. But this *unction of the Spirit* is in a certain measure required in all who are called, or to be called unto the Pastoral Office, *Ephes.* 4. 1. That there are Spiritual Powers, Gifts and Abilities required unto the Gospel Ministry, I have at large declared in *another Treatise*, as also what they are. And where there are none of these Spiritual Abilities which are necessary unto the Edification of the Church in the Administration of Gospel Ordinances, as in Prayer, Preaching, and the like, no outward Call or Order can constitute any Man an *Evangelical Pastor*. As unto particular Persons I will not contend, as unto an *absolute nullity* in the Office by reason of their deficiency in *Spiritual Gifts*, unless it be gross, and such as renders them utterly useless unto the Edification of the Church. I only say, that no Man can in an *orderly way and manner* be called or set apart unto this Office, in whom there are not some *Indications* of Gods designation of him thereunto by his furniture with Spiritual Gifts, of Knowledge, Wisdom, Understanding and utterance for *Prayer and Preaching*, with other Ministerial Duties, in some competent measure.

2. *COMPASSION and love* to the Flock, were gloriously eminent in this *great Shepherd of the Sheep*. After other evidences hereof, he gave them that signal confirmation in *laying down his Life for them*. This Testimony of his *love* he insists upon himself, *Joh.* 10. And herein also his example ought to lie continually before the eyes of them who are called unto the *Pastoral Office*. Their entrance should be accompanied with *love* to the Souls of Men; and if the discharge of their Office be not animated with *love* unto their Flocks, Wolves or Hirelings, or Thieves they may be, but *Shepherds* they are not. Neither is the glory of the Gospel-Ministry more lost or defaced in any thing, or by any means, than by the evidence that is given among the most, of an *inconformity* unto Jesus Christ in their love unto the Flock. Alas! it is scarce once thought of amongst the most of them, who in various degrees take
upon

upon them the *Pastoral Office*; where are the fruits of it? what evidence is given of it in any kind? It is well, if some instead of laying down their own lives for them, do not by innumerable ways *destroy their Souls*.

3. THERE is and was in this great Shepherd a *continual watchfulness over the whole Flock* to keep it, to preserve it, to feed, to lead and cherish it, to purify and cleanse it, until it be presented unspotted unto God. He doth never *slumber nor sleep*; he watereth his Vineyard *every moment*, keeps it Night and Day that none may hurt it; looseth nothing of what is committed to him; see *Is*. 40. 11. I speak not distinctly of previous *Qualifications* unto an outward call only, but with a mixture of those *Qualities* and *Duties* which are required in the discharge of this Office. And herein also is the Lord Christ to be our example. And hereunto do belong, (1) *Constant Prayer* for the Flock. (2.) *Diligence* in the dispensation of the Word, with Wisdom as unto Times, Seasons, the state of the Flock in general, their light Knowledge, Ways, Walking, Ignorance, Temptations, Trials, Defections, Weaknesses of all sorts, Growth and Decays, *&c.* (3.) *Personal Admonition*, Exhortation, Consolation, Instruction, as their particular cases do require. (4.) All with a design to keep *them from evil*; and to present them *without blame* before Christ Jesus at the great day. But these and things of the like nature, presenting themselves with some earnestness unto my mind, I shall at present discharge my self of the thoughts of them, hoping a more convenient place and season to give them a larger Treat; and somewhat yet farther shall be spoken of them in the next Chapter.

4. ZEAL *for the Glory of God* in his whole Ministry, and in all the *ends* of it, had its continual residence in the holy Soul of the *great Shepherd*. Hence it is declared in an *expression* intimating that it was *inexpressible*. The zeal of thy House hath *eaten me up*. This also must accompany the discharge of the *Pastoral Office*, or it will find no acceptance with him. And the want of it, is one of those things which hath filled the World with a dead, faithless, fruitless Ministry.

The Officers of the Church.

5. AS he was abfolutely in himfelf *Holy, Harmlefs, Undefiled, feparate from Sinners*; fo a conformity unto him in thefe things, and that in *some degree of eminency* above others, is required in them who are called unto this *Office*.

AGAIN, none can or may *take this Office upon him*, or difcharge the Duties of it, which are peculiarly its own, with Authority, but he who is *called and fet apart thereunto* according to the mind of Jefus Chrift. The continuation of all Church-Order and 'Power, of the regular Adminiftration of all facred Ordinances, yea, of the very Being of the Church as it is *Organical*, depends on this Affertion. Some deny the continuation of the *Office* it felf, and of thofe Duties which are peculiar unto it, as the Adminiftration of the Sacraments. Some judge, that Perfons neither *called* nor *fet apart* unto this Office, may difcharge all the Duties and the whole Work of it; fome, that a *temporary delegation* of Power unto any by the Church, is all the warranty is neceffary for the undertaking and difcharge of this Office. Many have been the contefts about thefe things, occafioned by the ignorance and diforderly affections of fome Perfons. I fhall briefly reprefent the Truth herein with the Grounds of it; and proceed to the confideration of the *call* it felf, which is fo neceffary.

1. CHRIST himfelf in his own Perfon, and by his own Authority, was the Author of this Office. He gave it, appointed it, erected it in the Church, by virtue of his Sovereign Power and Authority, *Ephef.* 4. 11, 12. 1 *Cor.* 12. 28. As he gave, appointed, ordained an extraordinary Office of *Apoftlefhip*; fo he ordained, appointed and gave the ordinary *Office* of *Paftorfhip* or Teaching. They have both the fame Divine Original.

2. HE appointed this *Office* for *continuance*, or to abide in the Church unto the confummation of all things, *Ephef.* 4. 13. *Matth.* 28. 19. And therefore he took order by his Apoftles, that for the continuation of this Office, *Paftors, Elders* or *Bifhops*, fhould be called and ordained unto the care and difcharge of it in all Churches; which was done by them accordingly, *Act.* 14. 22, 23. Chap. 20. 28. 1 *Tim.* 3. 1, 2. *Tit.* 1. 5.

Wherein

Wherein he gave Rule unto all Churches unto the end of the World, and prescribed them their Duty.

3. ON this *Office*, and the discharge of it, he hath laid the whole weight of the *Order, Rule* and *Edification* of his Church, in his Name and by virtue of his Authority, *Act.* 20. 28. *Col.* 4. 17. 1 *Tim.* 3. 15. 1 *Pet.* 5. 1, 2, 3, 4, 5, 6. *Rev.* 2. 1, 2, 3, 4, 5, *&c.* Hereon a double necessity of the *continuation* of this Office doth depend ; *First*, that which ariseth from the *precept* or command of it, which made it necessary to the Church, on the account of the obedience which it owes to Christ ; and *Secondly* of its being the principal *ordinary means* of all the ends of Christ in and towards his Church. Wherefore, although he can himself *feed his Church in the Wilderness*, where it is deprived of all outward instituted means of Edification ; yet where this Office fails through its *neglect*, there is nothing but disorder, confusion and destruction, that will ensue thereon ; no promise of Feeding or Edification.

4. THE Lord Christ hath given *Commands* unto the Church, for Obedience unto those who enjoy and exercise this Office among them. Now all these Commands are needless and superfluous, nor can any *obedience* be yielded unto the Lord Christ in their observance, unless there be a continuation of this Office. And the Church loseth as much in Grace and privilege, as it loseth in Commands. For in obedience unto the Commands of Christ, doth Grace in its exercise consist, 1 *Tim.* 5. 17. *Heb.* 13. 7, 17.

5. THIS Office is accompanied with *Power* and *Authority*, which none can take or assume to themselves. All *Power and Authority*, whether in things Spiritual or Temporal, which is not either founded in the law of Nature, or collated by Divine Ordination, is Usurpation and Tyranny. No Man can of himself *take either Sword*. To invade an Office which includes Power and Authority over others, is to disturb all Right, Natural, Divine and Civil. That such an Authority is included in this Office, is evident, (1.) From the *names* ascribed unto them in whom it is vested ; as *Pastors, Bishops, Elders, Rulers*, all of them requiring of it. (2.) From the *Work* prescribed unto

unto them, which is *feeding by Rule and Teaching*. (3.) From the execution of Church-Power in *Discipline*, or the exercise of the *Keys of the Kingdom of Heaven* committed unto them. (4.) From the Commands given for *Obedience* unto them which respect Authority. (5.) From their appointment to be the *means and instruments* of exerting the Authority of Christ in the Church, which can be done no other way.

6. CHRIST hath appointed a *standing Rule of the calling of Men* unto this *Office*, as we shall see immediately. But if Men may enter upon it, and discharge it, without any such *Call*, that Rule, with the way of the *Call* prescribed, are altogether in vain. And there can be no greater affront unto the Authority of Christ in his Church, than to act in it, in neglect of, or opposition unto the *Rule* that he hath appointed for the exercise of Power in it.

7. THERE is an *accountable Trust* committed unto those *who* undertake this Office. The whole Flock, the Ministry it self, the Truths of the Gospel as to the preservation of them all, are committed to them, *Col.* 4. 17. 1 *Tim.* 6. 20. 2 *Tim.* 2. 2, 16, 23. *Act.* 20. 28. 1 *Pet.* 5. 1, 2, 3, 4, 5. *Heb.* 13. 17. *They who must give an account.* Nothing can be more wicked or foolish, than for a Man to *intrude himself into a Trust*, which is not committed unto him. They are branded as profligately wicked, who attempt any such thing among Men, which cannot be done without impudent falsification: And what shall he be esteemed who *intrudes himself* into the *highest Trust* that any Creature is capable off in the Name of Christ, and take upon him to give an *account* of its discharge at the last day, without any divine call or warranty?

8. THERE are unto the discharge of this Office *especial promises* granted and annexed of present Assistances, and future eternal Rewards, *Matth.* 28. 19. 1 *Pet.* 5. 4. Either these promises belong unto them who take this Office on themselves *without any Call*, or they do not. If they do not, then have they neither any *especial assistance* in their Work, nor can expect any *Reward* of their Labours. If it be said they have an interest in them, then the worst of Men may obtain the

I   benefit

benefit of *divine promises*, without any divine designation.

9. THE general force of the *Rule*, *Heb.* 5. 4. includes a prohibition of undertaking any *sacred Office* without a *divine Call*; and so the instances of such prohibitions under the Old Testament, as unto the Duties annexed unto an Office, as in the case of *Uzziah invading the Priesthood*, or of taking a Ministerial *Office* without Call or Mission, as *Jerem.* 27. 9, 14, 15. having respect unto the order of Gods Institutions, may be pleaded in this case.

10. WHOEVER therefore takes upon him the *Pastoral Office* without a lawful outward Call, doth *take unto himself Power and Authority* without any divine Warranty, which is a foundation of all disorder and confusion; interests himself in an *accountable Trust*, no way committed unto him; hath *no promise* of Assistance in, or *Reward* for his Work, but ingageth in that which is destructive of all Church-Order, and consequently of the very Being of the Church it self.

11. YET there are *three things* that are to be annexed unto this Assertion by way of *Limitation*: As, (1.) Many things performed by virtue of *Office* in a way of *Authority*, may be performed by others not called to *Office*, in a way of *Charity*. Such are the moral Duties of Exhorting, Admonishing, Comforting, Instructing and Praying with, and for one another. (2.) *Spiritual Gifts* may be exercised unto the Edification of others, without Office-Power, where order and opportunity do require it. But the constant *exercise of Spiritual Gifts in Preaching*, with a refusal of undertaking a Ministerial Office, or without design so to do upon a lawful Call, cannot be approved. (3.) The *Rules* proposed concern only ordinary cases, and the ordinary state of the Church; extraordinary cases are accompanied with a warranty in themselves for extraordinary Actings and Duties.

12. THE *Call* of Persons unto the *Pastoral Office* is an Act and Duty of the Church. It is not an Act of the *political Magistrate*, not of the *Pope*, not of any *single Prelate*, but of the whole Church, unto whom the Lord Christ hath committed the *Keys of the Kingdom of Heaven*. And indeed, although there be great

The Officers of the Church.

great differences about the nature and manner of the Call of Men unto this *Office*, yet none who understand ought of these things, can deny, but that it is an *Act* and *Duty* of the Church; which the Church alone is impowered by Christ to put forth and exert. But this will more fully appear in the consideration of the nature and manner of this Call of Men unto the *Pastoral Office*, and the actings of the Church therein.

THE *Call of persons* unto the *Pastoral Office* in the Church consists of Two Parts. (1.) *Election*, (2.) *Ordination*, as it is commonly called, or sacred Separation by Fasting and Prayer. As unto the former, Four things must be enquired into. (1.) What is *previous* unto it or preparatory for it. (2.) *Wherein* it doth consist. (3.) Its *necessity*, or the demonstration of its Truth and Institution. (4.) What influence it hath into the *communication* of *Pastoral-Office-Power* unto a Pastor so chosen.

1. THAT which is *previous unto it*, is, the *Meetness* of the Person for his *Office* and *Work*, that is to be chosen. It can never be the Duty of the Church to call or choose an *unmeet*, an unqualified, an unprepared Person unto this *Office*. No pretended necessity, no outward motives can enable or warrant it so to do, nor can it by any *outward act*, whatever the Rule or Solemnity of it be, communicate *Ministerial Authority* unto Persons utterly unqualified for, and uncapable of the discharge of the Pastoral Office according unto the Rule of the Scripture. And this hath been one great means of debasing the *Ministery*, and almost ruining the Church it self; either by the neglect of those who suppose themselves entrusted with the *whole power of Ordination*, or by Impositions on them by *Secular Power*, and *Patrons of Livings* as they are called, with the stated Regulation of their Proceedings herein, by a defective Law, whence there hath not been a due regard unto the antecedent preparatory Qualifications of those who are called unto the Ministry.

TWO ways is the *Meetness* of any one made known and to be judged of. (1.) By an *evidence* given of the *Qualifications* in him before-mentioned. The Church is not to call or choose any one to *Office* who is not *known* unto them; of whose frame of spirit, and walking, they have not had some experience;

not a *Novice*, or one lately come unto them. He must be one who by his ways and walking hath obtained a *good Report*, even among *them that are without*, so far as he is known; unless they be enemies or scoffers; and one that hath in some good measure evidenced his *Faith*, *Love and Obedience* unto Jesus Christ in the Church. This is the chief *Trust* that the Lord Christ hath committed unto his Churches; and if they are negligent herein, or if at all-adventures they will impose an Officer in his House upon him without satisfaction of his *Meetness* upon due enquiry, it is a great dishonour unto him, and provocation of him. Herein principally are Churches made the *Overseers* of their own Purity and Edification. To deny them an *Ability* of a right judgment herein, or a *liberty* for the use and exercise of it, is Error and Tyranny. But that Flock which *Christ purchased and purified with his own blood*, is thought by some to be little better than an Herd of brute Beasts. Where there is a defect of this personal knowledge for want of opportunity, it may be supplied by Testimonies of unquestionable Authority. (2.) By a *trial of his Gifts for Edification*. These are those Spiritual Endowments which the Lord Christ grants, and the Holy Spirit Works in the Minds of Men, for this very end that the Church may be profited by them, 1 *Cor.* 12. 7. And we must at present take it for granted, that every true Church of Christ, that is so in the *matter* and form of it, is able to judge in some competent measure what Gifts of Men are suited unto their own Edification. But yet in making a judgment hereof, one *Directive means* is the Advice of other Elders and Churches, which they are obliged to make use off by virtue of the Communion of Churches, and the avoidance of offence in their walk in that Communion.

2. AS to the *nature of this Election*, Call or Choice of a Person known, tried, and judged, meetly qualified for the *Pastoral Office*, it is an Act of the whole Church, that is, of the *Fraternity* with their *Elders*, if they have any. For a *Pastor* may be chosen unto a Church which hath other Teachers, Elders, or *Officers* already instated in it. In this case their concurrence in the choice intended, is necessary by way of common suffrage.

The Officers of the Church.

suffrage, not of Authority or Office-Power. For *Election* is not an *Act of Authority*, but of Liberty and Power, wherein the whole Church in the Fraternity is equal. If there be no *Officers* stated in the Church before, as it was with the Churches in the Primitive Times, on the first Ordination of Elders among them, this *Election* belongs unto the Fraternity.

3. THAT therefore which we have now to prove, is this; That it is the Mind and Will of Jesus Christ, that *meet* Persons should be called unto the *Pastoral Office* (or any other Office in the Church) by the *Election and Choice* of the Church it self whereunto they are called, antecedently unto a sacred solemn separation unto their respective Offices: For,

1. UNDER the *Old Testament* there were three ways whereby Men were called unto *Office* in the Church. (1.) They were so *extraordinarily* and immediately by the nomination and designation of God himself. So *Aaron* was called unto the Priesthood, and others afterward, as *Samuel*, to be Prophets. (2.) By a *law of Carnal Generation*; so all the Priests of the *Posterity of Aaron* succeeded into the *Office* of the Priesthood, without any other call. (3.) By the *choice of the people*, which was the call of all the ordinary Elders and Rulers of the Church, *Deut.* 1. 13. הָבוּ לָכֶם. *Give to your selves.* It was required of the people, that they should in the first place, make a judgment on their Qualifications for the Office whereunto they were called. Men known unto them for Wise, Understanding, Righteous, walking in the *Fear of God*, they were to look out, and then to present them unto *Moses* for their separation unto *Office*, which is Election. It is true, that *Exod.* 13. 15. It is said that *Moses chose the Elders*. But it is frequent in the Scripture, that where any thing is done by many, where *one* is chief, that is ascribed indifferently either to the *many*, or to the chief Director. So is it said, *Israel sent Messengers, Numbers*, 21. 21. *Moses*, speaking of the same things, says, *I sent Messengers*, Deut. 2. 26. So 1 Chron. 19. 19. *They made peace with David and served him*; which is 2 *Sam.* 10. 19. *They made peace with Israel and served them.* See also 2 *King.* 11. 12. with 2 *Chron.* 23. 11. as also 1 *Chron.* 16. 1. with 2 *Sam.* 6. 17. and the same may be observed in

in other places. Wherefore the people *chose these Elders* under the conduct and guidance of *Moses*, which directs us unto the right interpretation of *Act* 14. 23. whereof we shall speak immediately.

THE First of these ways was repeated in the foundation of the *Evangelical Church*. Christ himself was *called unto his Office* by the Father, through the unction of the spirit, *Isa.* 60. *Heb.* 5. And he himself called the *Apostles* and *Evangelists*, in whom that call ceased. The second ordinary way by the *privilege of natural Generation* of the stock of the Priests, was utterly abolished. The *third way* only remained, for the ordinary continuation of the Church; namely, by the *Choice and Election* of the Church it self, with solemn Separation and Dedication by *Officers* extraordinary or ordinary.

THE first instance of the Choice of a Church-Officer had a mixture in it of the *first* and *later* way, in the case of *Matthias*. As he was able to be a *Church-Officer* he had the choice and consent of the Church; as he was to be an *Apostle* or an extraordinary *Officer*, there was an immediate divine disposition of him into his *Office*; the latter to give him Apostolical Authority, the former to make him a president of the future actings of the Church in the call of their *Officers*.

I say this being the *first example* and pattern of the calling of any Person unto *Office* in the Christian Church-State, wherein there was an interposition of the ordinary actings of Men, is established as a *Rule* and President not to be changed, altered or departed from, in any Age of the Church whatever. It is so, as unto what was of *common Right* and Equity, which belonged unto the whole Church. And I cannot but wonder, how Men durst ever reject and disanul this *divine Example* and Rule. It will not avail them to say, that it is only a *matter of Fact*, and not a precept or institution that is recorded. For, (1.) It is a *Fact* left on record in the holy Scripture for our Instruction and Direction. (2.) It is an *example* of the Apostles and the whole Church proposed unto us, which in all things, not otherwise determined, hath the force of an institution. (3.) If there was no more in it but this, that we have a matter of

common

The Officers of the Church. 63

common Right, determined and applied by the Wifdom of the Apoftles, and the entire Church of *Believers* at that time in the World, it were an impiety to depart from it, unlefs in cafe of the utmoft neceffity.

WHEREAS, what is here recorded was in the call of an *Apoftle*, it ftrengthens the Argument which hence we plead. For if in the *extraordinary call* of an Apoftle, it was the mind of Chrift, that the Fraternity or *Multitude* fhould have the liberty of their fuffrage, how much more is it certainly his mind, that in the *ordinary call* of their own peculiar Officers, in whom, under him, the concernment is their own only, that this *Right* fhould be continued unto them?

THE order of the proceeding of the Church herein is diftinctly declared. For, (1.) The number of the Church at that time, that is of the *Men*, was about *an Hundred and Twenty*, *v*. 15. (2.) They were *affembled all together* in one place, fo as that *Peter* ftood up in the midft of them, *v*. 15. (3.) *Peter* in the name of the reft of the Apoftles, declares unto them the neceffity of *choofing one* to be fubftituted in the room of *Judas*, *v*. 16, 17, 18, 19, 20. (4.) He limits the choice of him unto the efpecial Qualification of being a *meet witnefs of the Refurrection of Chrift*, unto thofe who conftantly accompanied him with themfelves from the *Baptifm of John*, that is, his being Baptized by him, whereon he began his publick Miniftry. (5.) Among thefe they were left at their liberty to nominate any *two*, who were to be left unto the *lot* for a determination whether of them God defigned unto the *Office*. (6.) Hereon the *whole multitude* ἔστησε δυὸ, appointed Two; that is the ἄνδρες ἀδελφοί, *the Men and Brethren*, unto whom *Peter* fpake, *v*. 16. did fo. (7.) The fame Perfons to promote the work, *prayed and gave forth their Lots*, *v*. 24. 26. (8.) Συνκατεληφίσθη, Ματθίας *Matthias was by the common fuffrage of the whole Church*, reckoned unto the number of the Apoftles.

I fay not that thefe things were done by the Difciples in diftinction from *Peter* and the reft of the Apoftles, but in conjunction with them. *Peter* did nothing without them; nor did they any thing without him.

THE

The Officers of the Church.

THE exception of *Bellarmine* and others, againſt this Teſtimony, is, that it was a *grant and a condeſcention in Peter, and not a declaration of the Right of the Church; that it was an extraordinary caſe; that the determination of the whole was by Lot;* are of no validity. The pretended conceſſion of *Peter* is a figment; the caſe was ſo extraordinary, as to include in it all ordinary caſes, for the ſubſtance of them. And although the ultimate determination of the *Individual Perſon*, which was neceſſary unto his *Apoſtleſhip*, was immediately Divine *by Lot*; yet here is all granted unto the people, in their *chooſing and appointing* Two, in their *Praying*, in their *caſting Lots*, in their *voluntary opprobatory Suffrage*, that is deſired.

THIS bleſſed Example given us by the Wiſdom of the Apoſtles, yea, of the ſpirit of God in them, being eminently ſuited unto the nature of the thing it ſelf, as we ſhall ſee immediately, compliant with all other directions, and Apoſtolical examples in the like caſe, is rather to be followed, than the practice of ſome *degenerate Churches*, who to cover the turpitude of acting in deſerting this Example and Rule, do make uſe of a mock-ſhew and pretence of that which really they deny, reject and oppoſe.

THE Second Example we have of the *practice of the Apoſtles* in this caſe, whereby the preceding Rule is confirmed, is given us, *Act.* 6. in the Election of the *Deacons*. Had there enſued after the choice of *Matthias* an inſtance of a diverſe practice, by an *excluſion* of the conſent of the people, the former might have been evaded, as that which was abſolutely extraordinary, and not obliging unto the Church. But this was the *very next inſtance* of the call of any *Church-Officer*; and it was the firſt appointment of any *ordinary Officers* in the Chriſtian Church. For it falling out in the *very year* of Chriſts Aſcenſion, there is no mention of any *ordinary Elders* diſtinct from the Apoſtles, ordained in that Church. For all the Apoſtles themſelves yet abiding there for the moſt part of this time, making only ſome occaſional Excurſions unto other places, were able to take care of the Rule of the Church, and the Preaching of the Word. They are indeed mentioned as thoſe
who

The Officers of the Church.

who were well known in the Church *not long afterwards*, *Chap.* 11. 30. But the first instance of the Call of Ordinary Teaching-Elders or Pastors is not recorded. That of *Deacons* is so by reason of the occasion of it. And we may observe concerning it unto our purpose,

1. THAT the *institution* of the Office it self was of Apostolical Authority, and that fulness of Church-Power wherewith they were furnished by Jesus Christ.

2. THAT they did not exert that Authority but upon such Reasons of it, as were *satisfactory* to the Church; which they declare, *v.* 2.

3. THAT the action is ascribed to the *Twelve* in general, without naming any person who spake for the rest; which renders the pretence of the *Romanists* from the former place, where *Peter* is said to have spoken unto the Disciples, whereon they would have the Actings of the Church which ensued thereon, to have been by his *concession and grant*, not of their own right, altogether vain. For the rest of the Apostles were as much interested and concerned in what was then spoken by *Peter*, as they were at this time, when the whole is ascribed unto the *Twelve*.

4. THAT the Church was greatly *multiplied* that time, on the account of the Conversion unto the Faith recorded in the foregoing Chapter. It is probable indeed, that many, yea, the most of them were returned unto their own Habitations; for the *next year* there were Churches in all *Judea*, *Galilee* and *Samaria*, *Chap.* 9. 31. And *Peter* went about throughout all Quarters to visit the *Saints* that dwelt in them, *ver.* 32. of whose Conversion we read nothing but that which fell out at *Jerusalem* at *Pentecost*; but a great multitude they were, *v.* 1, 2.

5. THIS whole *multitude* of the Church, that is the Brethren, *v.* 3. *assembled in one place*, being congregated by the Apostles, *v.* 2. who would not ordain any thing wherein they were concerned, without their own consent.

6. THEY *judged* on the whole matter proposed unto them, and gave their approbation thereof, before they entred upon

K   the

the practice of it, *v.* 5. *The saying pleased the whole Multitude.*

7. THE Qualifications of the Persons to be chosen unto the Office intended, are declared by the Apostles, *v.* 3. *of honest report, full of the Holy Ghost and Wisdom.*

8. THESE Qualities the multitude were to *judge upon*, and so absolutely of the *meetness* of any for this Office.

9. THE choice is *wholly committed* and left unto them by the Apostles, as that which of Right did belong unto them; *look you out among you;* which they made use of, choosing them unto the Office by their common suffrage, *v.* 5.

10. HAVING thus *chosen them*, they presented them as their chosen Officers unto the Apostles, to be by them *set apart* unto the exercise of their Office by Prayer and Imposition of hands, *v.* 6.

IT is impossible, there should be a more evident convincing instance and example of the *free choice* of *Ecclesiastical Officers* by the multitude or fraternity of the Church, than is given us herein. Nor was there any Ground or Reason why this Order and Process should be observed, why the Apostles would not themselves *nominate and appoint* Persons whom they saw and knew meet for this Office, to receive it, but that it was the *Right* and *Liberty* of the People, according to the mind of Christ, to choose their own Officers, which they would not abbridge, nor infringe.

SO was it then, οὕτω καὶ νῦν γίνεσθαι ἔδει, saith *Chrysostom* on the place, and *so it ought now to be*; but the usage began then to decline. It were well if some would consider how the Apostles at that time treated that *multitude* of the people, which is so much now despised, and utterly excluded from all concern in Church Affairs, but what consist in servile subjection. But they have, in this pattern and president for the future ordering of the calling of meet Persons to Office in the Church, their Interest, Power, and Privilege secured unto them, so as that they can never justly be deprived of it. And if there were nothing herein, but only a *Record* of the Wisdom of the Apostles in managing Church Affairs, it is marvellous to me, that any who would be thought to *succeed them* in any part of their Trust and Office,

should

The Officers of the Church.

should dare to depart from the example set before them by the Holy Ghost in them, preferring their own ways and inventions above it. I shall ever judge, that there is more safety, in a strict adherence unto this Apostolical Practice and Example, than in a compliance with all the *Canons* of *Councils* or Churches afterwards.

THE only Objection usually insisted on, that is by *Bellarmine* and those that follow him, is, That this being the Election of *Deacons* to manage the *Alms of the Church*, that is somewhat of their Temporals, nothing can thence be concluded unto the right or way of *Calling Bishops, Pastors or Elders*, who are to take care of the Souls of the People. They may indeed be able to judge of the *fitness* of them who are to be entrusted with their *Purses*, or what they are willing to give out of them; but it doth not thence follow, that they are able to judge of the fitness of those who are to be their *Spiritual Pastors*, nor to have the choice of them.

NOTHING can be weaker than this pretence or evasion. For, (1.) The Question is concerning the *Calling of Persons* unto *Office* in the Church in general, whereof we have here a Rule, whereunto no exception is any way entred. (2.) This cannot be fairly pleaded by them who *appoint Deacons to Preach, Baptize and Officiate* publickly in all holy things, excepting only the Administration of the *Eucharist*. (3.) If the people are meet and able to judge of them who are of *honest report*, and *full of the Holy Ghost and Wisdom*, which is here required of them, they are able to judge who are meet to be their Pastors. (4.) The Argument holds strongly on the other side; namely, that if it be *right and equal*, if it be of divine appointment and Apostolical practice, that the people should choose those who were to Collect and Distribute their Charitable Benevolence because of their concernment therein, much more are they to enjoy the same *Liberty, Right* and Privilege in the choice of their *Pastors*, unto whom they commit the care of their Souls, and submit themselves unto their Authority in the Lord.

3. ACCORDINGLY they did use the same liberty in the choice of their Elders, *Act.* 14. 23. Χειροτονήσαντες αὐτοῖς πρεσβυτέρους κατ'

The Officers of the Church.

κατ' ἐκκλησίαν, προσδεξάμενοι μετὰ νηστειῶν : That is, fay *Erafmus, Vatablus, Beza*, all our old *Englifh Tranflations*, appointing, ordaining, creating Elders *by Election or the fuffrage of the Difciples*, having prayed with Faftings. The whole Order of the facred feparation of Perfons qualified unto the Office of the Miniftry, that is, to be *Bifhops, Elders* or *Paftors*, is here clearly reprefented. For, (1.) They were *chofen by the people ;* the Apoftles who were prefent, namely *Paul* and *Barnabas* prefiding in the Action, directing of it and confirming that by their confent with them. (2.) A *time of Prayer and Fafting* was appointed for the Action, or difcharge of the Duty of the Church herein. (3.) When they were *fo chofen*, the Apoftles prefent *folemnly prayed*, whereby their *Ordination* was compleat. And *thofe* who would have the χειροτονία here mentioned to be, χειροθεσία, or an Authoritative impofition of hands, wherein this Ordination did confift, do fay there is an ὑπερβολογία in the words; that is they feign a *diforder* in them, to ferve their own *Hypothefis*. For they fuppofe that their compleat *Ordination* was effected, before there was *any Prayer with Fafting* ; for by *impofition of Hands* in their judgment, Ordination is compleated ; fo *Bellarmine, A Lapide*, on the place, with thofe that follow them. But firft to pervert the true fignification of the Word, and then to give countenance unto that wrefting of it by affigning a *diforder* unto the Words of the whole Sentence, and that *fuch a diforder* as makes in their judgment a *falfe Reprefentation* of the matter of Fact related, is a way of the Interpretation of Scripture which will ferve any turn. (4.) This was done in *every Church*, or in every Congregation, as *Tindal* renders the Word ; namely, in all the particular Congregations that were gathered in thofe parts ; for that Collection and Conftitution did always precede the Election and Ordination of their Officers, as is plain in this place ; as alfo *Tit.* 1. 5. So far is it from Truth, that the Being of Churches dependeth on the *Succeffive Ordination* of their Officers, that the Church effentially confidered, is always antecedent unto their Being and Call.

BUT becaufe it is fome Mens intereft to entangle things plain and clear enough in themfelves, I fhall confider the
Objections

The Officers of the Church.

Objections unto this rendition of the Words. The whole of it lies against the signification, use and application of χειροτονήσαντες. Now although we do not here argue meerly from the signification of the Word, but from the *representation of the matter of Fact* made in the context; yet I shall observe some things sufficient for the removal of that Objection: As,

1. THE *native signification* of χειροτονέω, by virtue of its Composition, is, to *lift up, or stretch forth the hands*, or an hand. And hereunto the LXX have respect, *Isa*. 58. 9. where they render שלח אצבע, *the putting forth of the finger*, which is used in an ill sence, by Χειροτονία. χειροτονεῖν is the same with τὰς χεῖρας αἴρειν, nor is it ever used in any other signification.

2. THE first constant use of it in things *Political or Civil*, and so consequently *Ecclesiastical*, is to *Choose, Elect*, Design or Create any Person an Officer, Magistrate or Ruler, by *Suffrage*, or common consent of those concerned. And this was usually done with making bare the hand and arm, with lifting up, as *Aristophanes* witnesseth. Ὅμως ὃ χειροτονητέον, ἐξωμισάμενος τ᾽ ἕτερον βραχίονα. He is a great stranger unto these things, who knoweth not that among the *Greeks*, especially the *Athenians*, from whom the use of this Word is borrowed or taken, χειροτονία was an act ὅλης τ. ἐκκλησίας *of the whole Assembly* of the people in the choice of their Officers and Magistrates. χειροτονέω is by *common Suffrage to decree* and determine of any Thing, Law, or Order; and when applied unto Persons, it signifies their Choice and Designation to Office. So is it used in the first sence by *Demosthenes, Orat. in Timoch.* ὁ δῆμος ταῖς ἐμαῖς γνώμαις περὶ σωτηρίας τ. πόλεως ἐχειροτόνει *The people confirmed my sayings by their Suffrage*: And in the other, *Philip.* 1. Οὔτε βουλῆς, οὔτε δήμου χειροτονησάντες αὐτόν; *Neither the Senate, nor the People choosing him to his Office.* So is the *Passive* Verb used to be created by Suffrages. Χειροτονία was the act of choosing, whose effect was ψήφισμα, the *determining* Vote or Suffrage. *Porrexerunt manus, Psephisma notum est*, saith *Cicero*, speaking of the manner of the *Greeks*. And when there was a division in choice, it was determined by the greater

The Officers of the Church.

greater Suffrage *Thucid. Lib.* 3. ἐχέιροντο ἢ ἐν τῇ χειροτονίᾳ ἀγχώμαλοι, ἑκατέρωσε ἢ ἡ ψῆφος δίδοτο. As many instances of this nature may be produced, as there are reports of calling Men unto Magistracy by Election in the *Greek Historians.* And all the farther compositions of the Word do signifie to *choose, confirm*, or to *abrogate* by common Suffrages.

3. THE Word is but once more used in the New Testament, 2 *Cor.* 8. 19. where it plainly signifies *Election* and Choice of a Person to an Employment, χειροτονηθεὶς ὑπὸ τῶν ἐκκλησιῶν συνέκδημος ἡμῶν: *He was chosen of the Churches to travel with us.*

4. IT is acknowledged, that after this was the *common use* of the Word, it was applied to signifie the *thing* it self, and not the manner of doing it. Hence it is used sometimes for the obtaining or collation of Authority, or Dignity or Magistracy, any manner of way, though not by Election. To *appoint*, to *create*. But this was by an *abusive application* of the Word, to express the thing it self intended, with ——— ard unto its signification and proper use. Why ——— a use of it should be here admitted, no Reason can be given. For in all other places on such occasions, the *Apostles* did admit and direct the Churches to use their liberty in their choice. So the *Apostles and Elders, with the whole Church, sent chosen Men of their own Company to Antioch*, such as they chose by common Suffrage for that end; so again *ver.* 25. *I will send whom you shall approve*, 1 *Cor.* 16. 3. The *Church chose them*, the Apostle sent him *who was chosen by the Church to be our Companion*, 2 *Cor.* 8. 19. *Look out from among your selves*, Act. 6. If on all these and the like occasions, the Apostles did guide and direct the people in their right and use of their Liberty, as unto the *Election* of Persons unto Offices and Employments, when the Churches themselves are concerned, what reason is there to depart from the proper and usual signification of the Word in this place, denoting nothing but what was the common practice of the Apostles on the like occasions?

5. THAT which alone is objected hereunto by *Bellarmine* and others who follow him, and borrow their whole in this case

The Officers of the Church.

case from him, namely that χειροτονησαντες *Grammatically* agreeing with and regulated by *Paul and Barnabas*, denotes their *act*, *and not any act of the people*, is of no force. For, (1.) *Paul* and *Barnabas* did preside in the whole action, helping, ordering and disposing of the people in the discharge of their Duty, as is meet to be done by some on all the like occasions. And therefore it is truly said of them, *that they appointed Elders by the Suffrage of the people*. (2.) I have shewed instances before out of the Scripture, that when a thing is done by the whole people, it is usual to ascribe it unto him or them who were chief therein, as elsewhere the same thing is ascribed unto the whole people.

THE same *Authors* contend that the liberty of choosing their own Officers or Elders, such as it was, was granted unto them or permitted by way of *condescention for a Season*; and not made use of by virtue of any right in them thereunto. But this permission is a meet imagination. It was according to the mind of Christ, that the Churches should choose their own Elders, or it was not. If it were not, the *Apostles* would not have permitted it; and if it were, they ought to ordain it, and practise according to it, as they did. Nor is such a constant Apostolical Practice proposed for the direction of the Church in all Ages, to be ascribed unto such an Original as *Condescension* and *Permission*. Yea, it is evident, that it arose from the most fundamental principles of the constitution and nature of the Gospel Churches, and was only a regular pursuit and practice of them: For,

1. THE Calling of Bishops, Pastors, Elders, is an Act of the *power of the Keys* of the Kingdom of Heaven. But these Keys are originally and *properly* given unto the *whole Church*, unto the Elders of it only *Ministerially*; and as unto exercise, Pastors are *eyes* to the Church: But God and Nature design, in the first place, *sight* to the whole Body, to the whole Person, thereunto it is granted both subjectively and finally, but *actually* it is peculiarly seated in the eye. So is it in the grant of Church-Power, it is given to the *whole Church*, though to be exercised only by its Elders.

THAT

The Officers of the Church.

THAT the grant of the *Keys unto Peter* was in the Person and as the reprefentative of the whole confeffing Church, is the known judgment of *Auftin* and a multitude of Divines that follow him. So he fully expreffeth himfelf, *Tractat.* 124. *in Johan.* "*Peter* the Apoftle bare in a general figure the perfon "of the Church. For as unto what belonged unto himfelf, "he was by Nature one Man, by Grace one Chriftian, and of "fpecial more abounding Grace, one and the chief Apoftle. "But when it was faid unto him, I will give unto thee the "Keys of the Kingdom of Heaven, *&c.* he fignified the whole "Church, *&c.* Again, the Church which is founded in Chrift, "received from him in (the perfon of) *Peter*, the Keys of "the Kingdom of Heaven, which is the power of binding and "loofing.

UNTO whom thefe *Keys* are granted, they according to their diftinct interefts in that grant, have the Right and Power of Calling their *Bifhops, Paftors or Elders*; for in the exercife of that Truft and Power, it doth confift. But this is made unto the *whole Church*. And as there are in a Church already conftituted feveral *forts of perfons*, as fome are Elders, others are of the people only, this *Right* refideth in them, and is acted by them according to their refpective capacities, as limited by the light of nature and divine inftitution, which is, that the *Election* of them fhould belong unto the body of the people, and their *Authoritative Defignation or Ordination* unto the Elders. And when in any place the fupream Magiftrate is a Member or Part of the Church, he hath alfo his peculiar Right herein.

THAT the *power of the Keys* is thus granted originally and fundamentally unto the whole Church, is undeniably confirmed by Two Arguments.

1. THE Church it felf is the *Wife*, the *Spoufe*, the *Bride*, the Queen of the *Husband* and *King* of the Church Chrift Jefus, *Pfal.* 45. 10. *John* 3. 29. *Revel.* 21. 9. Chap. 22. 17. *Matth.* 25. 1, 5, 6. Other *Wife* Chrift hath none, nor hath the Church any other *Husband*, Now to whom fhould the *Keys of the Houfe* be committed but unto the *Bride*? There is, I confefs, another who

claims

The Officers of the Church.

claims the *Keys* to be his own, but withal, he makes himself the *Head and Husband* of the Church, proclaiming himself, not only to be an Adulterer with that *Harlot* which he calleth the Church, but a *Tyrant* also, in that pretending to be her Husband he will not trust her with the *Keys of his House*, which Christ hath done with his Spouse. And whereas by the *Canon Law* every *Bishop* is the Husband or Spouse of his Diocesan Church, for the most part they commit an *open Rape* upon the people, taking them without their consent; at least are not chosen by them, which yet is essential unto a lawful Marriage. And the Bride of Christ comes no otherwise so to be, but by the voluntary choice of him to be her Husband.

FOR the Officers or Rulers of the Church, they do belong unto it as hers, 1 *Cor.* 3. 21. 22. And *Stewards in the House*, 1 *Cor.* 4. 1. the *Servants of the Church for Jesus sake*, 2 *Cor.* 4. 5.

IF the Lord Christ have the Keys of the Kingdom of Heaven, that is, of *his own House, Heb.* 3. If the Church it self be the *Spouse of Christ*, the *Mother of the Family*, Psal. 68. 13. the *Bride*, the *Lambs Wife*; and if all the Officers of the Church be but *Stewards* and *Servants* in the House and unto the Family; if the Lord Christ do make a grant of *these Keys* unto any, whereon the disposal of all things in this House and Family doth depend, the Question is, Whether he hath originally granted them unto his *holy Spouse* to dispose off according unto her judgment and duty, or unto any *Servants* in the House, to dispose of *her* and all *her* concernments, at their pleasure?

2. THE power of the *Keys* as unto *binding and loosing*, and consequently as unto all other acts thence proceeding, is expresly granted unto *the whole Church*, Matth. 18. 17, 18. *If he shall neglect to hear them, tell the Church; but if he neglect to hear the Church, let him be unto thee as an Heathen Man and a Publican; verily I say unto you, whatsoever ye shall bind on Earth shall be bound in Heaven; and whatsoever ye shall loose on Earth, shall be loosed in Heaven.* What Church it is that is here intended, we have proved before; and that the Church is intrusted with the power of binding and loosing. And what is the part of

the Body of the people herein, the Apoſtle declares; 1 *Cor.* 5. 4. 2 *Cor.* 2. 6.

SECONDLY, This Right exemplified in *Apoſtolical Practice*, is comprehended in the Commands given unto the *Church*, or Body of the People, with reſpect unto *Teachers* and *Rulers* of all ſorts; for unto them it is in a multitude of places given in charge that they ſhould *diſcern* and *try falſe Prophets*, *fly from them*; *try Spirits*, or ſuch as pretend Spiritual Gifts or Offices; reject them who Preach *falſe Doctrine*, to give teſtimony unto them that are to be in Office; with ſundry other things of the like nature, which all of them do ſuppoſe, or cannot be diſcharged without a *Right* in them to chooſe the worthy, and reject the unworthy, as *Cyprian* ſpeaks. See *Matth.* 7. 17. *Joh.* 5. 39. *Gal.* 11. 9. 1 *Theſſ.* 5. 19, 20, 21. 1 *Joh.* 4. 1. 2 *Joh.* 10. 11.

WHAT is objected hereunto from the *unfitneſs and diſability* of the people, to make a right judgment concerning them who are to be their Paſtors and Rulers, labours with a three-fold weakneſs. For, (1.) It reflects diſhonour upon the *Wiſdom* of Chriſt in Commanding them the obſervance and diſcharge of ſuch Duties, as they are no way meet for. (2.) It proceeds upon a ſuppoſition of that *degenerate ſtate of Churches* in their Members, as to Light, Knowledge, Wiſdom and Holineſs, which they are for the moſt part fallen into; which muſt not be allowed to have the force of Argument in it; when it is to be lamented, and ought to be reformed. (3.) It ſuppoſeth that there is no *ſupply of Aſſiſtance* provided for the people, in the diſcharge of their Duty to guide and direct them therein; which is otherwiſe; ſeeing the *Elders* of the Church wherein any ſuch Election is made, and thoſe of other Churches in Communion with that Church, are by the common advice and declaration of their judgment, to be Aſſiſtant unto them.

THIRDLY, The Church is a *voluntary Society*. Perſons otherwiſe abſolutely free, as unto all the Rules, Laws and Ends of ſuch a Society, do of their own Wills and free Choice coaleſce into it. This is the Original of all Churches, as hath been declared. *They gave their own ſelves to the Lord, and unto us by the Will of God*,

God, 2 Cor. 8. 5. Herein neither by Prescription, nor Tradition, nor Succession, hath any one more Power or Authority than another; but they are all *equal.* It is gathered into this *Society* meerly by the Authority of Christ; and where it is so Collected, it hath neither Right, Power, Privilege, Rules nor Bonds *as such,* but what are given, prescribed and limited by the Institution and Laws of Christ. Moreover, it abides and continues on the same Grounds and Principles, as whereon it was Collected, namely, the *Wills of the Members* of it subjected unto the Commands of Christ. This is as necessary unto its present continuance in all its Members, as it was in its first Plantation. It is not like the *Political Societies* of the World, which being first established by force or consent, bring a necessity on all that are born in them and under them, to comply with their Rule and Laws. For Men may, and in many cases ought to submit unto the disposal of temporal things, in a way, it may be, not convenient for them, which they judge not well off, and which in many things is not unto their advantage. And this may be *just* and *equal,* because the special *good* which every one would aim at, being not absolutely so, may be out-balanced by a *general* good, nor alterable, but by the prejudice of that which is good in particular. But with reference unto things Spiritual and Eternal it is not so. No Man can by any *previous Law* be concluded as unto his interest in such things; nor is there any *General Good* to be attained by the loss of any of them. None therefore can coalesce in such a Society, or adhere unto it, or be any way belonging unto it, but by his own *free choice* and consent. And it is enquired, how it is possible that any Rule, Authority, Power or Office, should arise or be erected in *such* a Society? We speak of that which is ordinary; for he by whom this Church-State is erected and appointed, may and did *appoint* in it, and over it, *extraordinary Officers* for a season. And we do suppose, that as he hath by his Divine Authority instituted and appointed that *such Societies* shall be, that he hath made grant of Privileges and Powers to them proper and sufficient for this end; as also that he hath given *Laws and Rules,* by the observance whereof, they

may

The Officers of the Church.

may be made partakers of those Privileges and Powers, with a Right unto their Exercise.

ON these suppositions in a Society absolutely *voluntary*, among those who in their conjunction into it, by their own consent, are every way *equal*, There can but three things be required unto the actual constitution of *Rule* and *Office* among them. And the First is, That there be some among them that are *fitted and qualified* for the Discharge of such an Office in a peculiar manner above others. This is previous unto all Government, beyond that which is purely natural and necessary. *Principio rerum, gentium nationumq; imperium penes Reges erat ; quos ad fastigium hujus Majestatis, non popularis Ambitio, sed spectata inter bonos moderatio provehebat. Just.* So it was in the World, so it was in the Church. *Præsident probati quique seniores, honorem istum non pretio sed testimonio adepti. Tertull.* This preparation and furniture of some Persons with Abilities and meet Qualifications for Office and Work in the Church, the Lord Christ hath *taken on himself*, and doth and will effect it in all Generations. Without this there can be neither *Office*, nor *Rule*, nor *Order* in the Church.

2. WHEREAS, there is a *new Relation* to be made or created between a *Pastor, Bishop or Elder, and the Church*, which was not before between them, (a Bishop and a Church, a Pastor and a Flock are *Relata's)* it must be introduced at the same time by the *mutual voluntary* acts of one another, or of each party. For one of the *Relata* can, as such, have no being or existence without the other. Now this can no otherwise be, but by the *consent and voluntary subjection* of the Church unto persons so antecedently qualified for Office, according to the Law and Will of Christ. For it cannot be done by the *Delegation of Power* and Authority from any other Superiour or Equal unto them that do receive it. Neither the nature of this Power, which is uncapable of such a *Delegation*, nor the *Relation* unto Christ of all those who are Pastors of the Church, will admit of an Interposition of Authority by way of *Delegation of Power* from themselves in other Men, which would make them *their Ministers*, and not Christs ; nor is it consistent with

The Officers of the Church.

with the nature of such a voluntary Society. This therefore can no way be done, but by *free Choice*, Election, Consent or Approbation. It cannot, I say, be so regularly. How far an *Irregularity* herein may vitiate the whole Call of a Minister, we do not now enquire.

NOW this *Choice* or *Election* doth not communicate a Power from them that *choose* unto them that are *chosen*, as though such a Power as that whereunto they are called, should be formally inherent in the *choosers*, antecedent unto such *choice*. For this would make those that *are chosen* to be *their Minister* only; and to act all things in their Name, and by virtue of Authority derived from them. It is only an *Instrumental, Ministerial* means to enstate them in that Power and Authority which is given unto such Officers by the Constitution and Laws of Christ, whose Ministers thereon they are. These *Gifts*, Offices, and Officers, being granted by Christ unto the Churches, *Ephes.* 4. 12. where-ever there is a Church called according to his Mind, they do in and by their Choice of them, *submit themselves unto them in the Lord*, according unto all the Powers and Duties wherewith they are by him intrusted, and whereunto they are called.

3. IT is required that Persons so chosen, so submitted unto, be so *solemnly separated, dedicated unto, and confirmed in their Office by Fasting and Prayer*. As this is consonant unto the Light of Nature, which directs unto a solemnity in the susception of publick Officers; whence proceeds the *Coronation of Kings*, which gives them not their *Title*, but solemnly proclaims it, which on many accounts is unto the advantage of Government; so it is prescribed unto the Church in this case by *especial Institution*. But hereof I shall speak farther immediately.

THIS Order of calling Men unto the Pastoral Office, namely by their *previous Qualifications* for the Ministry, whereby a general designation of the Persons to be called is made by Christ himself; the *orderly Choice or Election* of him in a voluntary subjection unto him in the Lord, according to the Mind of Christ, by the Church it self; followed with *solemn Ordination*, or setting apart unto the Office and discharge of it by

Prayer

Prayer with Fasting, all in obedience unto the Commands and Institution of Christ, whereunto the communication of Office-Power and Privilege, is by Law-constitution annexed, is suited unto the light of Reason, in all such cases, the nature of Gospel Societies in Order or Churches; the ends of the Ministry, the Power committed by Christ unto the Church, and confirmed by Apostolical Practice and Example.

HEREIN we rest, without any further dispute or limiting the *Formal Cause* of the Communication of Office-Power unto any one Act or Duty of the Church, or of the Bishops or Elders of it. All the three things mentioned are *essential* thereunto; and when any of them are utterly neglected, where they are neither formally nor virtually, there is no *lawful regular Call* unto the Ministry according to the Mind of Christ.

THIS Order was a long time observed in the *Ancient Church* inviolate; and the foot-steps of it may be traced through all Ages of the Church; although it first gradually decayed, then was perverted and corrupted, until it issued (as in the *Roman* Church) in a *Pageant* and Shew, instead of the Reality of the things themselves: For the *Trial and Approbation* of spiritual Endowments previously necessary unto the Call of any, was left unto the *Pedantick* Examination of the *Bishops Domesticks*, who knew nothing of them in themselves; the *Election and Approbation* of the people was turned into a mock-shew in the sight of God and Men, a *Deacon* calling out, That *if any had Objections against him who was to be Ordained*, they should come forth and speak; Whereunto another *cries out of* a corner by compact, He is *learned and worthy*; and *Ordination* was esteemed to consist only in the outward sign of *Imposition of Hands*, with some other Ceremonies annexed thereunto, whereby, without any other consideration, there ensued a flux of Power from the Ordainers unto the ordained.

BUT from the beginning it was not so. And some few Instances of the *Right of the* people, and the exercise of it in the Choice of their own Pastors, may be touched on in our Passage. *Clem. Epist. ad Corinth.* affirms, That the *Apostles* themselves appointed *approved Persons* unto the Office of the Ministry, συνευδοκησάσης τ͂ ἐκκλησίας πάσης, *by or with the consent or choice of the whole Church.* Συνευδοκεῖν, is to *enact by common consent*; which makes it somewhat strange, that a learned Man should think that the Right of the People in Elections is excluded in this very place by *Clemens,* from what is assigned unto the Apostles in Ordination.

IGNAT. Epist. ad Philadelph. Πρέπον ἐςιν ὑμῖν, ὡς ἐκκλησία Θεῦ, χειροτονῆσαι ἐπίσκοπον, writing to the Fraternity of the Church, It *becomes you, as a Church of God, to Choose or Ordain a Bishop.*

TERTULL. APOL. Præsident probati quiq; Seniores, honorem istum non pretio, sed Testimonio adepti. The Elders came unto their Honour or Office by the Testimony of the people; that is by their suffrage in their Election.

ORIGEN, in the close of his last Book against *Celsus,* discoursing expresly of the *Calling* and *Constitution* of Churches or *Cities of God,* speaking of the Elders and Rulers of them, affirms, That they are ἐκλεγόμενοι, *Chosen to their Office* by the Churches which they do Rule.

THE Testimony given by *Cyprian* in sundry places unto this *Right of the People,* especially in *Epist.* 68. unto the Elders and People of some Churches in *Spain,* is so known, so frequently urged and excepted against to so little purpose, as that it is no way needful to insist again upon it. Some few things I shall only observe concerning, and out of that Epistle: As,

1. IT was not a *single Epistle* of his own more ordinary occasions, but a determination upon a weighty Question made by a *Synod of Bishops* or Elders, in whose Name, as well as that of *Cyprian,* it was written and sent unto the Churches who had craved their advice.

2. HE doth not only assert the *Right of the people to choose worthy persons* to be their Bishops, and *reject* those that are unworthy; but also industriously proves it so to be their Right by *Divine Institution* and Appointment.

3. HE declares it to be the *Sin of the People,* if they neglect the use and exercise of their Right and Power in rejecting and

withdrawing themselves from the Communion of *Unworthy Pastors*, and choosing others in their room.

4. HE affirms that this *was the Practice*, not only of the Churches of *Africk*, but of those in most of the other Provinces of the Empire. Some passages in his Discourse, wherein all these things are asserted, I shall transcribe in the Order wherein they lie in the Epistle.

NEC sibi plebs blandiatur, quasi immunis esse a contagio delicti possit cum sacerdote peccatore communicans, & ad injustum & illicitum Præpositi sui Episcopatum consensum suum commodans. Propter quod plebs obsequens præceptis Dominicis & Deum metuens, a peccatore præposito separare se debet; nec se ad Sacrilegi Sacerdotis Sacrificia miscere; quando ipsa maxime habeat potestatem vel eligendi dignos sacerdotes, vel indignos recusandi; quod & ipsum videmus de Divina Authoritate descendere.

" FOR this cause the people obedient to the Commands of our
" Lord, and fearing God, ought to separate themselves from a
" wicked Bishop, nor mix themselves with the Worship of a
" Sacrilegious Priest. For they principally have the power of
" choosing the worthy Priests, and rejecting the unworthy;
" which comes from Divine Authority or Appointment; as he proves from the Old and New Testament. Nothing can be spoken more fully representing the Truth which we plead for. He assigns unto the people a *Right and Power* of separating from unworthy Pastors, of rejecting or deposing them, and that granted to them by Divine Authority.

AND this Power of *Election* in the people, he proves from the Apostolical Practice before insisted on. *Quod postea secundum Divina Magisteria observatur in Actis Apostolorum, quando in Ordinando in locum Judæ Episcopo, Petrus ad plebem loquitur. Surrexit, inquit, Petrus in medio discentium, fuit autem turba in uno. Nec hoc in Episcoporum tantum & Sacerdotum, sed in Diaconorum Ordinationibus observasse Apostolos, de quo & ipso in Actis eorum Scriptum est. Et convocarunt, inquit, duodecim, totam plebem Discipulorum, & dixerunt eis,* &c.

ACCORDING unto the Divine Commands the same course was observed in the Acts of the Apostles, whereof he gives instances in the

the Election of *Matthias*, *Act.* 1. and of the *Deacons*, Chap. 6.

AND afterwards speaking of Ordination, *De Vniversæ Fraternitatis Suffragio*, by the *Suffrage of the whole Brotherhood* of the Church; he says, *Diligenter de traditione Divina, & Apostolica observatione servandum est & tenendum apud nos quoque, ut fere per universas provincias tenetur*: According to which *Divine Tradition and Apostolical Practice, this custom is to be preserved and kept amongst us also, as it is almost through all the Provinces*.

THOSE who are not moved with his Authority, yet, I think have reason to believe him in a *matter of Fact*, of what was done *every where*, or almost every where, in his own days; and they may take *Time* to answer his *Reasons* when they can, which comprize the substance of all that we plead in this Case.

BUT the Testimonies in *following Ages* given unto this Right and Power of the People in choosing their own Church-Officers, Bishops and others, recorded in the *Decrees of Councils*, the *Writings* of the learned Men in them, the *Rescripts of Popes*, and *Constitutions of Emperours*, are so fully and faithfully Collected by *Blondellus* in the Third Part of his *Apology* for the judgment of *Hierom* about Episcopacy, as that nothing can be added unto his diligence, nor is there any need of farther confirmation of the Truth in this behalf.

THE pretence also of *Bellarmine*, and others who follow him, and borrow their conceits from him, that this *liberty of the people* in choosing their own Bishops and Pastors, was granted unto them at first by way of *Indulgence* or Connivence; and that being abused by them, and turned into disorder, was *gradually taken from them*, until it issued in that shameful mocking of God and Man, which is in use in the *Roman Church*, when at the Ordination of a *Bishop* or Priest one Deacon makes a demand, Whether the Person to be Ordained be approved by the people, and another answers out of a corner That the *people approve* him, have been so confuted by *Protestant* Writers of all sorts, that it is needless to insist any longer on them.

M   INDEED,

The Officers of the Church.

INDEED, the Conceſſions that are made, that this Ancient Practice of the Church, in the peoples chooſing their own Officers (which to deny, is all one as to deny that the Sun gives Light at Noon-day) is, as unto its *Right*, by various degrees transferred unto *Popes*, *Patrons* and *Biſhops*, with a Repreſentation in a meer Pageantry, of the peoples liberty to make Objections againſt them that are to be Ordained, are as fair a conceſſion of the *gradual Apoſtacy* of Churches from their Original Order and Conſtitution, as need be deſired.

THIS *Power* and *Right* which we aſſign unto the people, is not to act it ſelf only in a *ſubſequent conſent* unto one that is Ordained, in the acceptance of him to be their Biſhop or Paſtor. How far that may *ſalve* the defect and diſorder of the omiſſion of previous Elections, and ſo preſerve the Eſſence of the Miniſterial Call, I do not now enquire. But that which we plead for, is, the Power and Right of Election to be exerciſed *previouſly* unto the ſolemn Ordination or ſetting apart of any unto the Paſtoral Office, communicative of Office-Power in its own kind unto the perſon choſen.

THIS is part of that conteſt which for ſundry Ages filled moſt Countries of *Europe* with broils and diſorders. Neither is there yet an end put unto it. But in this preſent diſcourſe we are not in the leaſt concerned in theſe things. For our Enquiry is what State and Order of *Church*-Affairs is declared and repreſented unto us in the Scripture. And therein there is not the leaſt intimation of any of thoſe things from whence this Controverſy did ariſe, and whereon it doth depend. *Secular* Endowments, Juriſdictions, Inveſtiture, Rights of Preſentation, and the like, with reſpect unto the Evangelical Paſtoral Office, or its exerciſe in any place, which are the ſubject of theſe Conteſts, are foreign unto all things that are directed in the Scriptures concerning them, nor can be reduced unto any thing that belongs unto them. Wherefore, whether this *JUS PATRONATUS* be conſiſtent with Goſpel-Inſtitutions; whether it may be continued with reſpect unto Lands, Tythes and Benefices; or how it may be reconciled unto the Right of the People in the Choice of their own Eccleſiaſtical Officers,

from

The Officers of the Church. 83

from the different *Acts*, *Objects* and Ends required unto the one and the other, are things not of our present consideration.

AND this we affirm to be agreeable unto *natural Reason* and *Equity*, to the *nature of Churches* in their institution and ends, to all Authority and Office-Power in the Church, necessary unto its Edification, with the security of the Consciences of the *Officers* themselves, the preservation of due respect and obedience unto them, constituted by the Institution of Christ himself in his Apostles, and the practice of the Primitive Church. Wherefore, the utter *despoiling* of the Church, of the Disciples, of those gathered in Church Societies by his Authority and Command, of this Right and Liberty, may be esteemed a *Sacrilege* of an higher nature, than sundry other things which are reproached as criminal under that Name.

AND if any shall yet farther appear to justifie this deprivation of the Right laid claim unto, and the *exclusion* of the people from their Ancient Possession with sobriety of Argument and Reason, the whole cause may be yet farther debated from principles of *natural Light* and Equity, from *maxims* of *Law and Polity*, from the necessity of the *Ends* of Church-Order and Power, from the moral impossibility of any other way of the conveyance of *Ecclesiastical Office-Power*, as well as from Evangelical Institution and the practice of the first Churches.

IT will be Objected, I know, that the Restoration of this Liberty unto the people, will overthrow that *jus Patronatus*, or Right of *presenting unto Livings* and Preferments, which is established by Law in this Nation, and so under a pretence of restoring unto the people their Right in common, destroy other Mens undoubted Rights in their own enclosures.

BUT this Election of the Church, doth not actually and immediately instate the persons chosen in the *Office* whereunto he is chosen; nor give actual Right unto its Exercise. It is required moreover, that he be solemnly set apart unto his Office in and by the Church *with Fasting and Prayer*. That there should be some kind of *peculiar Prayer* in the dedication of any unto the *Office* of the Ministry, is a notion that could never be obliterated in the minds of Men concerned in these

M 2 things,

things, nor caſt out of their Practice. Of what ſort they have been amongſt many we do not now enquire. But there hath been leſs regard unto the other Duty, namely, that theſe Prayers ſhould be accompanied with *Faſting*. But this alſo is neceſſary by Virtue of Apoſtolical Example, *Act*. 14. 23.

THE Conduct of this Work belongs unto the *Elders or Officers of the Church*, wherein any one is to be ſo Ordained. It did belong unto *extraordinary Officers* whilſt they were continued in the Church. And upon the Ceſſation of their Office, it is devolved on the ordinary ſtated *Officers* of the Church. It is ſo, I ſay, in caſe there be any ſuch *Officer* before fixed in the Church, whereunto any one is to be only Ordained. And in caſe there be none, the Aſſiſtance of Paſtors or Elders of other Churches may and ought to be deſired, unto the Conduct and *Regulation* of the Duty.

IT is needleſs to enquire what is the Authoritative influence of this Ordination, into the *Communication of Office* or Office-Power; whilſt it is acknowledged to be indiſpenſably neceſſary and to belong eſſentially unto the *Call* unto *Office*. For when ſundry Duties, as theſe of *Election* and *Ordination*, are required unto the ſame End, by Virtue of Divine Inſtitution, it is not for me to determine what is the peculiar efficacy of the one or the other, ſeeing neither of them without the other, hath any at all.

HEREUNTO is added, as an *External Adjunct*, impoſition of hands ſignificant of the perſons ſo called to *Office*, in and unto the Church. For although it will be difficultly proved, that the uſe of this Ceremony was deſigned unto continuance, after a Ceſſation of the *Communication of the extraordinary Gifts of the Holy Ghoſt*, whereof it was the ſign and outward means, in *extraordinary Officers*; yet we do freely grant it unto the ordinary *Officers* of the Church; provided that there be no apprehenſion of its being the ſole Authoritative Conveyance of a ſucceſſive *flux of Office-Power*; which is deſtructive of the whole nature of the inſtitution.

AND this may at preſent ſuffice, as unto the *Call* of meet perſons unto the *Paſtoral Office*, and conſequently any other
Office

Office in the Church. The things following are *essentially* necessary unto it, so as that *Authority* and *Right* to Feed and Rule in the Church in the Name of Christ, as an Officer of his House, that may be given unto any one thereby by virtue of his Law, and the Charter granted by him unto the Church it self: The *First is*, That antecedently unto any actings of the Church towards such a person, with respect unto Office, he be furnished by the Lord Christ himself with *Graces and Gifts*, and Abilities, for the discharge of the Office whereunto he is to be called. This Divine Designation of the person to be called, rests on the Kingly Office and care of Christ towards his Church. Where this is *wholly* wanting, it is not in the power of any Church under Heaven, by virtue of any outward Order or Act, to communicate *Pastoral* or Ministerial Power unto any person whatever. *Secondly*, There is to be an *Exploration* or *Trial* of those Gifts and Abilities as unto their *Accommodation* unto the Edification of that Church, whereunto any person is to be Ordained a *Pastor* or Minister. But although the Right of judging herein, belong unto and reside in the Church it self, (for who else is able to judge for them, or is entrusted so to do?) yet is it their Wisdom and Duty to desire the *Assistance* and *Guidance* of those who are approved in the discharge of their Office in other Churches. *Thirdly*, The *first act of Power committed* unto the Church by Jesus Christ for the constitution of Ordinary Officers in it, is, that *Election* of a person qualified and tried, unto his Office, which we have now vindicated. *Fourthly*, There is required hereunto, the *Solemn Ordination, Inauguration, Dedication* or setting apart of the persons so chosen by the *Presbytery* of the Church *with Fasting* and Prayer, and the outward sign of the *Imposition* of Hands.

THIS is that Order which the Rule of the Scripture, the Example of the First Churches, and the nature of the things themselves, direct unto. And although I will not say that a defect in any of these, especially if it be from unavoidable hindrances, doth *disanull* the Call of a person to the Pastoral Office; yet I must say, that where they are not all duly attended unto, the Institution of Christ is neglected,

lected, and the Order of the Church infringed: Wherefore, THE Plea of the communication of all Authority for Office, and of Office it self, solely by a *flux of Power from the first Ordainers*, through the hands of their *pretended Successors* in all Ages, under all the innumerable Miscarriages whereunto they are subject, and have actually fallen into, without any respect unto the consent or call of the Churches, by Rule, Laws and Orders, foreign to the Scripture, is contrary to the whole nature of *Evangelical* Churches, and all the ends of their Institution; as shall be manifested, if it be needful.

CHAP. V.

The Especial Duty of Pastors of Churches.

WE have declared the *way* whereby *Pastors* are *given* unto, and instated in the Church. That which should ensue, is an account of *their Work and Duty* in the Discharge of their Office. But this hath been the subject of many large Discourses, both among the Ancient Writers of the Church, and of late. I shall therefore only touch on some things that are of most necessary consideration.

1. THE First and Principal Duty of a *Pastor*, is *to feed the flock* by diligent Preaching of the Word. It is a promise relating to the New Testament; that God *would give unto his Church Pastors according to his own heart, which should feed them with Knowledge and Understanding*, *Jer.* 3. 15. This is by Teaching, or Preaching the Word, and no otherwise. This *Feeding* is of the *Essence* of the *Office* of a Pastor, as unto the exercise of it; so that he who *doth* not, or *cannot*, or *will* not *feed the Flock*, is no Pastor, whatever outward call, or work he may have in the Church. The care of *Preaching the Gospel* was committed to *Peter*, and in him unto all true Pastors of the Church under the name of *Feeding*, *Joh.* 21. 15, 16. According

cording to the example of the Apostles they are to free themselves from all encumbrances, that they may give themselves wholly unto the *Word and Prayer*, Act. 6. Their work is *to labour in the Word and Doctrine*, 1 Tim. 5. 17. and thereby to *feed the Flock* over which the *Holy Ghost hath made them Overseers*, Act. 20. And it is that, which is every where given them in charge.

THIS Work and Duty, therefore, as was said, is *essential* unto the *Office* of a Pastor. A Man is a Pastor unto them whom he *feeds* by Pastoral Teaching, and to no more. And he that doth not *so feed*, is no Pastor. Nor is it required only that he *Preach now and then* at his leisure; but that he lay aside all other Employments, though *lawful*, all other Duties in the Church, as unto such a constant attendance on them, as would divert him from this work, that he *give himself unto it*, that he *be in these things labouring* to the utmost of his Ability. Without this, no Man will be able to give a *comfortable account* of the *Pastoral Office* at the last day.

THERE is indeed no more required of any Man than God giveth him Ability for. Weakness, Sickness, Bodily Infirmities, may *disenable Men* from the actual discharge of this Duty, in that assiduity and frequency which are required in ordinary cases. And some may through *Age* or other incapacitating Distempers, be utterly disabled for it, in which case it is their Duty to lay down and take a dismission from their Office; or, if their disability be but *partial*, provide a suitable supply, that the Edification of the Church be not prejudiced. But for Men to pretend themselves *Pastors of the Church*, and to be unable for, or negligent of this Work and Duty, is to live in open defiance of the Commands of Christ.

WE have lived to see, or hear of reproachful scorn and contempt cast upon *laborious* Preaching, that is *labouring in the Word and Doctrine*; and all manner of discouragements given unto it, with endeavours for its suppression in sundry instances. Yea, some have proceeded so far, as to declare that the work of Preaching is *unnecessary in the Church*, so to reduce all Religion to the Reading and Rule of the *Liturgy*. The next attempt,

attempt, so far as I know, may be to exclude *Christ himself* out of their Religion; which the denial of a necessity of Preaching the Gospel makes an entrance into, yea, a good Progress towards.

SUNDRY things are required unto this Work and Duty of *Pastoral Preaching:* As, (1.) *Spiritual Wisdom* and Understanding in the Mysteries of the Gospel; that they may declare unto the Church the *whole counsel of God,* and the unsearchable Riches of Christ; see *Act.* 20. 27. 1 *Cor.* 2. 4, 5, 6, 7. *Ephes.* 3. 8, 9, 10, 11. The generality of the Church, especially those who are grown in knowledge and experience have a spiritual insight into these things. And the Apostle prays that all Believers may have so, *Ephes.* 1. 17, 18, 19. And if those that instruct them, or should so do, have not some degree of *Eminency* herein, they cannot be *useful* to lead them on to perfection. And the little Care hereof or concernment herein, is that which in our days hath rendred the *Ministry* of many fruitless and useless. (2.) *Experience of the power of the Truth* which they Preach in and upon their own Souls. Without this, they will themselves be *lifeless* and *heartless* in their own work, and their labour for the most part *unprofitable* towards others. It is to such Men, attended unto, as a *task for their advantage;* or as that which carries some satisfaction in it from ostentation, and supposed Reputation wherewith it is accompanied. But a Man Preacheth that Sermon only well unto others, which Preacheth it self in his own Soul. And he that doth not *feed on,* and thrive in the *Digestion of the Food* which he provides for others, will scarce make it savoury unto them. Yea, he knows not but the *food* he hath provided may be *poyson,* unless he have really tasted of it himself. If the Word doth not dwell with power *in us,* it will not pass with power *from us.* And no Man lives in a more wofull condition than those who really *believe not themselves* what they perswade others to believe continually. The want of this *Experience* of the power of Gospel-Truth on their own Souls, is that which gives us so many lifeless, *sapless Orations,* queint in Words, and dead as to Power, instead of Preaching the Gospel in the

the *Demonſtration of the Spirit.* And let any ſay what they pleaſe, it is evident, that ſome *Mens Preaching* as well as others *not Preaching,* hath loſt the credit of their Miniſtry. (3.) *Skill to divide the Word aright,* 2 *Tim.* 2. 15. And this conſiſts in a *practical Wiſdom* upon a diligent attendance unto the Word of Truth, to find out what is real, ſubſtantial and meet food for the Souls of the Hearers, to give unto all ſorts of perſons in the Church that which is their proper portion. And this requires, (4.) A prudent and diligent *conſideration of the ſtate of the Flock,* over which any Man is ſet, as unto their ſtrength or weakneſs, their growth or defect in knowledge (the meaſure of their attainments requiring either *Milk* or *ſtrong Meat* ;) their Temptations and Duties, their Spiritual Decays or Thrivings ; and that not only in general, but as near as may be with reſpect unto all the Individual Members of the Church. Without a due regard unto theſe things, Men Preach at random, *uncertainly fighting like thoſe that beat the Air.* Preaching Sermons not deſigned for the advantage of them to whom they are Preached ; inſiſting on general Doctrines not levelled to the condition of the Auditory ; ſpeaking what Men *can,* without conſideration of what they *ought,* are things that will make Men weary of *Preaching,* when their minds are not influenced with outward advantages ; as much as make others weary in *hearing* of them. And, (5.) All theſe, in the whole diſcharge of their Duty are to be conſtantly accompanied with the evidence of *zeal* for the glory of God, and *compaſſion for the Souls of Men.* Where theſe are not in vigorous exerciſe, in the Minds and Souls of them that *Preach the Word,* giving a Demonſtration of themſelves unto the Conſciences of them that hear, the *quickening Form,* the *Life* and *Soul* of Preaching is loſt.

ALL theſe things ſeem *common,* obvious and univerſally acknowledged : But the ruine of the Miniſtery of the moſt for the want of them, or from *notable defects* in them, is, or may be no leſs evidently known. And the very naming of them, which is all at preſent which I deſign, is ſufficient to evidence how great a neceſſity there is incumbent on all *Paſtors of Churches,* to *give themſelves unto the Word and Prayer,* to labour *in the Word and Doctrine,* to be continually intent on this Work, to engage all the faculties of their Souls, to stir up all their Graces and Gifts unto constant exercise, in the discharge of their Duty. For *who is sufficient for these things.* And as the consideration of them is sufficient to stir up all Ministers unto *fervent Prayer* for supplies of Divine Aids and Assistance, for that Work which in their own strength they can no way answer; so is it enough to warn them of the avoidance of all things that would give them a Diversion or Avocation from the constant attendance unto the discharge of it.

WHEN Men undertake the *Pastoral Office,* and either judge it *not their Duty* to Preach, or are *not able* so to do, or attempt it only at some solemn Seasons, or attend unto it as a *task* required of them without that *Wisdom, Skill, Diligence, Care, Prudence, Zeal* and *Compassion,* which are required thereunto, the Glory and Use of the Ministry will be utterly destroyed.

2. THE Second Duty of a Pastor towards his Flock, is, *continual fervent Prayer for them.* Give our selves unto the *Word and Prayer.* Without this, no Man can, or doth Preach to them as he ought, nor perform any other Duty of his *Pastoral Office.* From hence may any Man take the best measure of the discharge of his Duty towards his Flock. He that doth constantly, diligently, fervently *Pray* for them, will have a Testimony in himself of his own sincerity in the discharge of all other Pastoral Duties; nor can he voluntarily omit or neglect any of them. And as for those who are negligent herein, be their Pains, Labour and Travel in other Duties, never so great, they may be influenced from other Reasons, and so give no evidence of sincerity in the discharge of their Office. In this *constant Prayer* for the Church, which is so incumbent on all Pastors, as that whatever is done without it, is of no esteem in the sight of Jesus Christ: Respect is to be had, (1.) Unto the *Success of the Word,* unto all the blessed ends of it among them. These are no less than the improvement and strengthening of all their Graces, the Direction of all their Duties, their Edification in Faith and Love, with the entire conduct of their Souls in the life of God, unto the enjoyment of him. To Preach

Jam 5.16.
Job. 17. 20.
Exod. 32. 11.
Deut. 9 18.
Levit. 16. 24.
1 *Sam.* 12. 23.
2 *Cor.* 13. 7, 9.
Ephes. 1. 15, 16, 17.
Ch. 3. 14.
Phil. 1. 4.
Col. 1. 3.
2 *Thess.* 1. 11.

The Duty of Pastors of Churches.

Preach the Word therefore, and not to follow it with constant and *fervent Prayer* for its success, is to dis-believe its use, neglect its end, and to cast away the Seed of the Gospel at random. (2.) Unto the *Temptations* that the Church is generally exposed unto. These greatly vary, according unto the outward circumstances of things. The *Temptations* in general that accompany a State of outward *Peace and Tranquility*, are of another nature, than those that attend a time of *Trouble*, Persecution, Distress and Poverty. And so it is as unto other Occasions and Circumstances. These the *Pastors of Churches* ought diligently to consider, looking on them as the means and ways whereby Churches have been ruined, and the Souls of many lost for ever. With respect unto them therefore, ought their *Prayers* for the Church to be fervent. (3.) Unto the *especial State* and condition of all the Members, so far as it is known unto them. There may be of them, who are spiritually sick and diseased, tempted, afflicted, bemisted, wandering out of the way, surprized in Sins and Miscarriages, disconsolate and troubled in Spirit in a peculiar manner. The remembrance of them all ought to abide with them, and to be continually called over in their daily *Pastoral Supplications*. (4.) Unto the *presence of Christ* in the Assemblies of the Church, with all the blessed Evidences and Testimonies of it. This is that alone which gives Life and Power unto all Church Assemblies; without which, all outward Order and Forms of Divine Worship in them, are but a *dead Carcass*. Now this *presence of Christ* in the Assemblies of his Church, is *by his Spirit*, accompanying all Ordinances of Worship with a gracious Divine Efficacy, evidencing it self by blessed Operations on the Minds and Hearts of the Congregation. This are Pastors of Churches continually to *Pray for*, and they will do so, who understand that all the success of their labours, and all the acceptance of the Church with God in their Duties, do depend hereon. (5.) To their *preservation* in Faith, Love and Fruitfulness, with all the Duties that belong unto them, &c.

IT were much to be desired, that all those who take upon them this *Pastoral Office*, did well consider and understand how great and necessary a part of their Work and Duty doth consist in their *continual fervent Prayer* for their Flocks. For besides that it is the only instituted way, whereby, they may by virtue of their Office *bless their Congregations*, so will they find their Hearts and Minds in and by the discharge of it, more and more filled with love, and engaged with diligence, unto all other Duties of their Office, and excited unto the Exercise of all Grace towards the whole Church on all occasions. And where any are negligent herein, there is no Duty which they perform towards the Church, but it is influenced with *false considerations*, and will not hold weight in the balance of the Sanctuary.

3. THE *Administration of the Seals of the Covenant* is committed unto them as the *Stewards of the House of Christ*. For unto them the *Authoritative Dispensation* of the Word is committed, whereunto the *Administration of the Seals* is annexed. For their principal end is, the peculiar Confirmation and Application of the Word Preached. And herein there are three things that they are to attend unto. (1.) The *Times* and Seasons of their Administration unto the Churches Edification, especially that of the *Lords Supper* whose frequency is enjoined. It is the Duty of Pastors to consider all the *necessary Circumstances* of their Administration, as unto Time, Place, Frequency, Order and Decency. (2.) To keep *severely* unto the Institution of Christ, as unto the way and manner of their Administration. The gradual introduction of *uninstituted Rites and Ceremonies* into the Church-Celebration of the Ordinance of the Lords Supper, ended at length in the Idolatry of the *Mass*. Herein then, alone, and not in bowing, cringing, and vestments, lies the Glory and Beauty of these Administrations; namely, that they are *compliant with, and expressive of the Institution of Christ*; nor is any thing done in them, but in express obedience unto his Authority. *I have received of the Lord, that which I delivered unto you*, saith the Apostle in this case, 1 *Cor.* 11. 23. (3.) To take care that these holy things be administred only unto those who are *meet* and *worthy*, according unto the Rule of the Gospel. Those who impose on Pastors the promiscuous Administration of these Divine Ordinances,

or

The Duty of Pastors of Churches.

or the Application of the Seals unto all without difference, do deprive them of one half of their Ministerial Office and Duty.

BUT here it is enquired by some, *Whether in case a Church have no Pastor at present, or a Teaching Elder with Pastoral Power, whether it may not delegate and appoint the Administration of these especial Ordinances, unto some Member of the Church at this or that season, who is meetly qualified for the outward Administration of them*; which for the sake of some I shall examine.

1. NO Church is compleat in *Order* without *Teaching Officers*; *Ephes.* 4. 11, 12. 1 *Cor.* 12. 27, 28.

A CHURCH not compleat in *Order* cannot be compleat in *Administrations*; because the Power of *Administrations* depends upon the Power of *Order* proportionably. That is, the *Power* of the Church depends upon the *Being* of the Church. Hence the *first Duty* of a Church without Officers, is to obtain them according to Rule. And to endeavour to *compleat Administrations*, without an antecedent compleating of Order, is contrary unto the Mind of Christ, *Act.* 14. 23. *Tit.* 1. 5. *That thou should'st set in Order the things that are wanting, and Ordain Elders in every Church.* The practice therefore proposed is irregular and contrary to the Mind of Christ.

THE *Order* of the Church is Two Fold; as *Essential,* as *Organical.* The Order of the Church as *Essential*, and its *Power* thence arising, is, First for its Preservation. Secondly for its Perfection. (1.) For its *Preservation*, in Admission and Exclusion of Members. (2.) For its *Perfection*, in the Election of Officers.

NO part of this Power which belongs to the Church as *essentially* considered, can be *delegated*, but must be acted by the whole Church. They cannot *delegate* Power to some to admit Members, so as it should not be an Act of the whole Church. They cannot *delegate* Power to any to Elect Officers; nor any thing else which belongs to them as a Church *essentially.* The Reason is; Things that belong unto the *essence* of any thing, belong unto it *formally* as such, and so cannot be transferred.

THE

THE Church therefore cannot *delegate* the Power and Authority inquired after, should it be supposed to belong to the Power of Order, as the Church is *essentially* considered; which yet it doth not.

IF the Church may delegate or substitute others for the discharge of all Ordinances whatsoever, without *Elders* or *Pastors*, then it may *perfect the Saints, and compleat the Work of the Ministry* without them, which is contrary to *Ephes.* 4. 11, 12. and Secondly, it would render the *Ministry* only *convenient*, and not absolutely *necessary* to the Church; which is contrary to the Institution of it.

A PARTICULAR Church, in Order, as *Organical*, is the adequate subject of all Ordinances, and not as *essential*; because as *essential* it never doth nor can enjoy all Ordinances, namely the *Ministry* in particular, whereby it is constituted *Organical*. Yet on this supposition the Church as *essentially* considered, is the sole adequate *subject* of all Ordinances.

THOUGH the Church be the only *Subject*, it is not the only *Object* of Gospel Ordinances; but that is various. For instance,

1. THE *Preaching of the Word*; its *first Object* is the *World*, for Conversion: Its next, Professors, for Edification.

2. *BAPTISM*; Its only Object is neither the *World* nor the Members of a Particular Church; but *Professors*, with those that are reckoned to them by Gods Appointment; that is their Infant Seed.

3. THE *Supper*; Its Object is a *Particular Church* only, which is acknowledged; and may be proved by the Institution, one special end of it, and the necessity of Discipline thereon depending.

ORDINANCES whereof the Church is the *only Subject* and the *only Object*, cannot be administred Authoritatively, but by Officers only. (1.) Because none but *Christs Stewards* have Authority in and towards his House as such, 1 *Cor.* 4. 1. 1 *Tim.* 3. 15. *Matth.* 24. 25. (2.) Because it is an *Act of Office-Authority* to represent Christ to the whole Church, and to feed the whole Flock thereby, *Act.* 20. 28. 1 *Pet.* 5. 2.

THERE

The Duty of Pastors of Churches.

THERE are no footsteps of any such practice among the Churches of God, who walked in Order; neither in the Scripture, nor in all Antiquity.

BUT it is Objected by those who allow this Practice, *That if the Church may appoint or send a person forth to Preach, or appoint a Brother to Preach unto themselves; then they may appoint him to Administer the Ordinance of the Supper.*

Answ. HERE is a mistake in the Supposition. The Church, that is the Body of it, cannot send out any Brother *Authoritatively* to Preach. Two things are required thereunto; *Collation of Gifts*, and *Communication of Office*; neither of which, the Church under that consideration can do to one that is sent forth. But where God *gives Gifts* by his Spirit, and a Call by his Providence, the Church only complies therewith; not in communicating Authority to the person, but in *praying* for a Blessing upon his Work.

THE same is the case in desiring a Brother to Teach among them. The Duty is moral in its own nature; the Gifts and Call are from God alone, the occasion of his exercise is only administred by the Church.

IT is farther added by the same persons, that, *If a Brother, or one who is a Disciple, only may Baptize, then he may also Administer the Lords Supper, being desired of the Church.*

Answ. THE supposition is not granted nor proved, but there is yet a difference between these Ordinances; the Object of one being *Professors* as such at large; the Object of the other being *Professors* as Members of a Particular Church. But to return:

4. IT is incumbent on them to *preserve the Truth or Doctrine of the Gospel*, received and professed in the Church; and to defend it against all opposition. This is *one principal end of the Ministry*, one principal means of the preservation of the *Faith once delivered unto the Saints*. This is committed in an especial manner unto the Pastors of the Churches, as the Apostle frequently and emphatically repeats the charge of it unto *Timothy*, and in him unto all, to whom the Dispensation of the Word is committed, 1 *Epist.* 1. 1, 3, 4. Chap. 4. 6, 7, 16.

Chap. 6. 20. 2 *Epist.* 1. 14, 22. Chap. 3. 14, 15, 16. The same he giveth in charge unto the *Elders of the Church of Ephesus*, *Act.* 20. 28, 29, 30. What he says of himself, that the *Glorious Gospel of the blessed God was committed unto his Trust*, 1 *Tim.* 1. 11. is true of all Pastors of Churches according to their measure and call; and they should all aim at the Account, which he gives of his Ministry herein; *I have fought a good Fight, I have finished my Course, I have kept the Faith*, 2 *Tim.* 3. 7. The Church is the *Ground and Pillar of Truth*; and it is so principally in its Ministry. And the sinful neglect of this Duty, is that which was the cause of most of the *pernicious Heresies and Errors* that have infested and ruined the Church. Those whose Duty it was *to preserve the Doctrine of the Gospel* entire in the publick profession of it, have many of them *spoken perverse things to draw away Disciples after them. Bishops, Presbyters, publick Teachers*, have been the ring-leaders in Heresies. Wherefore this Duty, especially at this time, when the fundamental Truths of the Gospel are on all sides impugned from all sorts of Adversaries, is in an especial manner to be attended unto.

SUNDRY things are required hereunto. As, (1.) A clear, sound *comprehensive knowledge* of the entire Doctrine of the Gospel, attained by all means useful and commonly prescribed unto that end, especially *diligent study of the Scripture*, with fervent Prayer for Illumination and Understanding. Men cannot preserve that for others, which they are ignorant of themselves. Truth may be lost by *weakness*, as well as by *wickedness*. And the defect herein in many is deplorable. (2.) *Love of the Truth*, which they have so learned and comprehended. Unless we look on Truth as a *Pearl*, as that which is valued at any rate, bought with any price, as that which is better than all the World, we shall not endeavour its preservation with that diligence which is required. Some are ready to part with Truth at an easie rate; or to grow indifferent about it, whereof we have multitudes of examples in the days wherein we live. It were easie to give instances of sundry important *Evangelical Truths*, which our fore-fathers in the Faith contended

contended for with all earnestness, and were ready to seal with their Blood, which are now *utterly disregarded* and opposed by some who pretend to succeed them in their Profession. If Ministers have not a sense of that Power of Truth in their own Souls, and a taste of its Goodness, the discharge of this Duty is not to be expected from them. (3.) A *conscientious care* and fear of giving countenance or encouragement unto *novel Opinions*, especially such as oppose any Truth, of whose Power and Efficacy, Experience hath been had among them that believe. Vain curiosity, boldness in conjectures, and readiness to vent their own conceits, have caused no small trouble and damage unto the Church. (4.) *Learning and ability of Mind* to discern and disprove the oppositions of the Adversaries of the Truth, and thereby to stop their Mouths, and convince gain-sayers. (5.) The *solid confirmation* of the most important Truths of the Gospel, and whereunto all others are resolved in their Teaching and Ministry. Men may, and do oft-times prejudice, yea, betray the Truth, by the weakness of their Pleas for it. (6.) A *diligent watch* over their own Flocks, against the crafts of Seducers from without, or the springing up of any *bitter root of error* among themselves. (7.) A *concurrent Assistance* with the Elders and Messengers of other Churches, with whom they are in Communion, in the declaration of the Faith which they all profess; whereof we must treat afterwards more at large.

IT is evident what Learning, Labour, Study, Pains, Ability and Exercise of the rational Faculties, are ordinarily required unto the right discharge of these Duties. And where Men may be useful to the Church in other things, but are defective in these, it becomes them to walk and act both circumspectly and humbly, frequently desiring and adhering unto the Advices of them whom God hath entrusted with more Talents and greater Abilities.

5. IT belongs unto their Charge and Office, *diligently to labour for the Conversion of Souls unto God.* The ordinary means of Conversion is left unto the Church, and its Duty it is to attend unto it. Yea, one of the *principal ends* of the Institution

and Preservation of Churches, is the *Conversion of Souls*; and where there are no more to be Converted, there shall be no more Church on the Earth. To enlarge the Kingdom of Christ, to diffuse the Light and Savour of the Gospel, to be subservient unto the Calling of the Elect, or gathering all the Sheep of Christ into his Fold, are things that God designs by his *Churches* in this World. Now the principal instrumental cause of all these, is the *Preaching of the Word*; and this is committed unto the *Pastors of the Churches*. It is true, Men may be, and often are Converted unto God by their occasional dispensation of the Word who are not called unto Office; for it is the *Gospel it self* that is *the Power of God unto Salvation*, by whomsoever it is Administred, and it hath been effectual unto that end, even in the necessary occasional *teaching of Women*. But it is so frequently in the exercise of Spiritual Gifts, by them who are not *stated Officers* of the Church, 1 Cor. 14. 24, 25. Phil. 1. 14, 15, 18. 1 Pet. 4. 10, 11. But yet this hinders not, but that the Administration of the Glorious Gospel of the blessed God, as unto all the ends of it, is committed unto the *Pastors of the Church*. And the *First Object* of the Preaching of the Gospel, is the *World*, or the Men of it for their Conversion. And it is so in the Preaching of all them unto whom that Work is committed by Christ. The Work of the Apostles and *Evangelists* had this Order in it. First, they were to make Disciples of Men, by the Preaching of the Gospel unto Conversion, and this was their principal Work, as *Paul* testifieth, 1 *Cor.* 1. 17. And herein were they gloriously instrumental, in laying the foundation of the Kingdom of Christ all the World over. The Second part of their Work, was, *to teach them that were Converted*, or made Disciples, to do, and observe, all that he did command them. In the pursuit of this part of their Commission, they gathered the Disciples of Christ into Churches, under ordinary Officers of their own. And although the Work of these Ordinary Officers, Pastors, and Teachers, be of the same nature with theirs, yet the *Method* of it is changed in them. For their first *ordinary Work* is to conduct and teach all the Disciples of Christ *to do and*

The Duty of Pastors of Churches.

and observe all things appointed by him; that is to Preach unto and Watch over their particular Flocks, unto whom they do relate. But they are not hereby discharged from an interest in the other *part of the Work* in Preaching the Word unto the Conversion of Souls. They are not indeed bound unto the *Method* of the *Apostles* and *Evangelists*; yea, they are by virtue of their Office, ordinarily excluded from it. After a Man is called to be a Pastor of a particular Church, it is not his Duty to leave that Church, and go up and down to Preach for the Conversion of Strangers. It is not, I say, *ordinarily* so, for many cases may fall out wherein the *Edification* of any particular Church is to give way unto the glory of Christ, with respect unto the calling of all the Members of the *Church Catholick*. But in the discharge of the *Pastoral Office*, there are many occasions of Preaching the Word unto the Conversion of Souls. As, (1.) When any that are Unconverted *do come into the Assemblies of the Church*, and are there wrought upon by the Power of the Word, whereof we have experience every day. To suppose that a Man at the same time, and in the same place Preaching unto one Congregation, should Preach to some of them, namely those that are of the Church whereunto he relates, as a Minister with *Ministerial Authority*; and to others only by virtue of a *Spiritual Gift*, which he hath received, is that which no Man can distinguish in his own Conscience, nor is there any colour of Rule or Reason for it. For though Pastors, with respect unto their whole Office, and all the Duties of it, whereof many can have the Church only for their Object, are *Ministers in Office unto the Church*, and so Ministers of the Church; yet are they Ministers of *Christ* also; and by him it is, and not by the *Church*, that the Preaching of the Gospel is committed unto them. And it is so committed, as that by virtue of their Office they are to *use it unto all its ends*, in his way and method, whereof the Conversion of Sinners is one. And for a Man to conceive of himself in a *double capacity* whilst he is Preaching to the same Congregation, is that which no Mans experience can reach unto. (2.) In *occasional Preaching* in other

other places, whereunto a *Paſtor of a Church* may be called and directed by Divine Providence. For, although we have no concernment in the figment of an *indelible Character* accompanying Sacred Orders; yet we do not think that the *Paſtoral Office* is ſuch a thing as a Man muſt *leave behind him* every time he goes from home; or that it is in his own power, or in the power of all Men in the World, to deveſt him of it, unleſs he be diſmiſſed or depoſed from it by Chriſt himſelf, through the Rule of his Word. Where-ever a true Miniſter Preacheth, he Preacheth as a Miniſter; for, as ſuch the Adminiſtration of the Goſpel is committed unto him, as unto all the ends of it; whereof, the chief as was ſaid, is the Converſion of Souls. Yea, of ſuch weight is it, that the Conveniency and Edification of particular Churches, ought to give place unto it. When therefore there are great Opportunities, and providential Calls for the Preaching of the Goſpel unto the Converſion of Souls, and the *Harveſt* being great there are *not Labourers* ſufficient for it; it is lawful, yea, it is the Duty of Paſtors of particular Churches, to leave their conſtant attendance on their Paſtoral Charge in thoſe Churches, at leaſt for a Seaſon, to apply themſelves unto the more publick Preaching of the Word unto the Converſion of the Souls of Men. Nor will any particular Church be unwilling hereunto, which underſtands that even the whole end of particular Churches is but the Edification of the *Church Catholick*; and that their good and advantage is to give place unto that of the Glory of Chriſt in the whole. The *good Shepherd will leave the Ninety and Nine* Sheep, to ſeek after *one* that wanders; and we may certainly leave a *few* for *a ſeaſon*, to ſeek after a great multitude of wanderers, when we are called thereunto by Divine Providence. And I could heartily wiſh that we might have a trial of it at this time.

THE Miniſters who have been moſt *celebrated*, and that deſervedly in the laſt Ages, in this and the neighbour Nations, have been ſuch as whoſe Miniſtry God made eminently ſucceſsful unto the Converſion of Souls. To affirm that they did not do their work *as Miniſters* and by virtue of their *Miniſterial Office*,

The Duty of Pastors of Churches.

Office, is to cast away the Crown, and destroy the principal glory of the Ministry. For my own part, if I did not think my self bound to Preach *as a Minister*, and *as a Minister* Authorized in all places, and on all occasions when I am called thereunto, I think I should never Preach much more in this World. Nor do I know at all what Rule they walk by, who continue *publick constant Preaching* for many years, and yet neither desire nor design to be called unto any Pastoral Office, in the Church. But I must not here insist on the debate of these things.

6. IT belongs unto Men on the account of their Pastoral Office, to be ready, willing, and able, to *comfort, relieve and refresh* those that are *tempted, tossed*, wearied with fears and grounds of disconsolation in times of trial and desertion. *The Tongue of the Learned* is required in them, that they should know how *to speak a word in Season unto him that is weary*. One excellent qualification of our Lord Jesus Christ, in the Discharge of his Priestly Office now in Heaven, is, That he is *touched with a sense of our Infirmities*, and *knows how to succour them that are tempted*. His whole Flock in this World, are a company of *tempted* ones. His own Life on the Earth, he calls the *time of his Temptation*. And those who have the charge of his Flock under him, ought to have a sense of their Infirmities, and endeavour in an especial manner to *succour* them that are tempted. But amongst them, there are some always that are cast under *darkness* and *disconsolations* in a peculiar manner; some at the entrance of their Conversion unto God, whilst they have a deep sense of the *terrour of the Lord*, the sharpness of Conviction, and the uncertainty of their Condition. Some are relapsed into Sin or omissions of Duties; some under great, sore and lasting Afflictions; some upon pressing, urgent, particular *Occasions*; some on Sovereign, Divine *Desertions*; some through the *buffetings of Satan*, and the injections of blasphemous Thoughts into their Minds, with many other occasions of an alike nature. Now the Troubles, Disconsolations, Dejections and Fears that arise in the Minds of Persons in these Exercises and Temptations, are various, oftentimes urged and fortified

fortified with subtil arguing, and fair pretences, perplexing the Souls of Men almost to Despair and Death. It belongs unto the Office and Duty of Pastors.

1. TO be able *rightly to understand the various cases* that will occurr of this kind, from such principles and grounds of Truth and Experience, as will bear a just confidence in a prudent Application unto the Relief of them concerned. The *Tongue of the Learned to know how to speak a Word in Season to him that is weary*. It will not be done by a *collection and determination of cases*, which yet is useful it its place. For hardly shall we meet with *two cases* of this kind, that will exactly be determined by the same Rule; all manner of *Circumstances* giving them variety. But a Skill, Understanding and Experience in the *whole nature of the Work of the Spirit of God* on the Souls of Men; of the Conflict that is between the *Flesh and the Spirit*; of the Methods and Wiles of *Satan*, of the Wiles of *Principalities and Powers* or wicked Spirits in *high places*; of the Nature, and Effects and Ends of Divine Desertions, with Wisdom to make Application out of such Principles, of fit Medicines and Remedies unto every Sore and Distemper, are required hereunto. These things are by some *despised*, by some *neglected*, by some looked after only in *stated cases of Conscience*; in which Work it is known that some have horribly debauched their own Consciences and others, to the scandal and ruine of Religion, so far as they have prevailed. But not to dispute how far such helps as *Books written of cases of Conscience*, may be useful herein, which they may be greatly unto those who know how to use them aright; the proper ways whereby *Pastors* and *Teachers* must obtain this Skill and Understanding, is, by diligent study of the Scriptures, Meditation thereon, fervent Prayer, Experience of Spiritual Things, and Temptations in their own Souls, with a prudent observation of the manner of Gods dealing with others, and the ways of the opposition made to the Work of his Grace in them. Without these things all pretences unto this Ability and Duty of the *Pastoral Office* are vain; whence it is, that the whole Work of it is much neglected.

2. TO

2. TO be ready and willing *to attend unto the especial cases that may be brought unto them,* and not to look on them as unnecessary Diversions; whereas a due Application unto them, is a principal part of their Office and Duty. To discountenance, to discourage any from seeking relief in *perplexities* of this nature, to carry it towards them with a seeming *moroseness* and unconcernedness, is to turn *that which is Lame out of the way, to push the Diseased,* and not at all to express the care of Christ towards his Flock, *Isa.* 40. 11. Yea, it is their Duty to hearken after them who may be so exercised, to seek them out, to give them their Counsel and Directions on all occasions.

3. TO bear *patiently* and tenderly with the *weakness, ignorance,* dulness, slowness to believe and receive satisfaction, yea, it may be, *Impertinencies* in them that are so tempted. These things will abound amongst them, partly from their *natural Infirmities,* many being weak, and perhaps froward; but especially from the *nature of their Temptations,* which are suited to disorder and disquiet their Minds, to fill them with perplexed Thoughts, and to make them jealous of every thing wherein they are spiritually concerned. And if much patience, meekness and condescention, be not exercised towards them, they are quickly *turned out of the way.*

IN the discharge of the whole *Pastoral Office,* there is not any Thing or Duty that is of *more importance,* nor wherein the Lord Jesus Christ is more concerned, nor more eminently suited unto the nature of the Office it self, than this is. But, whereas it is a *Work* or *Duty,* which because of the Reasons mentioned, must be accompanied with the exercise of Humility, Patience, Self-denial and Spiritual Wisdom, with Experience, with wearisome Diversions from other occasions; those who had got of old the *conduct of the Souls of Men* into their management, turned this whole part of their Office and Duty into an Engine they called *Aricular Confession,* whereby they wrested the Consciences of Christians to the promotion of their own Ease, Wealth, Authority, and oft-times to worse ends.

7. A *compassionate suffering,* with all the Members of the Church in all their trials and troubles, whether internal,

or external, belongs unto them in the discharge of their Office. Nor is there any thing that renders them more *like unto Jesus Christ*, whom to represent unto the Church, is their principal Duty. The view and consideration by Faith of the Glory of Christ in his *compassion with his suffering Members*, is the principal spring of Consolation unto the Church in all its Distresses. And the same Spirit, the *same Mind* herein, ought, according to their measure, to be in all that have the *Pastoral Office* committed unto them. So the *Apostle* expresseth it in himself: *Who is weak, and I am not weak? Who is offended, and I burn not?* 2 Cor. 11. 29. And unless this compassion and goodness do run through the discharge of their whole Office, Men cannot be said to be *Evangelical Shepherds*, nor the Sheep said in any sense to be *their own*. For those who pretend unto the *Pastoral Office*, to live, it may be, in wealth and pleasure, regardless of the Sufferings and Temptations of their Flock, or of the poor of it; or related unto such Churches, as wherein it is impossible that they should so much as be acquainted with the state of the greatest part of them, is not answerable unto the institution of their Office, nor to the design of Christ therein.

8. *CARE of the Poor*, and *visitation of the Sick*, are parts of this Duty, commonly known, though commonly neglected.

9. THE *principal care of the Rule of the Church* is incumbent on the Pastors of it. This is the second general head of the Power and Duty of this Office, whereunto many things in particular do belong. But because I shall treat afterwards of the Rule of the Church by it self distinctly, I shall not here insist upon it.

10. THERE is a *Communion to be observed among all the Churches of the same Faith and Profession* in any Nation. Wherein it doth consist, and what is required thereunto, shall be afterwards declared. The principal care hereof, unto the Edification of the Churches, is incumbent on the Pastors of them. Whether it be exercised by *Letters* of mutual advice, of congratulation or consolation, or in testimony of Communion with those who are

are called to Office in them, or whether it be by convening in Synods for confultation of their joint concernments, (which things made up a great part of the Primitive Ecclefiaftical *Polity*;) their Duty it is to attend unto it, and to take care of it.

11. THAT wherewith I fhall clofe thefe few inftances of the *Pafloral Charge* and Duty, is, that without which all the reft will neither be ufeful unto Men, nor be accepted with the great Shepherd Chrift Jefus. And that is an *humble, holy, exemplary converfation in all Godlinefs and Honefty.* The Rules and Precepts of the Scripture, the Examples of Chrift and his Apoftles, with that of the Bifhops or Paftors of the Primitive Churches, and the nature of the thing it felf, with the Religion which we do profefs, do undeniably prove this Duty to be neceffary and indifpenfable in a Gofpel Miniftry. It were an eafie thing to fill up a Volume with ancient *Examples* unto this purpofe; with *Teftimonies* of the Scripture and firft Writers among Chriftians, with Examples of publick and private mifcarriages herein, with evident demonftration, that the *ruine of Chriftian Religion* in moft Nations where it hath been profeffed, and fo of the Nations themfelves, hath proceeded from the *Ambition, Pride, Luxury, Uncleannefs, Profanenefs,* and otherways *vitious Converfations* of thofe who have been called the *Clergy*. And in daily obfervation, it is a thing written with the Beams of the Sun, that whatever elfe be done in Churches, if the Paftors of them or thofe who are fo efteemed, are not *Exemplary* in Gofpel Obedience and Holinefs, Religion will not be carried on and improved among the people. If Perfons, light or prophane in their Habits, Garbs and Converfe, corrupt in their Communication, Unfavoury and Barren as unto Spiritual Difcourfe; if fuch as are Covetous, Oppreffive and Contentious; fuch as are negligent in holy Duties in their own Families, and fo cannot ftir up others unto diligence therein; much more, if fuch as are openly fenfual, vitious and debauched, are admitted into this Office, we may take our leave of all the Glory and Power of Religion, among the people committed unto their charge.

P   TO

TO handle this property or *adjunct* of the Pastoral Office, it were necessary distinctly to consider and explain all the Qualifications assigned by the Apostle as necessary unto *Bishops* and *Elders*, evidenced as previously necessary unto the orderly Call of them unto this Office, 1 *Tim*. 3. 2, 3, 4, 5, 6, 7. *Tit*. 2. 6, 7, 8, 9. which is a Work not consistent with my present design to engage in.

THESE are some Instances of the things wherein the *Office-Duty* of Pastors of the Church doth consist. They are but *some* of them, and those only *proposed*, not *pursued* and pressed with the consideration of all those particular Duties, with the manner of their performance, way of management, motives and enforcements, defects and causes of them, which would require a large Discourse. These may suffice unto our present purpose; and we may derive from them the ensuing brief considerations.

1. A DUE meditation and view of these things, as proposed in the Scripture, is enough to make the wisest, the best of Men, and the most diligent in the discharge of the *Pastoral Office*, to cry out with the Apostle, *and who is sufficient for these things?* This will make them look well to their *Call* and *Entrance* into this Office, as that alone which will bear them out and justify them in the susception of it. For no sense of *insufficiency* can utterly discourage any in the undertaking of a Work, which he is assured that the Lord Christ calls him unto. For where he calls to a Duty, he gives competent strength for the performance of it. And when we say, Under a deep sense of our own weakness, *who is sufficient for these things*; he doth say, *My Grace is sufficient for you*.

2. ALTHOUGH all the things mentioned, do plainly, evidently and undeniably belong unto the discharge of the *Pastoral Office*, yet in point of Fact we find by the Success, that they are very little considered by the most that seek after it. And the present Ruine of Religion, as unto its Power, Beauty and Glory in all places, ariseth principally from this cause, that *Multitudes* of those who undertake this Office, are neither in any measure fit for it, nor do either conscientiously attend

attend unto, or diligently perform the Duties that belong unto it. It ever was, and every will be true in general; *like Priest, like People.*

3. WHEREAS the account which is to be given of this Office, and the discharge of it at the *last day* unto Jesus Christ, the consideration whereof had a mighty influence upon the *Apostles* themselves, and all the Primitive Pastors of the Churches, is frequently proposed unto us, and many warnings given us thereon in the Scripture; yet it is apparent they are but few who take it into due consideration. In the great day of Christs *Visitation*, he will proceed on such *Articles* as those here laid down, and others expressed in the Scripture, and not at all on those which are now enquired upon in our *Episcopal Visitations*. And if they may be minded of their true interest and concern, whilst they possess the places they hold in the Church, without offence, I would advise them to conform their *Enquiries* in their *Visitations*, unto those, which they cannot but know the Lord Christ will make in the great day of his *Visitation*, which doth approach: This I think but reasonable. In the mean time, for those who desire to give up their *account* with joy and confidence, and not with grief and confusion; it is their Wisdom and Duty continually to bear in Mind what it is that the Lord Christ requires of them in the discharge of their Office. To take *Benefices*, to perform *legal Duties by themselves or others*, is not fully compliant with what Pastors of Churches are called unto.

4. IT is manifest also from hence, how *inconsistent* it is with this Office, and the due discharge of it, for any one Man to undertake the relation of *a Pastor unto more Churches than one*, especially if far distant from one another. An evil this is, like that of *Mathematical Prognostications* at *Rome, always condemned and always retained*. But one view of the Duties incumbent on each Pastor, and of whose diligent performance he is to give an account at the last day, will discard this practice from all approbation in the Minds of them that are sober. However, it is as good to have Ten Churches at once, as having but one, never to discharge the Duty of a Pastor towards it.

5. ALL

5. ALL Churches may do well to confider the *weight and burden* that lies upon their Paftors and Teachers, in the difcharge of their Office, that they may be *conftant in fervent Prayers and Supplications* for them; as alfo to provide, what lies in them, that they may be *without trouble and cares about the things of this Life*.

6. THERE being fo many Duties neceffary unto the difcharge of their Office, and thofe of fuch *various forts and kinds*, as to require various Gifts and Abilities unto their due performance, it feems very difficult to find a concurrence of them in any one perfon, in any confiderable degree, fo as that it is hard to conceive how the Office it felf fhould be duly difcharged. I anfwer, (1.) The end both of the Office, and of the difcharge of it, is the *due Edification of the Church*: This therefore gives them their meafure. Where that is attained, the Office is duly difcharged, though the Gifts whereby Men are enabled thereunto, be not *eminent*. (2.) Where a Man is *called* unto this Office, and applieth himfelf fincerely unto the due difcharge of it, if he be evidently *defective* with refpect to any efpecial Duty or Duties of it, that *defect* is to be fupplied by calling any other unto his Affiftance in Office, who is qualified to make that fupply unto the Edification of the Church. And the like muft be faid concerning fuch Paftors, as through Age or Bodily weaknefs are difabled from attendance unto any part of their Duty; for ftill *the Edification of the Church* is that, which in all thefe things, is in the firft place to be provided for.

7. IT may be enquired, what is the State of thofe Churches, and what Relation, with refpect unto Communion, we ought to have unto them whofe Paftors are evidently *defective* in, or *neglective* of thefe things, fo as that they are not in any *competent meafure* attended unto. And we may in particular inftance in the *firft* and the *laft* of the Paftoral Duties before infifted on. Suppofe a Man be no way able to *Preach the Word* unto the Edification of them that are pleaded to be his Flock; or having any *ability*, yet doth not, will not give himfelf unto the *Word and Prayer*, or not *labour in the Word and Doctrine*, unto the great

The Duty of Pastors of Churches.

great prejudice of Edification: And suppose the same Person be openly *defective*, as unto an *exemplary Conversation*, and on the contrary, layeth the stumbling block of his *own Sins and Follies* before the eyes of others; what shall we judge of his Ministry, and of the state of that Church whereof he is a *constituent part*, as its Ruler? I Answer,

1. I DO not believe it is in the power of any Church really to conferr the Pastoral Office by virtue of any *Ordination* whatever, unto any who are openly and evidently destitute of all those previous Qualifications which the Scripture requireth in them who are to be called unto this Office. There is indeed a *Latitude* to be allowed in judging of them in times of necessity and great penury of able Teachers; so that Persons in holy Ministry, design the Glory of God and the Edification of the Church, according to their Ability. But otherwise there is a *nullity* in the pretended Office.

2. WHERE any such are admitted through *ignorance* or *mistake*, or the Usurpation of undue Power over Churches, in imposing Ministers on them, there is not an *absolute nullity in their Administrations*, until they are discovered and convicted by the Rule and Law of Christ. But if on evidence hereof, the people will voluntarily adhere unto them, they are partakers of their Sins, and do what in them lies to *Un-Church* themselves.

3. WHERE such Persons are by any means placed as Pastors in or over any Churches, and there is no way for the *Removal* or *Reformation*, it is Lawful unto, it is the **Duty** of every one who takes care of his own Edification and **Salvation**, to withdraw from the Communion of such Churches, and to join with such as wherein Edification is better provided for. For, whereas this is the sole end of Churches, of all their Offices, Officers and Administrations; it is the highest folly to imagine that any Disciple of Christ, can be, or is obliged by his Authority to abide in the Communion of such Churches, without seeking Relief in the ways of his Appointment; wherein that end is utterly overthrown.

4. WHERE

4. WHERE the generality of Churches in any kind of *Association* are headed by Pastors defective in these things, in the matter declared, there all *publick Church-Reformation* is morally impossible; and it is the Duty of *private Men* to take care of their own Souls, let Churches and Church-men say what they please.

SOME few things may yet be enquired into, with reference unto the *Office* of a Pastor in the Church: As,

1. WHETHER *a Man may be ordained a Pastor or a Minister, without Relation unto any particular Church, so as to be invested with Office-Power thereby.*

IT is usually said, that a Man may be Ordained a Minister unto, or of the *Catholick Church*, or to Convert Infidels, although he be not related unto any particular Flock or Congregation.

I SHALL not at present discuss sundry things about the power and way of *Ordination* which influence this *Controversy*, but only speak briefly unto the thing it self: And,

1. IT is granted, that a Man *endowed with Spiritual Gifts* for the Preaching of the Gospel, may be set apart by *Fasting and Prayer* unto that Work, when he may be orderly called unto it in the Providence of God. For, (1.) Such an one hath a *Call* unto it *materially* in the *Gifts* which he hath received, warranting him unto the exercise of them for the Edification of others, as he hath occasion, 1 *Pet.* 4. 10, 11. 1 *Cor.* 14. 12. Setting apart unto an important Work by Prayer is a *moral Duty*, and useful in Church Affairs in an especial manner, *Act.* 13. 12. (2.) A *publick Testimony* unto the Approbation of a Person undertaking the Work of Preaching, is necessary. (1.) Unto the *Communion of Churches*, that he may be received in any of them as is occasion; of which sort were the *Letters of Recommendation* in the Primitive Church, 1 *Cor.* 16. 3. 2 *Cor.* 3. 1. 3 *Joh.* 9. (2.) Unto the safety of them, amongst whom he may exercise his Gifts, that they be not imposed on by false Teachers or Seducers. Nor would the *Primitive Church allow*, nor is it allowable in the Communion of Churches, that any Person not so testified unto, not so sent

and

and warranted, should undertake constantly to Preach the Gospel.

2. SUCH Persons so *set apart and sent*, may be esteemed Ministers in the general notion of the Word, and may be useful in the calling and planting of Churches, wherein they may be instated in the *Pastoral Office*. This was Originally the Work of *Evangelists*, which Office being ceased in the Church, (as shall be proved elsewhere) the Work may be supplied by Persons of this sort.

3. NO Church whatever hath power to *Ordain* Men Ministers for the *Conversion of Infidels*. Since the Cessation of extraordinary *Officers* and *Offices*, the care of that Work is devolved meerly on the providence of God, being left without the verge of Church-Institutions. God alone can send and warrant Men for the undertaking of that Work. Nor can any Man know, or be satisfied in a Call unto that Work, without some previous guidance of Divine Providence leading him thereunto. It is indeed the Duty of all the ordinary Ministers of the Church, to diffuse the knowledge of Christ and the Gospel unto the Heathen and Infidels, among whom, or near unto whom their Habitation is cast; and they have all manner of Divine Warranty for their so doing; as many worthy Persons have done effectually in *New England*. And it is the Duty of every true Christian, who may be cast among them by the providence of God, to instruct them according unto his Ability in the knowledge of the Truth: But it is not in the power of any Church, or any sort of ordinary *Officers*, to Ordain a Person unto the Office of the Ministry for the Conversion of the Heathen, antecedently unto any designation by Divine Providence thereunto.

4. NO Man can be properly or compleatly Ordained unto the Ministry, but he is Ordained unto a *determinate Office*; as a *Bishop*, an *Elder*, a *Pastor*. But this no Man can be, but he who is Ordained in and unto a particular Church. For the contrary practice,

1. WOULD be contrary to the constant practice of the Apostles, who *Ordained no ordinary Officers*, but in and unto
particular

particular Churches, which were to be their proper charge and care, *Act.* 14. 23. *Tit.* 1. 5. Nor is there mention of any ordinary Officers in the whole *Scripture*, but such as were fixed in the particular Churches where-unto they did relate, *Act.* 20. 28. *Phil.* 1. 1. *Revel.* 2. 3. Nor was any such practice known or heard of in the *Primitive Church*: Yea,

2. IT was *absolutely forbidden* in the *Ancient Church*, and all such Ordinations declared *null*, so as not to communicate *Office-Power* or give any Ministerial Authority. So it is expresly in the First *Canon* of the *Council of Chalcedon*, and the Council Decrees, That all Imposition of Hands, in such cases, is *invalid and of no effect*. Yea, so exact and careful were they in this matter, that if any one, for any just cause, as he judged himself, did *leave his particular Church* or Charge, they would not allow him the Name or *Title of a Bishop*, or to Officiate occasionally in that Church, or any where else. This is evident in the case of *Eustathius* a Bishop of *Pamphilia*. The good Man finding the discharge of his *Office* very troublesome, by reason of *Secular Businesses* that it was incumbred withal, and much opposition, with Reproach that befell him from the Church it self, of *his own accord* laid down and resigned his Charge, the Church choosing one *Theodorus* in his room. But afterwards he desired, that though he had left his Charge, he might *retain the Name, Title and Honour of a Bishop*: For this end he made a Petition unto the *Council of Ephesus*, who, as themselves express it, in *meer commiseration* unto the Old Man, condescended unto his desire as unto the *Name and Title*, but not as unto any *Office-Power*, which they judge, related absolutely unto a particular Charge, *Epist. Can. Ephes.* 1. ad *Synod. in Pamphil.*

3. SUCH Ordination wants an *essential constitutive Cause*, and part of the Collation of *Office-Power*, which is the *Election* of the people, and is therefore invalid. See what hath been proved before unto that purpose.

4. A *BISHOP*, an *Elder*, a *Pastor*, being terms of Relation, to make any one so without *Relation* unto a Church, a People, a Flock, is to make him a Father who hath no Child, or an Husband who hath no Wife, a *Relate*

without

The Duty of Pastors of Churches.

without a *Correlate,* which is impossible, and implies a contradiction.

5. IT is inconsistent with the whole *nature* and *end* of the *Pastoral Office.* Whoever is duly Called, set Apart or Ordained unto that Office, he doth therein and thereby take on himself the *Discharge of all the Duties* belonging thereunto, and is obliged to attend diligently unto them. If then we will take a view of what hath been proved before to belong unto this Office, we shall find, that not the *least part,* scarce any thing of it, can be undertaken and discharged by such as are Ordained *absolutely* without Relation unto particular Churches. For any to take upon them to commit an Office unto others, and not at the same time charge them with all the *Duties* of that *Office* and their immediate attendance on them; or for any to accept of an *Office* and *Office-Power,* not knowing when or where to exert the *Power* or perform the *Duties* of it, is irregular. In particular, *Ruling* is an essential part of the *Pastoral Office,* which they cannot attend unto who have none to be ruled by them.

2. *MAY* a Pastor *remove from one Congregation unto another?*

THIS is a thing also which the *Ancient Church* made great Provision against. For when some Churches were encreased in Members, Reputation, Privileges and Wealth above others, it grew an ordinary practice for the *Bishops* to design and endeavour their own removal from a less unto a greater Benefice. This is so severely interdicted in the Councils of *Nice* and *Chalcedon,* as that they would not allow that a Man might be a *Bishop* or *Presbyter* in any other place, but only in the Church wherein he was *Originally Ordained:* And therefore, if any did so remove themselves, Decreed, that they should be *sent home again,* and there abide, or cease to be Church-Officers, *Council. Nice, Can.* 15, 16. *Chalced. Can.* 5, 20. *Pluralities,* as they are called, and open contending for *Ecclesiastical Promotions, Benefices* and *Dignities,* were then either unknown, or openly condemned.

YET it cannot be denied, but that there may be *just causes* of the Removal of a *Pastor* from one Congregation unto another;

another: For, whereas the end of all particular Churches is to *promote the Edification of the Catholick Church* in general; where, in any especial instance, such a removal is useful unto that end, it is equal it should be allowed. Cases of this nature may arise from the consideration of *Persons*, *Places*, *Times*, and many other Circumstances that I cannot insist on in particular. But that such removals may be without offence, it is required that they be made, (1.) With the *free consent of the Churches* concerned. (2.) With the *advice of other Churches*, or their Elders, with whom they walk in Communion. And of Examples of this kind, or of the Removal of *Bishops* or *Pastors* from one Church to another in an orderly manner, by Advice and Counsel for the good of the whole Church, there are many instances in the Primitive Times. Such was that of *Gregory Naz.* removed from *Casima* to *Constantinople*, though I acknowledge it had no good success.

3. MAY a Pastor *voluntarily, or of his own accord, resign and lay down his Office, and remain in a private Capacity?*

THIS also was judged inconvenient, if not unlawful, by the First *Synod of Ephesus*, in the case of *Eustathius*. He was, as it appears, an Aged Man, one that loved his one peace and quietness, and who could not well bear the Oppositions and Reproaches which he met withal from the Church or some in it; and thereon, solemnly upon his own judgment, without advice, laid down and renounced his Office in the Church, who, thereupon chose a good Man in his room. Yet did the *Synod* condemn this practice, and that not without weighty Reasons, whereby they confirmed their judgment.

BUT yet no *general Rule* can be established in this case; nor was the judgment or practice of the Primitive Church *precise* herein. *Clemens*, in his Epistle to the Church of *Corinth*, expressly adviseth those on whose occasion there was disturbance and divisions in the Church, to lay down their Office and withdraw from it. *Gregory Nazianzen* did the same at *Constantinople*, and protesteth openly, That although he were himself innocent and free from blame, as he *truly was*, and one of the greatest Men of his Age, yet he would depart or be cast out,

rather

rather than they should not have peace among them; which he did accordingly, *Orat.* 52. *& vit. Nazian.* And afterward a *Synod* at *Constantinople* under *Photius*, concluded, that in some cases it is lawful, *Can.* 5. Wherefore,

1. IT seems not to be lawful so to do, meerly on the account of *weakness of Work and Labour*, though occasioned by Age, Sickness, or Bodily Distempers. For no Man is any way obliged to do more than he is able, with the regular preservation of his Life; and the Church is obliged to be satisfied with the conscientious discharge of what Abilities a Pastor hath; otherwise providing for it self in what is wanting.

2. IT is not lawful, meerly on a *weariness* of, and *despondency* under opposition and reproaches; which a *Pastor* is called and obliged to undergo for the Good and Edification of the Flock, and not to faint in the warfare wereto he is called.

THESE two were the Reasons of *Eustathius* at *Perga,* which were disallowed in the *Council* at *Ephesus*: But,

3. IT is lawful in such an *incurable decay of Intellectual Abilities,* as whereon a Man can discharge no Duty of the *Pastoral Office* unto the Edification of the Church.

4. IT is lawful, in case of *incurable divisions* in the Church constantly obstructing its Edification, and which cannot be removed whilst such a one continues in his Office, though he be no way the cause of them. This is the case wherein *Clemens* gives advice, and whereof *Gregory* gave an Example in his own practice.

BUT this Case and its Determination, will hold only where the Divisions are *incurable* by any other ways and means. For if those who cause such Divisions may be *cast out of the Church,* or the Church may withdraw Communion from them; or if there be Divisions in fixed Parties and Principles, Opinions or Practices, they may separate into distinct Communion; in such cases this Remedy, by the Pastors laying down his Office, is not to be made use of; otherwise all things are to be done for Edification.

5. IT may be lawful, where the Church is *wholly negligent in its Duty,* and persists in that negligence after admonition, in

providing, according to their Abilities, for the outward necessity of their Pastor and his Family. But this Case cannot be determined without the consideration of many particular Circumstances.

6. WHERE all or many of these causes concurr, so as that a Man cannot cheerfully and comfortably go on in the discharge of his Office, especially, if he be pressed in point of *Conscience* through the Churches non-compliance with their Duty, with respect unto any of the Institutions of Christ: And if the Edification of the Church, which is at present obstructed, may be provided for in their own judgment after a due manner; there is no such grievous yoke laid by the Lord Christ on the necks of any of his Servants, but that such a Person may *peaceably* lay down his *Office* in such a Church, and either abide in a private station, or take the care of another Church, wherein he may discharge his *Office* (being yet of Ability) unto his own Comfort, and their Edification.

CHAP. VI.

Of the Office of Teachers in the Church, or an Enquiry into the State, Condition, and Work of those called Teachers in the Scripture.

THE Lord Christ hath given unto his Church *Pastors* and *Teachers*, Ephes. 4. 11. He hath *set in the Church, First, Apostles, Secondarily, Prophets, Thirdly, Teachers,* 1 Cor. 12. 28. In the Church that was at *Antioch* there were *Prophets* and *Teachers*, Act. 13. 1. And their *Work* is both described and assigned unto them, as we shall see afterwards.

BUT the thoughts of learned Men, about those who in the Scripture are called *Teachers*, are very various; nor is the Determination of their State and Condition easie or obvious, as we shall find in our Enquiry.

Of the Office of Teachers in the Church.

IF there were originally a distinct Office of *Teachers* in the Church, it was lost for many Ages: But yet there was always a *Shadow* or Appearance of it retained, First in publick *Catechists*, and then in *Doctors* or *Professors of Theology* in the Schools belonging unto any Church. But this, as unto the *Title of Doctor* or *Teacher*, is but a late Invention. For the occasion of it rose about the year of Christ, 1135. *Lotharius* the Emperor having found in *Italy* a Copy of the *Roman Civil Law*, and being greatly taken with it, he Ordained that it should be *publickly Taught and Expounded in the Schools*. This he began by the direction of *Imerius*, his Chancellor at *Bononia*; and to give encouragement unto this Employment, they Ordained, that those who were the publick Professors of it should be solemnly *created Doctors*, of whom *Bulgarus Hugolinus*, with others, were the First. Not long after, this Rite of *creating Doctors* was borrowed of the *Lawyers* by Divines, who publickly taught Divinity in their Schools. And this imitation first took place in *Bononia*, *Paris* and *Oxford*. But this Name is since grown a Title of Honour to sundry sorts of Persons, whether unto any good use or purpose, or no, I know not; but it is in use, and not worth contending about, especially, if as unto some of them, it be fairly reconcileable unto that of our Saviour, *Matth.* 23. 8.

BUT the custom of having in the Church *Teachers*, that did publickly explain and vindicate the principles of Religion, is far more Ancient, and of known usage in the Primitive Churches. Such was the Practice of the Church of *Alexandria* in their School, wherein the famous *Panlænus*, *Origen* and *Clemens* were Teachers; an imitation whereof was continued in all Ages of the Church.

AND indeed, the continuation of such a peculiar Work and Employment, to be discharged in manner of an *Office*, is an evidence, that Originally there was such a *distinct Office* in the Church. For, although in the *Roman* Church they had instituted sundry *Orders* of Sacred Officers, borrowed from the *Jews* or *Gentiles*, which have no resemblance unto any thing mentioned in the Scripture; yet sundry things abased and
corrupted

corrupted by them in Church-Officers, took their occasional rife from what is so mentioned.

THERE are Four Opinions concerning those who are called by this Name in the New Testament.

1. SOME say, that *no Office* at all is denoted by it; it being only a general Appellation of those that *taught others*, whether constantly or occasionally. Such were the *Prophets* in the Church of *Corinth*, that spake occasionally and in their turns, 1 *Cor.* 14. Which is that which all might do who had ability for it, *v.* 5. 24, 25.

2. SOME say, it is only *another name* for the *same Office* with that of a *Pastor*, and so not to denote any distinct Office; of which mind *Hierom* seems to be, *Ephes.* 4.

3. OTHERS allow, that it was a *distinct Office*, whereunto some were called and set apart in the Church, but it was only to *Teach* (and that in a peculiar manner) the Principles of Religion, but had no Interest in the *Rule* of the Church, or the Administration of the Sacred Mysteries; so the *Pastor* in the Church was to *Rule and Teach*, and *Administer* the *Sacred Mysteries*: The *Teacher* to Teach or Instruct only, but not to Rule, nor Dispense the Sacraments; and the *Ruling Elder* to Rule only, and neither to Preach nor Administer Sacraments; which hath the appearance of Order, both useful and beautiful.

4. SOME judge, that it was a *distinct Office*, but of the same nature and kind with that of the *Pastor*, endowed with all the same Powers, but differenced from it with respect unto Gifts, and a peculiar kind of Work allotted unto it: But this Opinion hath this seeming disadvantage, that the *difference* between them is so *small*, as not to be sufficient to give a distinct denomination of Officers, or to constitute a distinct Office. And it may be, such a distinction in *Gifts* will seldom appear, as that the Church may be guided thereby in their choice of meet Persons unto *distinct Offices*. But Scripture-Testimony and Rule must take place; and I shall briefly examine all these Opinions.

1. THE First is, That this is *not the name of any Officer*, nor is a *Teacher, as such*, any Officer in the Church; but it is used

Of the Office of Teachers in the Church. 119

used only as a general Name for any that *Teach* on any account the Doctrine of the Gospel. I do not indeed know of any who have in particular contended for this Opinion; but I observe that very many *Expositors* take no farther notice of them, but as such. This seems to me to be most remote from the Truth.

IT is true, that in the First Churches, not only *some*, but *all* who had received Spiritual Light in the Gifts of knowledge and utterance, did teach and instruct others as they had opportunity, 1 *Pet.* 5. 8, 9, 10, 11. Hence, the Heathen Philosophers, as *Celsus* in particular, objected to the Christians of old, that they suffered *Sutlers*, and *Weavers*, and *Coblers* to teach among them, which, they who knew that *Paul* himself, their great Apostle, wrought at a Trade not much better, were not offended at. Of this sort were the *Disciples* mentioned, *Act.* 8. 4. So was *Aquila, Act.* 18. 26. and the many *Prophets* in the Church of *Corinth*, 2 *Epist.* Chap. 1. 14. But,

1. THE Name διδάσκαλος, is not used in the New Testament but for a *Teacher with Authority*. The Apostle *John* tells us, that διδάσκαλος is the same with ῥαββουνί, *Chap.* 20. 16. or as it is written, ῥαββονί, *Mark*, 10. 51. which in mixed dialect was the same with *Rabbi*: And רבא and רבי, רב, were then in use for the *Hebrew* מורה; of which see *Job* 36. 22. *Isa.* 30. 20. Now the constant signification of these words, is, a *Master in Teaching*, a *Teacher with Authority*. Nor is διδάσκαλος used in the New Testament, but for such a one. And therefore those who are called *Teachers*, were such as were set apart unto the Office of Teaching, and not such as were so called from an occasional Work or Duty.

2. TEACHERS are numbred among the *Officers*, which Christ hath given unto, and set in the Church, *Ephes.* 4. 11. 1 *Cor.* 12. 28. So that Originally *Church-Officers* were intended by them, is beyond contradiction.

3. THEY are mentioned as those, who with others did *preside* in the Church, and join in the publick ministrations of it, *Act.* 15. 1, 2.

4. THEY

Of the Office of Teachers in the Church.

4. THEY are charged to *attend unto the Work of Teaching*, which none can be, but they whose *Office* it is to Teach, *Rom.* 12. 7. It is therefore undeniable, that there is such an *Office* as that of a *Teacher* mentioned in the *Scripture*.

THE Second Opinion is, that *although a Teacher be a Church-Officer, yet no distinct Office is intended in that denomination.* It is, say they, only *another Name* for a *Pastor*, the Office being one and the same, the same Persons being both *Pastors and Teachers*, or called by these several Names, as they have other *Titles* also ascribed unto them.

SO it is fallen out, and so it is usual in things of this nature, that Men run into extreams; Truth pleaseth them not. In the First Deviation of the Church from its Primitive Institution, there were introduced sundry *Offices* in the Church that were not of *Divine Institution*, borrowed partly of the *Jews*, and partly of the *Gentiles*, which issued in the *Seven Orders of the Church of Rome.* They did not utterly reject any that were of a Divine Original, but retained some kind of Figure, Shadow or Image of them. But they brought in others that were meerly of their own invention. In the rejection of this Exorbitancy, some are apt to run into the other extreme. They will deny and reject *some of them* that have a Divine Warranty for their Original. Howbeit, they are not many, nor burthensome: Yea, they are all such, as without the continuation of them, the Edification of the Church cannot be carried on in a due manner. For unto the Beauty and Order of the Church in its Rule and Worship, it is required, not only that there be many Officers in each Church, but also that they be of sundry sorts; all Harmony in things Natural, Political and Ecclesiastical, arising from variety with proportion. And he that shall with *Calmness*, and without *Prejudice*, consider the whole Work that is to be done in Churches, with the end of their institution, will be able to understand the necessity of *Pastors, Teachers, Ruling-Elders* and *Deacons*, for those ends, and no other. And this I hope I shall demonstrate in the consideration of these respective *Offices*, with the Duties that belong unto them, as I have considered one of them already.

Of the Office of Teachers in the Church.

already. Wherefore, as unto the opinion under present consideration, I say,

1. IN the Primitive Church, about the end of the *Second Century*, before there was the least attempt to introduce new Officers into the Church, there were Persons called unto the Office and Work of *publick Teaching*, who were not Pastors, nor called unto the Administration of other Ordinances. Those of this sort, in the Church of *Alexandria*, were, by reason of their extraordinary Abilities, quickly of great fame and renown. Their constant Work was publickly unto all comers, Believers and Unbelievers, to explain and teach the Principles of Christian Religion, defending and vindicating it from the opposition of its Heathen Adversaries, whether *Atheists* or *Philosophers*. This had never been so exactly practised in the Church, if it had not derived from Divine Institution. And of this sort is the ὁ κατηχῶν the *Catechist*, intended by the Apostle, *Gal.* 6. 6. For it is such an one as constantly labours in the Work of Preaching, and hath those who depend upon his Ministry therein; οἱ κατηχούμενοι, those that are *Taught* or *Catechised* by him. For, hence alone it is that *Maintenance* is due unto him for his Work. *Let the Catechised communicate unto the Catechist*, the taught unto the Teacher *in all good things*. And it is not the *Pastor* of the Church that he intends, for he speaks of him in the same case in another manner, and no where only with respect unto teaching alone.

2. THERE is a *plain distinction* between the Offices of a Pastor and a Teacher, *Ephes.* 4. 11. *Some Pastors and Teachers*. This is one of the instances wherein Men try their Wits, in putting in exceptions unto plain Scripture Testimonies, as some, or other do in all other cases; which if it may be allowed, we shall have nothing left us certain in the whole Book of God. The Apostle enumerates distinctly all the *Teaching Officers* of the Church, both extraordinary and ordinary. It is granted, that there is a difference between Apostles, Prophets and Evangelists, but there is none, say some, between *Pastors and Teachers*; which are also named distinctly. Why so? Because there is an *interposition of the Article* τοὺς between

those

those of the former sort, and not between *Pastors and Teachers*; a very weak consideration to controul the evidence of the design of the Apostle in the Words. We are not to prescribe unto him how he shall express himself. But this I know, that the *discretive* and *copulative* conjunction ϗ, *and*, between *Pastors and Teachers*, doth no less distinguish them the one from the other, than the τὰς μὲν and τὰς δ̀ before made use of. And this I shall confirm from the words themselves.

1. THE Apostle doth not say *Pastors or Teachers*, which in congruity of speech should have been done, if the *same Persons*, and the *same Office* were intended. And the *discretive* Particle in the close of such an enumeration of things distinct, as that in this place, is of the same force with the other notes of distinction before used.

2. AFTER he hath named *Pastors* he nameth *Teachers* with a note of distinction. This must contain either the addition of a *New Office*, or be an interpretation of what went before; as if he had said *Pastors*, that is, *Teachers*. If it be the latter, then the name of *Teachers* must be added, as that which was better known than that of *Pastors*, and more expressive of the Office intended. It is declared who are meant by *Pastors* in calling them *Teachers*; or else the addition of the word is meerly superfluous. But this is quite otherwise; the name of *Pastor* being more known as unto the Indigitation of Office-Power and Care, and more appropriated thereunto than that of *Teacher*; which is both a common name, not absolutely appropriated unto Office, and respective of one part of the Pastoral Office and Duty only.

3. NO instance can be given in any place where there is an *enumeration of Church-Officers*, either by their *Names*, as 1. *Cor.* 12. 28. or by their Work, as *Rom.* 12. 5, 6, 7. or by the *Offices* themselves, as *Phil.* 1. 1. of the same Officer, at the same time to be expressed under various names, which indeed must needs introduce confusion into such an enumeration. It is true, the *same Officers* are in the *Scripture* called by *several Names*, as *Pastors, Bishops, Presbyters*, but if it had been said any where, that there were in the Church *Bishops* and *Presbyters*;

it

it must be acknowledged that they were *distinct Officers*, as *Bishops* and *Deacons* are, *Phil.* 1. 1.

4. THE words in their First notion, are not *Synonymous*; for all *Pastors* are *Teachers*, but all *Teachers* are not *Pastors*; and therefore the latter cannot be *exegetical* of the former.

3dly. AS these *Teachers* are so called and named in contradistinction unto *Pastors* in the same place, so they have *distinct Office-Works* and Duties assigned unto them in the same place also; *Rom.* 12. 18. *He that teacheth on teaching; he that exhorteth on exhortation.* If they have especial Works to attend unto distinctly, by virtue of their Offices, then are their Offices distinctly also; for from one there is an especial obligation unto one sort of Duties, and to another sort from the other.

4thly. THESE Teachers are *set in the Church* as in a distinct Office from that of Prophets; *Secondarily*, *Prophets*, *Thirdly*, *Teachers*, 1 *Cor.* 12. 28. And so they are mentioned distinctly in the Church of *Antioch*, Act. 13. 1. *There were in the Church at Antioch Prophets and Teachers.* But in both places *Pastors* are comprized under the name of Prophets; Exhortation being an especial branch of *Prophecy*, *Rom.* 12. 6, 7, 8.

5. THERE is a peculiar *institution of Maintenance* for these *Teachers*, which argues a *distinct Office*, Gal. 6. 6.

FROM all these considerations, it appears, that the *Teachers* mentioned in the *Scripture*, were *Officers* in the Church distinct from Pastors. For they are distinguished from them, (1.) By their *Name*, declarative of the especial nature of their Office. (2.) By their *peculiar Work*, which they are to attend unto, in Teaching by virtue of Office. (3.) By the *distinct placing* in the Church as peculiar Officers in it, distinct from Prophets or Pastors. (4.) By the especial *constitution* of their necessary Maintenance. (5.) By the *necessity of their Work* to be distinctly carried on in the Church. Which may suffice for the removal of the Second Opinion.

THE Third is, that Teachers are a *distinct Office in the Church*, but such whose Office, Work and Power, is confined unto *Teaching* only, so as that they have no interest in *Rule* or the Administration of the Sacraments. And,

1. I

Of the Office of Teachers in the Church.

1. I ACKNOWLEDGE that this seems to have been the way and practice of the Churches after the Apostles. For they had *ordinary Catechists and Teachers* in Assemblies like *Schools*, that were not called unto the whole Work of the Ministry.

2. THE name of a *Teacher*, neither in its native signification, nor in its ordinary application, as expressive of the Work of this *Office*, doth extend it self beyond, or signifie any thing but the meer Power and Duty of *Teaching*. It is otherwise as unto the names of *Pastors, Bishops* or *Overseers, Elders,* which as unto the two former, their constant use in Scripture suited unto their signification, includes the whole Work of the Ministry; and the latter is a name of Dignity and Rule. Upon the proposal of Church-Officers under these names, the whole of Office-Power and Duty is apprehended as included in them. But the name of a *Teacher*, especially, as significant of that of *Rabbi* among the *Jews*, carries along with it a confinement unto an especial Work or Duty.

3. I DO judge it lawful for any Church, from the nature of the thing it self, Scripture, general Rules and Directions, to choose, call and set apart meet Persons unto the *Office, Work* and *Duty* of *Teachers*, without an interest in the *Rule of the Church,* or the Administration of the Holy Ordinances of Worship. The same thing is practised by many for the substance of it, though not in due order. And, it may be, the practice hereof duly observed, would lead us unto the Original Institution of this *Office*. But,

4. WHEREAS a Teacher, meerly as such, hath no right unto Rule or the Administration of Ordinances, no more than the *Doctors* among the *Jews* had right to *Offer Sacrifices in the Temple*; yet he who is called to be a *Teacher,* may also at the same time be called to be an *Elder*; and a *Teaching Elder* hath the power of all holy Administrations committed to him.

5. BUT he that is called to be a *Teacher* in a peculiar manner, although he be an *Elder* also, is to attend peculiarly unto that part of his Work from whence he receiveth his Denomination. And so I shall at present dismiss this

Third

Of the Office of Teachers in the Church.

Third Opinion unto farther confideration, if there be any occafion for it.

THE *Fourth Opinion* I rather embrace than any of the other, namely, upon a fuppofition that a *Teacher* is a diftinct Officer in the Church, his Office is *of the fame kind with that of the Paftor*, though diftinguifhed from it as unto degrees, both materially and formally: For,

1. THEY are *joined with Paftors* in the fame Order as their Affociates in Office, *Ephef.* 4. 1. So they are with *Prophets*, and fet in the Church as they are, 1 *Cor.* 12. 28. *Act.* 13. 1. (2.) They have a *peculiar Work* of the fame general nature with that of Paftors affigned unto them, *Rom.* 12. 7. Being to Teach or Preach the Gofpel by virtue of Office, they have the fame Office for fubftance with the Paftors. (3.) They are faid λειτυργῆσαι in the Church, *Act.* 13. 1. which comprizeth all *Sacred Adminiftrations*.

WHEREFORE, upon the confideration of all that is fpoken in the Scripture concerning *Church-Teachers*, with the various conjectures of all forts of Writers about them, I fhall conclude my own Thoughts in fome few obfervations, and then enquire into the *ftate of the Church*, with reference unto thefe *Paftors* and *Teachers*. And I fay,

1. THERE may be *Teachers* in a Church called only unto the Work of Teaching, without any farther intereft in Rule or Right unto the Adminiftration of the Sacraments. Such they feem to be who are mentioned, *Gal.* 6. 6. They are there called peculiarly κατηχοῦντες, *Catechifts*; and παιδαγωγοὶ, 1 *Cor.* 4. 15. *Inftructors* of thofe that are young in the Rudiments of Religion. And fuch there were in the Primitive Churches; fome whereof were eminent, famous and ufeful. And this was very neceffary in thofe days when the Churches were great and numerous. For, whereas the whole Rule of the Church, and the Adminiftration of all Ordinances in it, is originally committed unto the *Paftor*, as belonging entirely unto his Office; the difcharge of it in all its parts, unto the Edification of the Church, efpecially when it is numerous, being impoffible for any one Man, or it may be more, in the fame Office
where

Of the Office of Teachers in the Church.

where all are obliged unto an especial attendance on one part of it, namely, the *Word and Prayer*, it pleased the Lord Christ to appoint such as in distinct *Offices* should be associated with them, for the discharge of sundry parts of their Duty. So were *Deacons* Ordained to take care of the poor, and the outward concerns of the Church, without any interest in Rule or Right to *Teach*. So were, as we shall prove, *Elders* Ordained to assist and help in *Rule*, without any call to Preach or Administer the Sacraments. And so were *Teachers* appointed to instruct the Church and others in the Truth, who have no Right to *Rule*, or the Administration of other Ordinances. And thus, although the whole Duty of the Edification of the Church be still incumbent on the Pastors, yet being supplied with assistance to all the parts of it, it may be comfortably discharged by them. And if this Order were observed in all Churches, not only many inconveniences would be prevented, but the Order and Edification of the Church greatly promoted.

2. HE who is *peculiarly called to be a Teacher*, with reference unto a distinction from a *Pastor*, may yet at the same time be called to be an *Elder* also, that is to be a *Teaching Elder*. And where there is in any *Officer* a concurrence of both these, a *Right unto Rule* as an *Elder*, and *power to Teach*, or Preach the Gospel, there is the same *Office* and *Office-Power*, for the substance of it, as there is in the *Pastor*.

3. ON the foregoing supposition there yet remains a *distinction* between the *Office* of a *Pastor* and *Teacher*; which, as far as light may be taken from their Names and distinct Ascriptions unto them, consists *materially* in the different Gifts which those to be called unto *Office* have received, which the Church in their call ought to have respect unto; and *formally* in the peculiar exercise of those Gifts in the discharge of their *Office*, according unto the Assignation of their especial Work unto them, which themselves are to attend unto.

UPON what hath been before discoursed concerning the *Office* of *Pastors* and *Teachers*, it may be enquired, *Whether there may be many of them in a particular Church, or whether there ought only to be one of each sort*: And I say,

1. TAKE

no *Office* in the Church. For although I do grant, that those who have once been regularly or solemnly set Apart or Ordained unto the Ministry, have the *Right of constant Preaching* inherent in them, and the Duty of it incumbent on them, though they may be separated from those Churches, wherein and unto whom they were peculiarly Ordained; yet for Men to give themselves up constantly unto the Work of *Teaching* by Preaching the Gospel, who never were set apart by the Church thereunto, I know not that it can be justified.

2. If there be but *one sort of Elders* mentioned in the Scripture, it is out of all question, that there may be many Pastors in the same Church. For there were *many Elders* in every Church; *Act.* 14. 22. *Act.* 20. 28. *Phil.* 1. 1. *Tit.* 1. 5. But if there are *sundry sorts of Elders* mentioned in the Scripture, as *Pastors*, who peculiarly feed the Flock, those *Teaching Elders* of whom we have spoken, and those *Rulers* concerning whom we shall treat in the next place; then no determination of this enquiry can be taken from the multiplication of them in any Church.

3. It is certain, that the Order very early observed in the Church was *one Pastor*, ὁ προέστως, *Præses*, quickly called *Episcopus* by way of distinction, with many *Elders* assisting in Rule and Teaching, and *Deacons* Ministring in the things of this Life, whereby the Order of the Church was preserved, and its Authority represented. Yet I will not deny, but that in each particular Church there may be *many Pastors*, with an *equality of power*, if the Edification of the Church doth require it.

4. IT was the alteration of the state of the Church from its Primitive Constitution, and Deviation from its First Order, by an occasional coalescency of many Churches into one, by a new form of Churches never appointed by Christ, which came not in until after the end of the *Second Century*, that gave

occasion

occasion to corrupt this Order into an *Episcopal Preheminence*, which degenerated more and more into confusion under the Name of Order. And the absolute equality of many *Pastors* in one and the same Church, is liable unto many inconveniencies, if not diligently watched against.

5. WHEREFORE, let the state of the Church be preserved and kept unto its *Original Constitution*, which is *Congregational*, and no other; and I do judge, that the Order of the *Officers*, which was so early in the Primitive Church, namely, of one *Pastor* or *Bishop* in one Church, assisted in Rule and all holy Administrations, with *many Elders* Teaching or Ruling only, doth not so overthrow Church-Order, as to render its Rule or Discipline useless.

6. BUT whereas there is *no difference* in the *Scripture*, as unto Office or Power intimated between *Bishops* and *Presbyters*, as we have proved, where there are *many Teaching Elders* in any Church, an equality in Office and Power is to be preserved. But yet this takes not off from the due preference of the *Pastoral Office*, nor from the necessity of precedency for the observation of Order in all Church Assemblies, nor from the consideration of the peculiar advantages, which Gifts, Age, Abilities, Prudence and Experience, which may belong unto some according to Rule, may give.

CHAP. VII.

Of the Rule of the Church; or, of Ruling Elders.

1. THE Rule and Government of the Church, or the *execution of the Authority of Christ therein;* is in the hand of the *Elders*. All *Elders* in Office have Rule; and none have *Rule* in the Church but *Elders*. As *such*, Rule doth belong unto them. The Apostles, by virtue of their especial *Office*, were intrusted with *all Church-Power*; but therefore they were *Elders* also; 1 *Pet.* 5. 1. 2 *Joh.* 1. 3 *Joh.* 1.

See

Of the Rule of the Church; or, of Ruling Elders.

See *Act.* 21. 17. 1 *Tim.* 5. 17. They are *some of them* on other accounts, called *Bishops, Pastors, Teachers, Ministers, Guides*, but what belongs unto any of them in *point of Rule*, or what interest they have therein, it belongs unto them as *Elders*, and not otherwise.; *Act.* 20. 17, 18.

SO under the Old Testament, where the Word doth not signifie a difference in *Age*, but is used in a moral sence, *Elders* are the same with *Rulers* or Governours, whether in Offices *Civil* or *Ecclesiastical*; especially the *Rulers* of the Church were constantly called its *Elders*. And the use of the Word, with the abuse of the Power or Office intended by it, is traduced to signifie Men in Authority *(Signeiores, Eldermani)* in all places.

2. CHURCH-Power acted in its Rule, is called the *Keys of the Kingdom of Heaven*, by an expression derived from the *Keys* that were a sign of Office-Power in the Families of Kings, *Isa.* 22. 22. and used by our Saviour himself to denote the communication of Church-Power unto others, which was absolutely and universally vested in himself under the Name of the *Key of David*; *Revel.* 3. 7. *Mat.* 16. 19.

3. THESE *Keys* are usually referred unto Two Heads; namely, the one of *Order*, the other of *Jurisdiction*.

4. BY the *Key of Order*, the *Spiritual Right, Power, and Authority* of Bishops or Pastors to Preach the Word, to Administer the Sacraments, Doctrinally to bind and loose the Consciences of Men, are intended.

5. BY *Jurisdiction*, the Rule, Government, or Discipline of the Church is designed, though it was never so called or esteemed in the *Scripture*, or the Primitive Church, until the whole nature of Church-Rule or Discipline was depraved and changed. Therefore, neither the *Word*, nor any thing that is signified by it, or which it is applied unto, ought to be admitted unto any consideration in the things that belong unto the *Church* or its Rule; it being expressive of, and directing unto that corrupt Administration of things *Ecclesiastical*, according unto the *Canon Law*, by which all Church-Rule and Order is destroyed. I do therefore at once dismiss all disputes about it,

as of things Foreign to the Gospel and Christian Religion, I mean as unto the Institutions of Christ in his Church. The *Civil Jurisdiction* of Supreme Magistrates about the externals of Religion, is of another consideration. But that these *Keys* do include the two-fold distinct Powers of *Teaching* and *Rule*, of *Doctrine* and *Discipline*, is freely granted.

6. IN the Church of *England*, (as in that of *Rome*) there is a peculiar distribution made of these *Keys*. Unto some, that is unto *one special sort* or order of Men, they are both granted, both the Key of *Order* and of *Jurisdiction* ; which is unto *Diocesan Bishops*, with some others under various Canonical restrictions and limitations, as *Deans* and *Arch-Deacons*. Unto some is granted the *Key of Order* only, without the least interest in *Jurisdiction* or Rule by virtue of their Office ; which are the *Parochial Ministers*, or meer *Presbyters*, without any additional Title or Power, as of *Commissary Surrogates*, or the like. And unto a third sort, there is granted the *Key of Rule* or *Jurisdiction* almost *plenipotent*, who have no share in the *Key of Order*, that is, were never *Ordained*, Separated, Dedicated unto any Office in the Church ; such as are the *Chancellors*, &c.

7. THESE *Chancellors* are the *only Lay-Elders* that I know any where in any Church ; that is, Persons entrusted with the *Rule of the Church*, and the *Disposition* of its Censures, who are not *Ordained* unto any Church-Office ; but in all other things continue in the Order of the *Laity* or the People. All *Church Rulers*, by institution, are *Elders*. To be an *Elder* of the Church, and a *Ruler* in it, is all one. Wherefore, these Persons being *Rulers* in the Church, and yet thus continuing in the Order of the People, are *Lay-Elders* ; whom I wonder how so many of the Church came so seriously to oppose, seeing this Order of Men is owned by none but themselves. The Truth is, and it must be acknowledged, that there is no *known Church* in the World, (I mean whose Order is known unto us, and is of any publick consideration,) but they do dispose the Rule of the Church in part, into the hands of Persons, who have not the *power of Authoritative Preaching* of the Word, and Administration of the Sacraments committed unto them. For even those who

Of the Rule of the Church; or, of Ruling Elders.

who place the whole *external Rule* of the Church in the *Civil Magistrate*, do it, as they judge him an Officer of the Church, *entrusted by Christ with Church-Power*. And those who deny any such *Officers* as are usually called *Ruling Elders* in the Reformed Churches to be of Divine Institution, yet maintain that it is *very necessary* that there should be such *Officers* in the Church, either appointed by the *Magistrate*, or *chosen by the people*, and that with cogent Arguments. See *Grot. de Jure Potestat. Cap.*

8. BUT this distribution mentioned of Church-Power, is *unscriptural*; nor is there any foot-steps of it in *Antiquity*. It is so as unto the two latter Branches of it. That any one should have the *power of Order*, to Preach the Word, to Administer the Seals, to bind and loose the Conscience *Doctrinally*; or Ministerially to bind and loose in the Court of Conscience, and yet by the virtue of that *Office* which gives them this power, not to have a Right and Power of *Rule* or *Discipline* to bind and loose in the Court of the Church, is that, which neither the Scripture, nor any example of the Primitive Church doth give countenance unto. And as by this means, those are abridged and deprived of their power, to whom it is granted by the Institution and Law of Christ, as it is with *all Elders* duly called unto their Office; so in the Third Branch there is a grant of Church-Power unto such, as by the Law of Christ, are excluded from any Interest therein. The enormity of which constitution, I shall not at present insist upon. But Enquiry must be made what the Scripture directs unto herein: And,

1. THERE is a *Work and Duty of Rule* in the Church, distinct from the Work and Duty of *Pastoral Feeding*, by the Preaching of the Word and Administration of the Sacraments. All agree herein, unless it be *Erastus* and those that follow him, who seem to oppose it. But their Arguments are not against *Rule* in general, which were brutish, but only *Rule by external Jurisdiction* in the Elders of the Church. So they grant the general Assertion of the necessity of Rule, for who can deny it? only they contend about the subject of power required thereunto. A *Spiritual Rule by virtue of mutual voluntary confederation*, for the preservation of Peace, Purity

S 2 and

and Order in the Church, few of that opinion deny; at least it is not that which they do oppose. For to deny all *Rule and Discipline* in the Church, with all Administration of Censures in the exercise of a Spiritual Power internally inherent in the Church, is to deny the Church to be a Spiritual Political Society, overthrow its Nature, and frustrate its Institution in direct opposition unto the Scripture. That there is such a *Rule* in the Christian Church, see *Act.* 20. 28. *Rom.* 12. 8. 1 *Cor.* 12. 28. 1 *Tim.* 9. 5. Chap. 5. 17. *Heb.* 13. 7, 17. *Revel.* 2. 3.

2. *DIFFERENT and distinct Gifts* are required unto the discharge of these *distinct Works and Duties.* This belongs unto the Harmony of the dispensation of the Gospel. *Gifts* are bestowed to answer all Duties prescribed. Hence they are the First Foundation of all Power, Work and Duty in the Church. *Unto every one of us is given, Grace according to the measure of the Gift of Christ,* that is, Ability for Duty, according to the measure wherein Christ is pleased to grant it; *Ephes.* 4. 7. *There are diversities of Gifts, but the same spirit; and the manifestation of the spirit is given to every Man to profit withal,* 1 Cor. 12. 4, 7, 8, 9, 10. *Having then Gifts differing according to the Grace given unto us,* &c. *Rom.* 12. 6, 7, 8. *Wherefore, as every Man hath received the Gift, so are they to minister the same, as good Stewards of the manifold Grace of God,* 1 Pet. 4. 10. Hence are they called the *Powers of the World to come,* Heb. 6. 4, 5. Wherefore, differing Gifts, are the first foundation of differing Offices and Duties.

3. THAT *differing Gifts* are required unto the different Works of *Pastoral Teaching* on the one hand, and *practical Rule* on the other, is evident, (1.) From *the Light of Reason,* and the nature of the Works themselves being so different. And, (2.) From *experience*; Some Men are fitted by Gifts, for the Dispensation of the Word and Doctrine in a way of *Pastoral Feeding,* who have no *useful Ability* in the Work of *Rule*; And some are fitted for *Rule,* who have no Gifts for the discharge of the Pastoral Work in *Preaching.* Yea, it is very seldom that both these sorts of Gifts do concurr in any eminency in the same Persons, or without some notable defect. Those
who

Of the Rule of the Church; or, of Ruling Elders.

who are ready to assume all things unto themselves, are for the most part fit for nothing at all. And hence it is, that most of those who esteem both these Works to belong principally unto them, do almost totally decline the *one*, or that of *Pastoral Preaching*, under a pretence of attending unto the other, that is, *Rule*, in a very preposterous way; for they omit that which is *incomparably the greater* and more worthy, for that which is less and inferior unto it, although it should be attended unto in a due manner.

BUT this, and sundry other things of the like nature, proceed from the corruption of that *Traditional notion*, which is true in it self and continued among all sorts of Christians; namely, that there ought to be some on whom the *Rule of the Church* is in an especial manner incumbent, and whose principal Work it is to attend thereunto. For the great depravations of all Church Government, proceed from the Corruption and Abuse of this notion, which in it self, and its original, is true and sacred. Herein also, *Malum habitat in alieno fundo*. There is no corruption in Church-Order or Rule, but is corruptly derived from; or is set up as an Image of some Divine Institution.

4. THE *Work of Rule*, as distinct from Teaching, is in general *to watch over the walking or conversation of the Members of the Church with Authority*, Exhorting, Comforting, Admonishing, Reproving, Incouraging, Directing of them, as occasion shall require. The Gifts necessary hereunto, are *Diligence, Wisdom, Courage* and *Gravity*, as we shall see afterwards. The *Pastoral Work*, is principally *to reveal the whole Counsel of God, to divide the Word aright*, or to *labour in the Word and Doctrine*, both as unto the general Dispensation, and particular Application of it, in all seasons, and on all occasions.

HEREUNTO Spiritual *Wisdom, Knowledge, Sound Judgment, Experience* and *Utterance* are required, all to be improved by continual study of the Word and Prayer. But this difference of Gifts, unto these distinct Works, doth not of it self constitute distinct Offices, because the same Persons may be meetly furnished with those of both sorts.

5. YET

5. YET *distinct Works and Duties*, though some were furnished with *Gifts* for both, was a ground in the Wisdom of the Holy Ghost, for distinct Offices in the Church, where one sort of them were as much as those of one Office could ordinarily attend unto, *Act.* 6. 2, 3, 4. *Ministration unto the poor of the Church*, for the supply of their Temporal Necessities, is an Ordinance of Christ. The Administration hereof, the Apostles were furnished for with Gifts and Wisdom above all others: But yet, because there was another part of their Work and Duty *superior* hereunto, and of greater necessity unto the Propagation of the Gospel and Edification of the Church, namely, a *diligent attendance unto the Word and Prayer*, the Wisdom of the Holy Ghost in them thought meet to erect a *New Office* in the Church, for the discharge of that part of the Ministerial Duty which was to be attended unto; yet, not so as to be any obstruction unto the other. I do not observe this, as if it were lawful for any others after them to do the same; namely, upon a supposition of an *especial Work*, to erect an *especial Office*. Only I would demonstrate from hence, the equity and reasonable ground of that Institution, which we shall afterwards evince.

6. THE *Work of the Ministry in Prayer, and Preaching of the Word*, or labour in the Word and Doctrine, whereunto the Administration of the Seals of the Covenant is annexed, with all the Duties that belong unto the especial Application of these things before insisted on, unto the Flock; are ordinarily sufficient to take up the *whole Man*, and the utmost of their endowments who are called unto the *Pastoral Office* in the Church. The very nature of the Work in it self is such, as that the Apostle giving a short description of it, adds as an intimation of its greatness and excellency, *Who is sufficient for these things?* 2 *Cor.* 2. 16. And the manner of its performance adds unto its weight. For not to mention that intension of Mind in the exercise of Faith, Love, Zeal and Compassion, which is required of them in the discharge of their whole Office; the diligent consideration of the state of the Flock, so as to provide Spiritual Food convenient for them; with a constant attendance

Of the Rule of the Church; or, of Ruling Elders.

tendance unto the issues and effects of the Word in the Consciences and Lives of Men; is enough for the most part to take up their whole time and strength.

IT is gross *ignorance* or *negligence* that occasioneth any to be otherwise minded. As the Work of the Ministry is generally discharged, as consisting only in a *Weekly provision of Sermons*, and the performance of some stated Offices by Reading, Men may have time and liberty enough to attend unto other occasions. But in such Persons we are not at present concerned. Our *Rule* is plain, 1 *Tim.* 4. 12, 13, 14, 15, 16.

7. IT doth not hence follow, that those who are called unto the Ministry of the Word, as *Pastors and Teachers*, who are *Elders* also, are devested of the *Right of Rule* in the Church, or discharged from the exercise of it, because others not called unto their Office, are appointed to be assistant unto them; that is, *Helps in the Government*. For the Right and Duty of *Rule* is inseparable from the *Office of Elders* which all *Bishops or Pastors* are. The *Right* is still in them, and the *exercise* of it consistent with their more excellent Work, is required of them. So was it in the First Institution of the *Sanhedrim* in the Church of *Israel*; *Exod.* 18. 17, 18, 19, 20, 21, 22, 23. *Moses* had before the sole Rule and Government of the People. In the addition that was made of an *Eldership* for his assistance, there was no diminution of his Right, or the exercise of it according to his precedent power. And the Apostles, in the constitution of *Elders* in every Church, derogated nothing from their own Authority, nor discharged themselves of their care. So when they appointed *Deacons* to take care of Supplies for the Poor, they did not forgo their own Right, nor the exercise of their Duty as their other Work would permit them, *Gal.* 2. 9, 10. And in particular, the Apostle *Paul* manifested his concernment herein, in the care he took about *Collection for the Poor* in all Churches.

8. AS we observed at the entrance of this Chapter, the whole *Work* of the Church, as unto Authoritative Teaching and Rule, is committed unto the *Elders*. For Authoritative Teaching and Ruling, is Teaching and Ruling by virtue of
Office:

Office: And this Office whereunto they do belong, is that of *Elders*, as it is undeniably attested, *Act*. 20. 17, *&c*. All that belongs unto the Care, Inspection, Oversight, Rule and Instruction of the Church, is committed unto the *Elders* of it expresly. For *Elders* is a Name derived from the *Jews*, denoting them that have *Authority* in the Church. The First signification of the Word in all Languages respects *Age*. *Elders* are *Old Men*, well stricken in years; unto whom respect and reverence is due by the Law of Nature and Scripture Command; unless they forfeit their Privilege by levity or wickedness, which they often do. Now *Ancient Men* were originally judged, if not only, yet the most meet for *Rule*, and were before others constantly called thereunto. Hence, the Name of *Elders* was appropriated unto them, who did *Preside* and *Rule* over others in any kind.

ONLY it may be observed, that there is in the *Scripture* no mention of *Rulers* that are called *Elders*, but such as are in a subordinate Power and Authority only. Those who were in supream absolute power, as *Kings* and *Princes*, are never called *Elders*. But *Elders by Office*, were such only as had a *Ministerial Power* under others. Wherefore, the highest *Officers* in the Christian Church being called *Elders*, even the Apostles themselves, and *Peter* in particular, 1 *Epist*. Chap. 5. v. 1. 2. it is evident, that they have only a *Ministerial Power*; and so it is declared *ver*. 4. The *Pope* would now scarce take it well to be esteemed only an *Elder* of the Church of *Rome*; unless it be in the same sence wherein the *Turkish Monarch* is called the *Grand Signior*. But those who would be in the Church above *Elders*, have no Office *in it*, whatever usurpation they may make *over it*.

9. TO the compleat constitution of any particular Church, or the perfection of its *Organical State*, it is required that there be *many Elders* in it; at least more than one. In this proposition lies the next foundation of the Truth which we plead for, and therefore it must be distinctly considered. I do not determine *what their number ought to be*; nor is it determinable, as unto all Churches. For the Light of Nature sufficiently directs,

Of the Rule of the Church; or, of Ruling Elders. 137

directs, that it is to be proportioned unto the Work and End designed. Where a Church is *numerous*, there is a necessity of encreasing their number proportionable unto their Work. In the days of *Cyprian* there was in the Church of *Carthage* Ten or Twelve of them that are mentioned by Name; And at the same time, there were a great many in the Church of *Rome* under *Cornelius*. Where the Churches are small, the number of *Elders* may be so also. For no Office is appointed in the Church for *pomp* or *show*, but for *labour* only. And so many are necessary in each Office as are able to discharge the Work which is allotted unto them. But that Church, be it small or great, is not compleat in its state, is defective, which hath not *more Elders than one*; who have not so many as are sufficient for their Work.

10. THE Government of the Church, in the judgment and practice of some, is absolutely *Democratical* or *Popular*. They judge that all Church-Power or Authority, is seated and setled in the *Community of the Brethren* or Body of the People. And they look on *Elders* or Ministers, only as *Servants of the Church*; not only *materially* in the Duties they perform, and *finally* for their Edification, serving for the good of the Church, in the things of the Church; but *formally* also, as acting the Authority of the Church by a meer delegation, and not any of their own received directly from Christ, by virtue of his Law and Institution. Hence, they do occasionally appoint Persons among themselves not called unto, not vested with any Office, to Administer the *Supper of the Lord*, or any other solemn Offices of Worship. On this principle and supposition, I see no necessity of *any Elders at all*, though usually they do conferr this Office on some with solemnity. But as among them, there is no direct necessity of *any Elders for Rule*, so we treat not at present concerning them.

11. SOME place the Government of many particular Churches in a *Diocesan Bishop*, with those that act under him, and by his Authority, according unto the Rule of the *Canon Law*, and the civil constitution of the Land. These are so far from judging it necessary that there should be *many Elders for Rule*

T in

in every particular Church, as that they allow no Rule *in them* at all, but only assert a Rule *over them*. But a Church, where there is no Rule in it self, to be exercised in the Name of Christ by its own Rulers, Officers, Guides, immediately presiding in it, is unknown to Scripture and Antiquity. Wherefore, with these we deal not in this Discourse; nor have any apprehension, that the power of presenting Men, for any pretended Disorder, unto the *Bishops* or *Chancellors Court*, is any part of Church-Power or Rule.

12. OTHERS place the Rule of particular Churches, especially in cases of greatest moment, in an *Association, Conjunction* or *Combination* of all the Elders of them in one Society, which is commonly called a *Classis*. So in all Acts of Rule, there will be a conjunct acting of many Elders. And, no doubt it is the best provision that can be made on a supposition of the continuance of the present *Parochial Distribution*. But those also of this judgment, who have most weighed and considered the nature of these things, do assert the necessity of *many Elders* in every particular Church, which is the common judgment and practice of the *Reformed Churches* in all places.

13. AND some there are, who begin to maintain, That there is no need of any more but *One Pastor, Bishop*, or *Elder*, in a particular Church, which hath its Rule in its self; other Elders for Rule being unnecessary. This is a *Novel Opinion*, contradictory to the sence and practice of the Church in all Ages. And I shall prove the contrary.

1. THE pattern of the First Churches constituted by the Apostles, which it is our Duty to imitate and follow as our Rule, constantly expresseth and declares, That *many Elders* were appointed by them in every Church, *Act.* 11. 30. Chap. 14. 23. Chap. 15. 2, 4, 6, 22. Chap. 16. 4. Chap. 20. 17, *&c.* 1 *Tim.* 5. 17. *Phil.* 1. 1. *Tit.* 1. 5. 1 *Pet.* 5. 1. There is no mention in the Scripture, no mention in Antiquity, of any Church wherein there was not *more Elders than One*, nor doth that Church answer the *Original Pattern*, where it is otherwise.

2. WHERE there is *but one Elder* in a Church, there cannot be an *Eldership* or *Presbytery*; as there cannot be a *Senate* where

Of the Rule of the Church; or, of Ruling Elders.

where there is but one *Senator*; which is contrary unto 1 *Tim.* 4. 14.

3. THE *continuation* of every Church in its original State and Constitution, is, since the ceasing of extraordinary Offices and Powers, committed to the Care and Power of the Church it self. Hereunto the Calling and Ordaining of ordinary *Officers*, Pastors, Rulers, Elders, Teachers, doth belong. And therein, as we have proved, both the *Election* of the People, submitting themselves unto them in the Lord, and the solemn setting of them apart by *Imposition* of Hands, do concurr. But if there be but One Elder only in a Church, upon his Death or Removal, this Imposition of Hands must either be left unto the People, or be supplied by Elders of other Churches, or be wholly omitted, all which are irregular. And that Church-Order is *defective*, which wants the *Symbol* of Authoritative Ordination.

4. IT is difficult, if not impossible, on a supposition of One Elder only in a Church, to preserve the Rule of the Church from being *Prelatical* or *Popular*. There is nothing more frequently objected unto those who dissent from *Diocesan Bishops*, than that they would every one be *Bishops* in their *own Parishes*, and unto their own People. All such pretences are excluded on our principles, of the Liberty of the People, of the necessity of *many Elders* in the same Church in an equality of Power, and the Communion of other Churches in Association: But practically where there is but One Elder, one of the extreams can be hardly avoided. If he *Rule by himself*, without the *previous Advice* in some cases, as well as the *subsequent consent* of the Church, it hath an eye of unwarrantable Prelacy in it: If every thing be to be Originally Transacted, Disposed, Ordered by the *whole Society*, the *Authority of the Elder* will quickly be insignificant, and he will be little more in point of Rule, than any other Brother of the Society. But all these Inconveniencies are prevented by the fixing of *many Elders* in each Church, which may maintain the Authority of the *Presbytery*, and free the Church from the *Despotical* Rule of any *Diotrephes*. But in case there be *but one* in any Church, unless he have

T 2   Wisdom

Wisdom to maintain the Authority of the *Eldership* in his own Person and Actings, there is no Rule but Confusion.

5. THE nature of the Work whereunto they are called, requires, that in every Church consisting in any considerable number of Members, there should be *more Elders than One*. When God first appointed *Rule* in the Church under the Old Testament, he assigned unto every *Ten Persons*, or *Families*, a *distinct Ruler*, *Deut.* 1. 15. For the Elders are to take care of the *Walk* or Conversation of all the Members of the Church, that it be according unto the Rule of the Gospel. This Rule is eminent as unto the holiness that it requires, above all other Rules of moral Conversation whatever. And there is in all the Members of the Church great Accuracy and Circumspection required in their walking after it and according unto it. The *Order* also and *Decency* which is required in all Church-Assemblies, stands in need of exact care and inspection. That all these things can be attended unto, and discharged in a due manner in any Church by One Elder, is for them only to suppose who know nothing of them. And, although there may be an appearance for a season of all these things in such Churches, yet there being not therein a due compliance with the Wisdom and Institution of Christ, they have no present Beauty, nor will be of any long continuance.

THESE considerations, as also those that follow, may seem *jejune* and contemptible unto such as have another frame of *Church-Rule* and *Order* drawn in their Minds and Interests. A Government vested in some few Persons, with Titles of Preheminence and Legal Power, exercised in Courts with Coercive Jurisdiction, by the Methods and Processes of *Canons* of their own framing, is that which they suppose doth better become the *Grandeur* of Church-Rulers, and the State of the Church, than these *Creeping Elders* with their Congregations. But, whereas our present enquiry after these things, is only in and out of the Scripture, wherein there is neither shadow nor appearance of any of these *practices*, I beg their pardon, if at present I consider them not.

10. WE

10. WE shall now make Application of these things unto our present purpose. I say then, (1.) Whereas there is a *Work of Rule* in the Church, distinct from that of *Pastoral Feeding*. (2.) Whereas this Work is to be attended unto with *diligence*, which includes the whole Duty of him that attends unto it. And, (3.) That the *Ministry of the Word and Prayer*, with all those Duties that accompany it, is a *full Employment* for any Man, and so consequently his principal and proper Work, which it is unlawful for him to be remiss in by attending on another with *Diligence*. And, (4.) Whereas there ought to be *many Elders* in every Church, that both the Works of *Teaching* and *Ruling* may be constantly attended unto. (5.) That in the Wisdom of the Holy Ghost, *distinct Works* did require *distinct Offices* for their discharge; all which we have proved already; our enquiry hereon is, *Whether the same Holy Spirit, hath not distinguished this Office of Elders into those two sorts, namely, those who are called unto Teaching and Rule also; and those who are called unto Rule only,* which we Affirm.

THE *Testimonies* whereby the Truth of this Assertion is confirmed, are generally known and pleaded; I shall insist on some of them only, beginning with that which is of *uncontroulable evidence*, if it had any thing to conflict withal but prejudices and interest; and this is 1 *Tim.* 5. 17. οἱ καλῶς προεστῶτες πρεσβύτεροι διπλῆς τιμῆς ἀξιούσθωσαν· μάλιστα οἱ κοπιῶντες ἐν λόγῳ καὶ διδασκαλίᾳ. Προΐστημι or προΐσταμαι, is *Præsum, Præsidio*; to Preside, to Rule. *Præsident probati Seniores.* Tertull. And the *Bishop* or *Pastor* in *Justin Martyr*, is ὁ προεστώς. So is the Word constantly used in the New Testament, *Rom.* 12. 8. ὁ προϊστάμενος, *that Ruleth*; 1 *Thess.* 5. 12. προϊσταμένους ὑμῶν, *that are over them*, that is, *in place of Rule*, 1 *Tim.* 3. 4, 5, 12. It is applied unto *Family Rule* and Government, as it is also unto care and diligence about good Works, *Tit.* 3. 8. 14. Προστασία is the whole *Presidency* in the Church, with respect unto its Rule. Translators agree in the reading of these Words, so the *Hebrew of Munster*, זקני־העדה אשר מטיבים רנהג, *The Elders of the Congregation who well discharge their Rule or Conduct.* So the *Syriack*, קשושא אילין, *Those Elders. Qui bene præsunt*

Of the Rule of the Church; or, of Ruling Elders.

præsunt Presbyteri; *Vul. Lat.* *Seniori che Governano bene*; *Ital.* All agree that it is the *Governours* and the *Government* of the Church in general that is here intended. Μάλιϛα is the Word most controverted. All Translators esteem it *distinctive*, *Heb.* יתרה, *Eminently*; *Syr.* יתיראית, *Chiefly*, *Principally*; *Maxime*. οἱ κοπιῶντες, היוגעים, *who labour painfully*, labour to weariness; travail in the Word and Doctrine.

THE Elders *or Presbyters in Office,* Elders *of the Church* that Rule well, *or discharge their Presidency for Rule in due manner*, are worthy, *or ought to be reputed worthy* of double honour; especially those *of them* who labour, *or are ingaged in the great labour and travail of* the Word and Doctrine.

AND some things may be observed in general concerning these words.

1. THIS Testimony relates directly unto the *Rules and Principles* before laid down, directing unto the practice of them. According unto the *Analogy* of those Principles, these Words are to be interpreted. And unless they are overthrown, it is to no purpose to put in exceptions against the sense of this or that Word; the Interpretation of them is to be suited unto the *Analogy* of the things which they relate unto. If we consider not what is spoken here in consent with other Scriptures treating of the same matter, we depart from all sober Rules of Interpretation.

2. ON this supposition, the Words of the Text have a *plain and obvious signification*, which at first view presents it self unto the common sense and understanding of all Men. And where there is nothing contrary unto any other Divine Testimony, or Evident Reason, such a sense is constantly to be embraced. There is nothing here of any Spiritual Mystery; but only a direction concerning *outward Order* in the Church. In such cases the *literal sense* of the Words rationally apprehended, is all that we are concerned in. But on the first Proposal of this Text, That *the Elders that Rule well, are worthy of double honour, especially those who labour in the Word and Doctrine*; a rational

Man

Of the Rule of the Church; or, of Ruling Elders. 143

Man who is unprejudiced, who never heard of the Controversy about *Ruling Elders*, can hardly avoid an Apprehension that there are *two sort of Elders*, some that labour in the Word and Doctrine, and some who do not so do. The Truth is, it was Interest and Prejudice that first caused some *learned Men* to strain their wits to find out evasions from the evidence of this Testimony: Being so found out, some others of meaner Abilities have been entangled by them. For there is not one new Argument advanced in this cause, not one exception given in unto the sence of the place which we plead for, but what was long since coined by *Papists* and *Prelatists*, and managed with better Colours than some now are able to lay on them, who pretend unto the same judgment.

3. THIS is the substance of the Truth in the Text. There are *Elders in the Church*; there are or ought to be so in every Church. With these Elders the *whole Rule of the Church* is intrusted; all these, and only they, do Rule in it. Of these Elders there are *two sorts*, for a description is given of one sort *distinctive* from the other, and *comparative* with it. The First sort doth *Rule*, and *also labour in the Word and Doctrine*. That these Works are distinct and different was before declared. Yet, as distinct Works, they are not incompatible, but are committed unto the same Person. They are so unto them, who are not Elders *only*, but moreover Pastors or Teachers. Unto Pastors and Teachers, as such, there belongs no Rule; although, by the institution of Christ, the Right of Rule be inseparable from their Office. For all that are rightfully called thereunto are Elders also, which gives them an Interest in Rule. They are Elders with the Addition of Pastoral or Teaching Authority. But there are Elders which are not Pastors or Teachers. For there are some who *Rule well, but labour not in the Word and Doctrine*; that is, who are not Pastors or Teachers.

ELDERS *that Rule well, but labour not in the Word and Doctrine, are Ruling Elders only*; and such are in the Text.

THE most learned of our *Protestant* Advocates in this case, are *Erastus*, *Bilson*, *Sarravia*, *Downham*, *Scultetus*, *Mead*, *Grotius*,

Grotius, Hamond; who agree not at all among themselves about the sence of the Words : For,

1. THEIR whole design and endeavour is to *put in Exceptions* against the obvious sence and interpretation of the Words, not fixing on any determinate exposition of it themselves, such as they will abide by in opposition unto any other sence of the place. Now this is a most *sophistical* way of arguing upon Testimonies, and suited only to make Controversies endless. Whose Wit is so barren, as not to be able to raise one exception or other against the plainest and most evident Testimony? So the *Socinians* deal with us, in all the Testimonies we produce to prove the *Deity* or *Satisfaction* of Christ. They suppose it enough to evade their force, if they can but pretend that the Words are *capable of another sence* ; although they will not abide by it, that this or that is their sence. For if they would do so, when that is overthrown the Truth would be established. But every Testimony of the Scripture hath *one determinate sence*. When this is contended about, it is equal that those at difference do express their Apprehensions of the mind of the Holy Spirit in the Word which they will abide by. When this is done, let it be examined and tried, whether of the *two sences* pretended unto, doth best comply with the *signification* and use of the Words, the context or scope of the place, other *Scripture Testimonies*, and the *Analogy* of Faith. No such *Rule* is attended unto in this case by our Adversaries. They think it enough to oppose our sence of the Words, but will not fix upon any of their own, which if it be disproved, ours ought to take place. And hence,

2. THEY do not in the least *agree among themselves*, scarce any *Two of them*, on what is the *most probable sence* of the Words, nor are any of them *singly*, well resolved what Application to make of them, nor unto what persons; but only propose things as their conjecture. But of very many opinions or conjectures that are advanced in this case, all of them but of *one*, are accompanied with the modesty of granting that *divers sorts of Elders* are here intended, which, without more than ordinary confidence, cannot be denied. But,

SOME

SOME by *Elders that Rule well*, do underſtand *Biſhops* that are *Dioceſans*; and by thoſe that *labour in the Word and Doctrine*, ordinary Preaching *Presbyters*; which plainly gives them the advantage of Preheminence, Reverence and Maintenance above the other.

SOME by *Elders that Rule well*, underſtand *ordinary Biſhops* and *Presbyters*; and by thoſe that *labour in the Word and Doctrine, Evangeliſts*; ſo carrying the Text out of the preſent concernment of the Church, *Deacons* are eſteemed by ſome to have an Intereſt in the Rule of the Church, and ſo to be intended in the firſt place; and *Preaching Miniſters* in the latter.

SOME ſpeak of two *ſorts of Elders*, both of the ſame Order, or Miniſters; ſome that Preach the Word and Adminiſter the Sacraments; and others that are Imployed about *inferior Offices*, as *Reading*, and the like, which is the conceit of *Scultetus*.

Mr. *MEDE* weighs moſt of theſe conjectures, and at length prefers one of his own before them all; namely, that by Elders that Rule well, *Civil Magiſtrates* are intended; and by thoſe that *labour in the Word and Doctrine*, the *Miniſters of the Goſpel*.

BUT ſome diſcerning the weakneſs and improbability of all theſe Conjectures; and how eaſily they may be diſproved, betake themſelves unto a direct denial of that which ſeems to be plainly aſſerted in the Text; namely, that there are two ſorts of Elders here intended and deſcribed, which they countenance themſelves in, by exception unto the application of ſome Terms in the Text, which we ſhall immediately conſider.

GROTIUS, 'as was before intimated, Diſputes againſt the Divine Inſtitution of ſuch Temporary *Lay-Elders* as are made uſe of in ſundry of the Reformed Churches. But when he hath done, he affirms, That it is highly neceſſary that ſuch conjunct Aſſociates in Rule from among the people, ſhould be in every Church; which he proves by ſundry Arguments. And theſe he would have either nominated by the Magiſtrate, or choſen by the People.

WHEREFORE, omitting all conteſts about the forementioned *conceits*, or any other of the like nature, I ſhall propoſe

One Argument from thefe Words, and vindicate it from the exceptions of thofe of the latter fort.

PREACHING Elders, although they Rule well, are not worthy of double Honour, unlefs they labour in the Word and Doctrine.
BUT there are Elders who Rule well that are worthy of double Honour, though they do not labour in the Word and Doctrine.
THEREFORE, there are Elders that Rule well, who are not Teaching or Preaching Elders, that is who are Ruling Elders only.

THE *Propofition* is evident in *its own light* from the very Terms of it. For to *Preach*, is to *labour in the Word and Doctrine* : Preaching or Teaching Elders, that do not labour in the Word and Doctrine, are Preaching or Teaching Elders. that do not Preach or Teach. And to fay that *Preachers*, whofe Office and Duty is to Preach, are worthy of that double honour which is due on the account of Preaching, though they do not Preach, is uncouth and irrational. It is contrary to the Scripture, and the Light of Nature, as implying a contradiction, that a Man whofe Office it is to Teach and Preach, fhould be efteemed worthy of double honour on the account of his Office, who doth not as an Officer *Teach or Preach.*

THE *Affumption* confifts upon the matter, in the very Words of the Apoftle. For he who fays, *The Elders who Rule well, are worthy of double Honour, efpecially they who labour in the Word and Doctrine*, faith there are, or may be Elders *who Rule well, who do not labour in the Word and Doctrine*, that is, who are not obliged fo to do.

THE Argument from thefe Words may be otherwife framed, but this contains the plain fence of this Teftimony.

SUNDRY things are *excepted* unto this Teftimony and our *Application* of it. Thofe which are of any weight confift in a conteft about Two Words in the Text, μάλιςα and κοπιῶντες; fome place their confidence of Evafion in *one of them*, and fome in *another*; the Argument from both being inconfiftent. If that fence of one of thefe Words which is pleaded as a Relief againft
this

Of the Rule of the Church; or, of Ruling Elders.

this Testimony be embraced, that which unto the same purpose is pretended to be the sence of the other, must be rejected. Such shifts doth an opposition unto the Truth, put Men to.

1. SOME say that μάλιστα, *especially*, is not *Distinctive*, but *Descriptive* only; that is, it doth not distinguish one sort of Elders from another; but only *describes* that single sort of them by an adjunct of their Office, whereof the Apostle speaks. The meaning of it, they say, is as much as, *seeing that*. The Elders that Rule well, are worthy of double Honour; *seeing that they also labour*; or especially considering that they Labour, *&c.*

THAT this is the sence of the *word*, that it is thus to be interpreted, must be proved from the Authority of *Ancient Translations*, or the *use of it* in other places of the New Testament, or from its *precise Signification* and Application in other Authors learned in this Language; or that it is inforced from the *Context*, or Matter treated of.

BUT none of these can be pretended.

1. THE rendring of the word in *old Translations* we have before considered. They agree in *maxime illi qui*; which is *distinctive*.

2. THE use of it in other places of the New Testament is constantly *distinctive*, whether applied to *Things* or *Persons*, *Act.* 20. 39. οδυνώμενοι, μάλιστα ἐπὶ τῷ λόγῳ, *Sorrowing chiefly at the word*, of seeing his face no more. Their sorrow herein was *distinct* from all their other trouble, *Gal.* 6. 10. *Let us do good unto all*; μάλιστα δὲ πρὸς τοὺς οἰκείους τῆς πίστεως, *but chiefly, especially, unto the houshould of Faith*. It puts a *distinction* between the *houshold of Faith* and all *others*, by virtue of their especial privilege; which is the direct use of the word in that place of the same Apostle, *Phil.* 4. 22. *All the Saints salute you*; μάλιστα ᾑ οἱ ἐκ τῆς Καίσαρος οἰκίας, *especially they that are of Cæsar's House*. Two sorts of Saints are plainly expressed; first such as were so in general; such as were so also, but under this especial Privilege and Circumstance, that they were of *Cæsar's House*, which the others were not; as it is here

with

with respect unto Elders: *All Rule well, but some moreover labour in the Word and Doctrine,* 1 *Tim.* 5. 8. εἰ δέ τις τῶν ἰδίων, ϰ μάλιςα τῶν οἰκείων ȣ πϱονοεῖ· *If a man provide not for his own, especial those of his own House*; especially Children or Servants, which live in his own House, and are thereby distinguished from others of a more remote Relation. 2 *Tim.* 4. 13. *Bring the Books*; μάλιςα τὰς μεμβράνας, *especially the Parchments*; not because they are Parchments; but among the Books, the Parchments in particular, and in an especial manner. 2 *Pet.* 2. 9, 10. *The Lord knows how to reserve the Wicked to the Day of Judgment to be punished*; μάλιςα ʝ τȣς ὀπίσω σαρϰος, &c. *especially those that walk after the Flesh*; who shall be singled out to exemplary Punishment. It is but once more used in the New Testament; namely, *Act.* 26. 3. where it includes a distinction in the thing under consideration.

WHEREAS this is the *constant use of the word* in the Scripture, (being principally used by this Apostle in his Writings) wherein it is *distinctive* and *comparative* of the things and persons, that respect is had unto; it is to no purpose to pretend that it is *here used* in another sence, or is otherwise applied; unless they can prove from the Context that there is a necessity of their peculiar Interpretation of it.

3. THE use of the word, in other Authors, is concurrent with that of it in the Scripture, *Herodian. Lib.* 2. φιλέορ͗οι δὲ φύσει σύροι, μάλιςα ʝ ἡ Ἀντιοχέαν ϰατοικȣῆ͗ες, *The Syrians are naturally lovers of Festivals; especially they that dwell at* Antioch. It is the same phrase of Speech with that here used. For all they that dwelt at *Antioch* were *Syrians*; but all the *Syrians* dwelt not at *Antioch*. There is a *distinction* and *distribution* made of the *Syrians* into two sorts: Such as were *Syrians* only, and such as being *Syrians*, dwelt at *Antioch*, the Metropolis of the Country. If a Man should say, that all English Men were Stout and Couragious, especially the *Londoners*; he would both affirm the *Londoners* to be *Englishmen*, and distinguish them from the rest of their Countrymen. So, all that *labour in the Word and Doctrine*, are Elders; but all Elders do not labour in the Word and Doctrine,

Of the Rule of the Church; or, of Ruling Elders.

ctrine, nor is it their Duty so to do; these we call *Ruling Elders*; and, as I judge, rightly.

4. THE sence which the words will give being so interpreted, as that a *distinction of Elders* is not made in them, is absurd; the *subject and predicate* of the Proposition being terms convertible; it must be so, if the Proposition be not allowed to have a Distinction in it. One sort of Elders only, it is said are here intended. I ask who they are, and of what sort? it is said, the same with *Pastors* and *Teachers*, or *Ministers of the Gospel*. For if the one sort of Elders intended, be of another sort, we obtain what we plead for, as fully as if two sorts were allowed. Who then are these Elders, these Pastors and Teachers, these Ministers of the Church? Are they not those who *labour in the Word and Doctrine?* Yes, it will be said, it is they and no other. Then this is the sence of the words; Those who labour in the Word and Doctrine, that Rule well, are worthy of double honour, especially if they labour in the Word and Doctrine. For if there be but one sort of Elders; then Elders, and those that labour in the Word and Doctrine, are terms convertible. But Elders, and labour in the Word and Doctrine, are *subject* and *predicate* in this Proposition.

WHEREFORE, there are few of any Learning or Judgment, that make use of this Evasion; but allowing a *Distinction* to be made, they say, That it is as to *Work* and *Employment*, and not as unto *Office*. Those who in the discharge of their Office as Elders do *so labour* as is intended and included in the word κοπιῶντες, which denotes a *peculiar* kind of work in the Ministry: Yea, say some, this word denotes the Work of an *Evangelist*, who was not confined unto any one place; but *travelled* up and down the World to Preach the Gospel. And those of this mind do allow, That *two sorts of Elders* are intended in the Words. Let us see whether they have any better success in this their *Conjecture*, than the others have in the former Answer.

1. I GRANT, That κοπιῶν, the word here used, signifies to *Labour with Pains* and Diligence, *ad ultimum virium, usque ad fatigationem*; unto the utmost of Mens Strength, and unto Weariness. But,

2. SO

2. SO to labour in the Word and Doctrine, is the *Duty of all Pastors and Teachers*; and who-ever doth not *so labour*, is negligent in his Office, and worthy of *severe Blame*, instead of double Honour. For,

1. Κόπ©, whence is κοπιάω, is the *Labour of a Minister*; and so of any Minister in his Work of Teaching and Preaching the Gospel, 1 *Cor.* 3. 8. ἕκαστ@ δὲ τ̅ ἴδιον μισθὸν λήψεται κ̅τ̅ τ̅ ἴδιον κόπον, *Every one* (that is every one employed in the Ministry, whether to Plant or to Water; to Convert Men, or to Edifie the Church) *shall receive his own Reward, according to his own Labour.* He that doth not strive, κοπιᾶν, in the Ministry, shall never receive a Reward, κ̅τ̅ τ̅ ἴδιον κόπον, according to his own Labour; and so is not *worthy of double Honour.*

2. IT is a general word used to express the *work of any*, in the Service of God; whereon it is applied unto the Prophets and Teachers under the Old Testament, *Joh.* 4. 38. *I sent you to Reap that whereon you bestowed no Labour*; ἄλλοι κεκοπιάκασι κ̅ ὑμεῖς εἰς τ̅ κόπον αὐτῶ̅ εἰσεληλύθατε, *others have laboured, and you have entered into their Labours:* That is of the Prophets and *John the Baptist.* Yea, it is so unto the Labour that Women may take in the serving of the Church, *Rom.* 16. 6. *Salute Mary*, ἥτις πολλὰ ἐκοπίασε, *who laboured much*; which is more than simply κοπιᾶν, *Vers.* 12. *Salute Tryphæna and Tryphosa*, τὰς κοπιώσας ἐν κυρίῳ, *who laboured in the Lord.* *Vers.* 13. *Salute the beloved Persis*, ἥτις πολλὰ ἐκοπίασεν ἐν κυρίῳ, *who laboured much in the Lord.* So wide from Truth is it, that this word should signifie a Labour peculiar to some sorts of Ministers, which all are not in common obliged unto.

3. IF the labour of *Evangelists*, or of them who travelled up and down to Preach the Word be intended, then it is so, either because this is the *proper signification of the word*, or because it is *constantly used* elsewhere to express that kind of Labour. But the contrary unto both of these is evident from all places wherein it is used. So is it expresly applied to *fixed Elders*, 1 *Thess.* 5. 12. *We exhort you, Brethren, to know*, τοὺς κοπιῶντας ἐν ὑμῖν, *them that labour among you*; who are the Rulers and Instructers.

Of the Rule of the Church; or, of Ruling Elders.

IT is therefore evident, that this Word expresseth no more but what is the *ordinary Indispensable Duty* of every Teaching Elder, Pastor or Minister. And if it be so, then those Elders, that is Pastors or Teachers, that do not perform and discharge it, are not worthy of double Honour. Nor would the Apostle give any countenance unto them, who were any way remiss or negligent, in comparison of others, in the discharge of their Duty; see 1 *Thess.* 5. 12.

THERE are therefore *Two sorts of Duties* confessedly here mentioned and commanded; the First is *Ruling well*, the other *Labouring in the Word and Doctrine*. Suppose that both these, Ruling, and Teaching, are committed to *one sort of Persons only*, having one and the same Office absolutely, then are some commended who do not discharge their whole Duty, at least not comparatively unto others; which is a vain imagination. That both of them are committed unto one sort of Elders, and one of them only unto another, each discharging its Duty with respect unto its Work, and so both *worthy of Honour*, is the mind of the Apostle.

THAT which is objected from the following verse, namely, that *maintenance* belongs unto this double Honour, and so, consequently, that if there be Elders that are employed in the *Work of Rule only*, that *maintenance* is due unto them from the Church; I answer, It is so no doubt; *if,* (1.) The Church be *able* to make them an Allowance. (2.) If their Work be such as to *take up the whole or the greatest part of their industry*; and, (3.) If they *stand in need* of it: Without which Considerations, it may be dispensed withal; not only in them, but in Teaching Elders also.

OUR next Testimony is from the same Apostle, *Rom.* 12. 6, 7.

8. *HAVING then Gifts differing according unto the Grace given unto us, whether Prophecy, let us Prophesy according to the proportion of Faith; or Ministry, let us wait on our Ministry; or he that Teacheth on Teaching; or he that Exhorts on Exhortation, he that giveth let him do it with simplicity, he that Ruleth with diligence, he that sheweth mercy with cheerfulness.*

OUR

Of the Rule of the Church; or, of Ruling Elders.

OUR Argument from hence is this; There is in the Church ὁ προϊστάμενος *one that Ruleth*; προΐστημι is *to Rule with Authority by virtue of Office*, whence is πρέσβυς, and προϊστάμενος, one that *Presides* over others with Authority. For the discharge of their Office, there is χάρισμα διάφορον, a *differing peculiar Gift* bestowed on some; ἔχοντες χαρίσματα διάφορα, ver. 7. and there is the *especial manner* prescribed for the discharge of this especial Office, by virtue of that especial Gift; ἐν σπουδῇ, it is to be done with peculiar *diligence*. And this *Ruler* is distinguished from him that *Exhorteth,* and him that *Teacheth*, with whose especial Work, as such, he hath nothing to do; even as they are distinguished from those *who give* and *shew mercy*. That is, there is an Elder by Office in the Church, whose Work and Duty it is to *Rule,* not to *Exhort* or *Teach* Ministerially, which is our *Ruling Elder*.

IT is Answered, that the Apostle doth not treat in this place of *Offices, Functions,* or *distinct Officers*; but of *differing Gifts*, in all the Members of the Church, which they are to exercise according as their different nature doth require.

SUNDRY things I shall return hereunto, which will both explain the Context, and vindicate our Argument.

1. THOSE with whom we have to do principally, allow no exercise of *Spiritual Gifts* in the Church, but by virtue of *Office*. Wherefore, a distinct exercise of them is here placed in distinct Officers; one, as we shall see, being expresly distinguished from another.

2. GIVE such a probable enumeration of the *distinct Offices* in the Church, which they assert, namely, of *Arch-Bishops, Bishops, Presbyters,* and *Chancellors,* &c. and we shall yield the cause.

3. GIFTS *alone* do no *more*, give *no other* Warranty nor Authority, but only *render Men meet* for their exercise, as they are called, and as occasion doth require. If a Man hath received a *Gift of Teaching*, but is not called to Office, he is not obliged nor warranted thereby, to attend on *publick Teaching*, nor is it required of him in a way of Duty, nor given in charge unto him, as here it is.

4. THERE

Of the Rule of the Church; or, of Ruling Elders. 153

4. THERE is *in One*, Rule required with *diligence*. He is ὁ προϊστάμενος, a *Ruler*; and it is required of him that he attend unto his Work with *diligence*. And there are but two things required unto the confirmation of our *Thesis*. (1.) That this Rule is an Act of *Office-Power*. (2.) That he unto whom it is ascribed, is *distinguished from them* unto whom the *Pastoral* and other *Offices* in the Church are committed.

FOR the First, it is evident that *Rule* is *an Act of Office* or of Office-Power: For it requires, (1.) An especial *Relation*; there is so between him that Ruleth, and them that are Ruled; and this is the *Relation of Office*, or all confusion will ensue. (2.) Especial *Brelation*. He that Rules, is over, is above them that are Ruled; *Obey them that are over you in the Lord:* This in the Church cannot be in any, but by virtue of Office. (3.) *Especial Authority*. All lawful Rule is an Act of Authority; and there is no Authority in the Church, but by virtue of Office. Secondly, That this Officer is distinct from all others in the Church, we shall immediately demonstrate, when we have a little further cleared the Context. Wherefore,

5. IT is confessed that respect is had unto *Gifts*; having *different Gifts*, ver. 6, 7. As all Office-Power in the Church is founded in them, *Ephes.* 4. 7, 8, 9, 11, 12. But Gifts, absolutely with reference unto common use, are not intended,. as in some other places. But they are spoken of with respect unto *Offices* or *Functions*, and the communication of them unto *Officers*, for the discharge of their *Office*. This is evident from the Text and Context, with the whole design of the place: For,

1. THE *Analysis* of the place directs unto this Interpretation. Three sorts of Duties are prescribed unto the Church in this Chapter. (1.) Such as are *Universal*, belonging absolutely unto all, and every one that appertains unto it; which are declared *ver.* 1. 2. (2.) Such as are *peculiar* unto some, by virtue of that especial place which they have in the Church, *ver.* 3, 4, 5, 6, 7, 8. This can be nothing but Office. (3.) Such as are *general* or common, with respect unto occasions, from *ver.* 8. to the end of the Chapter. Hence the same Duty is doubly prescribed; to some in way of especial Office, to others in the

X way

way of a Gracious Duty in general. So here, *He that gives, let him do it with simplicity,* Verſ. 8. is the same Duty or Work for the ſubſtance of it, with *Diſtributing unto the neceſſity of the Saints,* Verſ. 13. And the Apoſtle doth not repeat his Charge of the ſame Duty in ſo few words, as required in the *ſame manner,* and of the *ſame perſons.* But in the firſt place, he ſpeaks of the manner of its Performance, by virtue of *Office*; and in the latter of its diſcharge as to the Subſtance of it, as a *Grace* in all Believers. The Deſign of the Apoſtle lies plain in the *Analyſis* of this Diſcourſe.

2. THE *Context* makes the ſame Truth evident. For,

1. THE whole *ordinary Publick work of the Church,* is diſtributed into προφητεία, and διακονία; *Prophecy* and *Miniſtry.* For the extraordinary *Gift of Prophecy* is not here intended; but only that of the Interpretation of the Scripture, whoſe Rule is the *Analogy of Faith*; εἴτε προφητείαν, κ̄ τὴν ἀναλογίαν τῆς πίστεως. It is ſuch *Prophecy* as is to be regulated by the *Scripture* it ſelf; which gives the Proportion of Faith. And there is not any thing, in any, or both of theſe, *Prophecy* and *Miniſtry,* but it belongs unto *Office* in the Church. Neither is there any thing *belonging unto Office* in the Church, but may be reduced unto one of theſe, as they are all of them here, by the Apoſtle.

2. THE Gifts ſpoken of, are in general, referred unto all them who are intended. Now theſe are either the *whole Church,* and all the Members of it, or all the *Officers* of the Church only. Hence it is expreſſed in the Plural number, ἔχοντες χαρίσματα, *we having;* that is, all we that are concerned herein. This cannot be *all of the Church;* for all the Church have *not received the Gifts of Prophecy and Miniſtry.* Nor can any diſtinction be made of who doth receive them, and who doth not, but with reſpect unto Office. And therefore,

3. IN the Diſtribution which enſues of *Prophecy,* into *Exhorting* and *Teaching;* and of *Miniſtry* into *Shewing, Mercy, Rule,* and *Giving;* having ſtated theſe Gifts in general, in the Officers in general, making diſtinct Application of them unto diſtinct Officers, he ſpeaks in the *Singular* number,

ὁ διδάσκων, ὁ παρακαλῶν, ὁ προϊστάμενος. *He that Teacheth, he that Exhorteth, he that Ruleth.*

6. IT is then evident that *Offices* are intended; and it is no less evident, that *distinct Offices* are so, which was to be proved in the Second place. For, (1.) The *distributive Particle* ὅτι, and the *indicative Article* ὁ, prefixed unto each Office in particular, do shew them distinct, so far as Words can do it. As by the Particle ὅτι, *whether*, they are distinguished in their nature; whether they be of this or that kind; so by the *Article* prefixed to each of them in exercise, they are distinguished in their *Subjects*. (2.) The *Operations*, Work, and Effects ascribed unto these Gifts, require distinct *Offices* and *Functions* in their exercise. And if the Distribution be made unto all promiscuously without respect unto distinct Offices, it were the only way to bring *confusion* into the Church, whereas, indeed here is an accurate Order in all Church Administrations represented to us. And it is farther evident that distinct Offices are intended. (1.) From the comparison made unto the *Members of the Body*, ver. 4. *All the Members have not the same Office;* the eye hath one, the ear hath another. (2.) Each of the Duties mentioned and given in charge, is sufficient for a distinct Officer, as is declared *Act.* 6.

7. IN particular, *He that Ruleth*, is a distinct Officer. An Officer, because *Rule* is an Act of Office, or Office-Power. And he is expresly distinguished from all others. But, say some, *he that Ruleth*, is he that doth so, be who he will, that is the *Pastor* or *Teacher*, the Teaching Elder. But the contrary is evident. (1.) He that says, *He that Exhorteth*, and then adds, *He that Ruleth*, having distinguished before between *Prophecy*, whereunto *Exhortation* doth belong, and *Ministry* whereof *Rule* is a part; and prefixing the *Prepositive Indicative Article* to each of them, doth as plainly put a difference between them, as can be done by Words. (2.) *Rule* is the principal Work of him that *Ruleth*. For he is to attend unto it, ἐν σπουδῇ, with *Diligence*, that is such as is peculiar unto *Rule*, in contradistinction unto what is principally required in other Administrations. But *Rule* is not the principal Work of the *Pastor*, re-

quiring constant and continual attendance. For his *labour in the Word and Doctrine*, is ordinarily sufficient for the utmost of his *Diligence* and Abilities.

8. WE have therefore in this Context the *beautiful Order* of things in and of the Church. All the Duties of it, with respect unto its Edification, derived from distinct *differing Spiritual Gifts*, exercised in and by *distinct Officers*, unto their peculiar ends. The distinction that is in the nature of those Gifts, their use and end being provided for in distinct Subjects. The mind of no *One Man*, at least ordinarily, is meet to be the seat and subject of all those differing Gifts in any eminent degree; the *Person of no Man* being sufficient, meet, or able to *exercise* them in a way of Office towards the whole Church; especially those who *labour in the Word and Doctrine*, being obliged to give themselves wholly thereunto, and those that *Rule* to *attend thereto with diligence* ; so many distinct Works, Duties and Operations, with the Qualifications required in their discharge, being inconsistent in the same Subject; all things are here distributed into their proper Order and Tendency, unto the Edification of the Church. Every *distinct Gift* required to be exercised in a peculiar manner, unto the publick Edification of the Church, is distributed unto *peculiar Officers*, unto whom an especial Work is assigned to be discharged by virtue of the Gifts received, unto the Edification of the whole Body. No Man alive is able to fix on any thing which is necessary unto the *Edification of the Church*, that is not contained in these Distributions, under some of the Heads of them. Nor can any Man find out any thing in *these Assignations* of distinct Duties unto distinct Offices, that is *superfluous, redundant*, or not directly necessary unto the Edification of the whole, with all the Parts and Members of it; nor do I know any wise and sober Man who knows any thing how the Duties enjoined are to be performed, with what Care, Diligence, Circumspection, Prayer and Wisdom, suited unto the nature, ends and objects of them, can ever imagine that they can all of them belong unto *one and the same Office*, or be discharged by one and the same Person.

LET

Of the Rule of the Church; or, of Ruling Elders. 15

LET Men advance any other *Church Order* in the room of that here declared; so suited unto the principles of Natural Light, Operations and Duties of *diverse natures*, being distributed and assigned to such *distinct Gifts*; acted in distinct *Offices*, as renders those unto whom they are prescribed meet and able for them; so correspondent to all *Institutions*, Rules and Examples of Church-Order in other places of Scripture; so suited unto the Edification of the Church, wherein nothing which is necessary thereunto is omitted, nor any thing added above what is necessary; and it shall be cheerfully embraced.

THE Truth is, the ground of the different Interpretations and Applications of this Context of the Apostle, ariseth meerly from the prejudicate Apprehensions, that Men have concerning the *State of the Church and its Rule*. For if the State of it be *National* or *Diocesan*, if the *Rule* of it be by *Arbitrary Rules and Canons*, from an Authority exerting it self in *Courts Ecclesiastical*, Legal or Illegal, the Order of things here described by the Apostle, doth no way belong, nor can be accommodated thereunto. To suppose that we have a full Description and Account in these Words of all the *Offices* and *Officers* of the Church, of their Duty and Authority, of all they have to do, and the manner how they are to do it, is altogether unreasonable and sencelefs unto them, who have *another Idea* of Church-Affairs and Rule, conceived in their Minds, or received by Tradition, and riveted by Interest. And on the other hand; those who know *little or nothing* of what belongs unto the *due Edification of the Church*, beyond Preaching the Word and reaping the Advantage that is obtained thereby, cannot see any necessity of the distribution of these several *Works and Duties* unto *several Officers*; but suppose all may be done well enough by One or Two in the same Office. Wherefore, it will be necessary, that we treat briefly of *the Nature of the Rule of the Church* in particular, and what is required thereunto, which shall be done in the close of this Discourse.

9. THE *Exceptions* which are usually put in unto this Testimony, have not the least countenance from the Text or Context, nor the matter treated of, nor Confirmation from

any

any other Divine Testimony. It is therefore in vain to contend about them, being such as any Man may multiply at his pleasure on the like occasion; and used by those who on other considerations, are not willing that things should be as they are here declared to be by the Apostle. Yet we may take a brief *Specimen* of them. Some say it is *Gifts absolutely* without respect unto *distinct Offices*, that the Apostle Treats of; which hath been disproved from the *Text* and *Context* before. Some say that *Rule* is included in the *Pastoral Office*, so as that the Pastor only is here intended. But, (1.) *Rule* is not his principal Work, which he is to attend unto in a peculiar manner with *diligence* above other parts of his Duty. (2.) *The care of the Poor of the Flock* belongs also to the *Pastoral Office*, yet is there *another Office* appointed to attend unto it in a peculiar manner, *Act.* 6. (3.) *He that Ruleth*, is in this place expresly distinguished from *him that Exhorteth*, and *him that Teacheth*. Some say, that *he that Ruleth*, is he that *Ruleth his Family*. But this is disproved by the *Analysis* of the Chapter before declared. And this Duty, which is common unto all that have Families, and confined unto their Families, is ill placed among those *publick* Duties, which are designed unto the Edification of the whole Church. It is objected, that *he that Ruleth*, is here placed after him that *giveth*, that is, the *Deacon*; I say then it cannot be the *Pastor* that is intended; if we may prescribe Methods of expressing himself unto the Apostle. But he useth his Liberty, and doth not oblige himself unto any *Order* in the annumeration of the *Offices* of the Church; see 1 *Cor.* 12. 8, 9, 10, 28. And some other Exceptions are insisted on of the same nature and importance, which indeed deserve not our consideration.

10. THERE is the same Evidence given unto the Truth argued for, in another Testimony of the same Apostle, 1 *Cor.* 12. 28. *God hath set some in the Church, First Apostles, Secondarily Prophets, Thirdly Teachers, after that Miracles, then Gifts of Healings, Helps, Governments, Diversities of Tongues.* I shall not insist on this *Testimony* and its Vindication in particular, seeing many things would be required thereunto, which have

have been Treated of already. Some things may be briefly observed concerning it. That there is here an Annumeration *of Officers and Offices* in the Church, both *extraordinary* for that season, and *ordinary* for continuance, is beyond exception. Unto them is added, the present exercise of some *extraordinary Gifts*, as *Miracles*, *Healing*, *Tongues*. That by *Helps*, the *Deacons* of the Church are intended, most do agree, because their Original Institution was as *helpers* in the Affairs of the Church. *Governments*, are Governours or *Rulers*, the *Abstract* for the *Concrete*; that is, such as are distinct from Teachers; such hath *God placed in the Church*, and such there ought to be. But it is said that *Gifts*, not *Offices* are intended; the *Gift of Goverment*, or Gift for Government. If so, then these Gifts are either *ordinary* or *extraordinary*; if *ordinary*, how come they to be reckoned among *Miracles*, *Healing*, and *Tongues*? if *extraordinary*, what extraordinary *Gifts for Government* were then given distinct from those of the Apostles; and what instance is any where given of them in the Scripture? Again, If God hath given *Gifts for Government* to abide in the Church, distinct from those given unto *Teachers*, and unto other Persons than the Teachers, then is there a distinct *Office of Rule or Government* in the Church, which is all we plead for.

11. THE Original Order in these things is plain in the Scripture. The Apostles had all *Church-Power* and *Church-Office* in themselves, with Authority to exercise all Acts of them every where on all occasions. But considering the nature of the Church, with that of the Rule appointed by the Lord Christ in it or over it; they did not, they would not ordinarily exercise their power by themselves or in their own persons alone. And therefore, when the First Church consisted of a small number, the Apostles acted all things in it, by the *consent of the whole Multitude* or the *Fraternity*, as we have proved from *Acts* the First. And when the number of Believers encreased, so as that the Apostles themselves could not in their own Persons attend unto all the Duties that were to be performed towards the Church by virtue of Office, they added by the direction of the Holy Ghost, the Office of the *Deacons*; for the especial discharge

discharge of the Duty which the Church oweth unto its poor Members. Whereas therefore it is evident, that the Apostles could no more *personally* attend unto the *Rule of the Church*, with all that belongs thereunto, without an entrenchment on that *labour in the Word and Prayer*, which was incumbent on them, than they could attend unto the *Relief of the Poor*, they appointed *Elders*, to help and assist in that part of Office-Work, as the *Deacons* did in the other.

THESE Elders are first mentioned, *Act.* 11. 30. where they are spoken of as those which were well known, and had now been of some time in the Church. Afterwards they are still mentioned in conjunction with the Apostles, and *distinction* from the Church it self, *Acts* 15. 2, 4, 6, 22. Chap. 16. 4. Chap. 21. 18. Now the *Apostles* themselves were *Teaching Elders*, that is such as had the *Work of Teaching and Rule* committed to them, 1 *Pet.* 5. 1. 2 *Joh.* 1. And *these Elders* are constantly distinguished from them; which makes it evident, that they were not *Teaching Elders*. And therefore in all the mention that is made of them, the Work of *Teaching* or Preaching is no where ascribed unto them; which at *Jerusalem* the Apostles reserved to themselves, *Act.* 6. 2, 3. but they are every where introduced as joining with the Apostles in the *Rule* of the Church, and that in distinction from the Church it self or the Brethren of it. Yea, it is altogether improbable, that whilst the Apostles were at *Jerusalem*, giving themselves wholly unto the *Word and Prayer*, that they should appoint in the same Church many more *Teaching Elders*; though it is plain that the *Elders* intended were *many*.

I SHALL add for a close of all, that there is no sort of Churches in being but are of *this perswasion*, that there ought to be *Rulers* in the Church, that are not in *Sacred Orders*, as some call them; or have no interest in the *Pastoral* or *Ministerial Office*, as unto the dispensation of the Word, and Administration of the Sacraments. For as the Government of the *Roman Church* is in the hands of such Persons in a great measure, so in the *Church of England*, much of the Rule of it is managed by *Chancellors*, *Officials*, *Commissaries*, and the like Officers,

Officers, who are absolutely *Lay-Men*, and not at all in their *holy Orders*. Some would place the *Rule* of the Church in the *Civil Magistrate*, who is the only *Ruling Elder*, as they suppose. But the generality of all *Protestant* Churches throughout the World, both *Lutherans* and *Reformed*, do both in their judgment and practice assert the necessity of the *Ruling Elders* which we plead for; and their Office lies at the foundation of all their Order and Discipline, which they cannot forgo without extream confusion, yea, without the ruine of their Churches. And although some among us, considering particular Churches only as *small Societies*, may think there is no need of any such *Office* or Officers for Rule in them; yet when such Churches consist of *some Thousands*, without any opportunity of distributing themselves into several Congregations, as at *Charenton* in *France*, it is a weak imagination, that the Rule of Christ can be observed in them by *Two or Three Ministers* alone. Hence, in the Primitive Times we have instances of *Ten*, *Twenty*, yea, *Forty* Elders in a particular Church, wherein they had respect unto the Institution under the Old Testament, whereby *each Ten Families* were to have a peculiar Ruler. However, it is certain that there is such a Reformation in all sorts of Churches, that there ought to be some *attending unto Rule*, that are not called to labour in the Word and Doctrine.

CHAP. VIII.

The Nature of Church-Polity or Rule; with the Duty of Elders.

HAVING declared *who are the Rulers of the Church*, something must be added concerning the *Rule* it self, which is to be exercised therein. Hereof I have Treated before in general: That which I now design, is, what in particular respects them who are *called unto Rule only*;

only; whereunto some Considerations must be premised.

1. THERE is *Power, Authority*, and *Rule* granted unto and residing in some Persons of the Church, and not in the Body of the Fraternity or Community of the People. How far the Government of the Church may be denominated *Democratical* from the necessary *consent of the people* unto the principal Acts of it in its exercise, I shall not determine. But whereas this consent, and the liberty of it is absolutely necessary according to the Law of Obedience unto Christ, which is prescribed unto the Church, requiring that all they do in compliance therewith be *voluntary*; as unto the manner of its exercise, being in *dutiful compliance* with the guidance of the Rule, it changeth not the State of the Government. And therefore, where any thing is Acted and Disposed in the Church, by *Suffrage*, or the plurality of Voices, the *Vote of the Fraternity* is not Determining and *Authoritative*, but only *declarative of consent and obedience*. It is so, in all Acts of Rule where the Church is *Organical*, or in compleat Order.

2. THAT there is such an *Authority* and *Rule* instituted by Christ in his Church, is not liable unto dispute. Where there are *Bishops, Pastors, Elders, Guides, Rulers, Stewards, instituted, given, granted, called, ordained*; and some to be Ruled, *Sheep, Lambs, Brethren*, obliged by command to *obey* them, *follow* them, *submit* unto them in the Lord, *regard them as over them*: There is *Rule* and *Authority* in some persons, and that committed unto them by Jesus Christ. But all these things are frequently repeated in the Scripture. And when in the practical Part or Exercise of Rule, due respect is not had unto their *Authority*, there is nothing but Confusion and Disorder. When the People judge that the *Power of the Keys* is committed unto them as such only, and in them doth the *Right* of their Use and Exercise reside; that their *Elders* have no interest in the disposing of Church Affairs, or in Acts of Church Power, but only their own suffrages, or what they can obtain by reasoning, and think there is no Duty incumbent on them to acquiesce in *their Authority* in any thing (an Evil apt to grow in Churches) it overthrows all that *beautiful Order*, which Jesus Christ

with the Duty of Elders.

Christ hath ordained: And if any shall make Advantage of this Complaint, That where the *People* have their due Liberty granted unto them, they are apt to *assume that Power* unto themselves which belongs not unto them; an evil attended with troublesome Impertinencies and Disorder, tending unto *Anarchy*; let them remember, on the other hand, how upon the confinement of Power and Authority unto the *Guides*, *Bishops* or *Rulers* of the Church, they have changed the nature of Church-Power, and enlarged their Usurpation, until the whole Rule of the Church issued in absolute *Tyranny*. Wherefore, no fear of consequents that may ensue and arise from the darkness, ignorance, weakness, lusts, corruptions or secular interests of Men ought to entice us unto the least Alteration of the Rule by any *prudential Provisions* of our own.

3. THIS *Authority* in the Rulers of the Church, is neither *Autocratical* or *Sovereign*, nor *Nomothetical* or *Legislative*, nor *Despotical* or *Absolute*; but *Organical* and *Ministerial* only. The endless Controversies which have sprung out of the mystery of iniquity, about an *Autocratical and Monarchical* Government in the Church, about *power* to *make Laws* to bind the Consciences of Men, yea, to *kill* and destroy them, with the whole manner of the execution of this Power, we are not concerned in. A pretence of any such Power in the Church, is destructive of the *Kingly Office of Christ*, contrary to express Commands of Scripture, and condemned by the Apostles, *Isa.* 33. 22. *Jam.* 4. 12. *Mat.* 17. 5. Chap. 23. 8, 9, 10, 11. *Luke* 22. 25, 26. 2 *Cor.* 1. 24. 1 *Cor.* 3. 21, 22, 23. 2 *Cor.* 4. 5. 1 *Pet.* 5. 1, 2 5.

4. AS the Rule of the Church, in those by whom it is exercised, is meerly *Ministerial*, with respect unto the Authority of Christ, his Law, and the Liberty of the Church, wherewith he hath made it free; so in its nature it is *spiritual*, purely and only. So the Apostle Affirms expresly, 2 *Cor.* 10. 4, 5, 6. For its *object* is spiritual; namely, the Souls and Consciences of Men whereunto it extends, which no other Humane Power doth; nor doth it reach those other concerns of Men that are subject unto any political Power: Its *end* is Spiritual, namely,

the Glory of God, in the guidance and direction of the Minds, and Souls of Men, to live unto him, and come to the enjoyment of him; the *Law* of it is spiritual, even the Word, Command and Direction of Christ himself alone; the *Acts* and *Exercise* of it in binding and loosing, in remitting and retaining Sin, in opening and shutting the Kingdom of Heaven, are all *Spiritual* meerly and only. Neither can there be an Instance given of any thing belonging unto the Rule of the Church, that is of another nature. Yea, it is sufficient eternally to exclude any Power or Exercise of it, any Act of Rule or Government from any Interest in Church-Affairs, that it can be proved to be *Carnal, Political, Despotical,* of external Operaration, or not entirely Spiritual.

5. THE *Change of this Government* of the Church, fell out and was introduced *gradually*, upon an advantage taken from the *unmeetness of the People* to be lead under this Spiritual Rule. For the greatest part of them that made up Christian Churches, being become ignorant and carnal, that Rule which consists in a spiritual influence on the Consciences of Men, was no way able to retain them within the bounds of outward obedience, which was at last only aimed at. There was therefore *another kind of Rule* and Government judged necessary to retain them in any Order or *Decorum*. And it must be acknowledged, that where the Members of the Church are not in some degree *Spiritual*, a Rule that is meerly Spiritual will be of no great use unto them. But principally, this change was introduced by those that were in possession of the Rule it self; and that on two grounds. (1.) Their *unskilfulness* in the management of this *Spiritual Rule*, or weariness of the Duties which are required thereunto: This made them willing to desert it; with that perpetual labour and exercise of all sorts of Graces which are required in it, and to embrace another more easie, and more suited unto their Inclinations. (2.) A desire of the Secular advantages of Profit, Honour and Veneration, which tendered themselves unto them in another kind of Rule: By these means was the *Original Government* of the Church, which was of Divine Institution, utterly lost; and a Worldly Domination introduced

with the Duty of Elders.

introduced in the room thereof. But the brief delineation given of it before, with what shall now be added, will demonstrate sufficiently, that all these Disputes and Contests which are in the World, between the *Church of Rome* and others about *Church-Power and Rule,* are utterly foreign unto Christian Religion.

6. I SHALL therefore briefly enquire into these three things, (1.) What is the *Skill* and *Polity* that is required unto the Exercise, or Administration of the Government of the Church? (2.) What is the sole *Law and Rule* of it ? (3.) What are the *Acts and Duties* of it? What it is conversant about.; especially those wherein the Office of *Ruling Elders* doth take place.

1. THE *Polity* of Church-Government *subjectively* considered, is generally supposed to consist, (1.) In a *skill,* learning or understanding in the *Civil,* and especially the *Canon Law,* with the additional *Canons,* accomodating that Law unto the present state of things of the Nation, to be interpreted according unto the general Rules of it. (2.) *Knowledge* of and Acquaintance with the Constitution, Power, Jurisdiction and Practice of some *Law Courts*; which being in their original, grant of Power, manner of Proceeding, Pleas and Censures meerly Secular, are yet called *Ecclesiastical* or *Spiritual.* (3.) A good *Discretion* to understand a-right the extent of their Power, with the bounds and limits of it; that on the *one* hand they let none escape whom they can reach by the discipline of their Courts, and on the *other* not entrench so far on the *Civil-Power* and the *Jurisdiction* of other Courts according to the Law of the Land, as to bring themselves into charge or trouble. (4.) An acquaintance with the *Table of Fees,* that they may neither lose their own profit, nor give advantage unto others to question them for taking more than their due. But in these things we are not at present concerned.

8. THE skill then of the Officers of the Church for the Government of it, is a *spiritual Wisdom and Understanding in the Law of Christ, for that end, with an Ability to make application of it in all requisite Instances, unto the Edification of the whole Church, and all its Members, through a ministerial Exercise*

ercife of the *Authority of Chrift himfelf, and a due Reprefen-tation of his Holinefs, Love, Care, Compaffion and Tendernefs to-ward his Church*.

1. THE fole *Rule and Meafure* of the Government of the Church being the Law of Chrift; that is, the Intimation and Declaration of his Mind and Will, in his Inftitutions, Commands, Prohibitions and Promifes; an *Underftanding* herein, with Wifdom, from that Underftanding, is and muft be the whole of the *Skill* enquired after. How this *Wifdom* is beftowed as a fpiritual Gift, how it is to be acquired in a way of Duty, by Prayer, Meditation and ftudy of the Word, hath been intimated before, and fhall fully be declared, in our *Difcourfe of fpiritual Gifts*. All Decrees and Decretals, *Canons* and *Gloffes* come properly in this matter under one Title of them, namely *Extravagant*. The utmoft Knowledge of them, and Skill in them will contribute nothing unto this Wifdom. Neither are any fort of Men more ftrangers unto it, or unacquainted with it, than they are, for the moft part, who are eminently cunning in fuch Laws, and the Jurifdiction of *Ecclefiaftical Courts*. But *Wifdom* in the knowledge of the Will of Chrift as revealed in the Scripture, is that alone which is of ufe in the Government of the Church.

2. A PART of this Wifdom confifteth in an *Ability* of Mind to make *Application* of the Law of Chrift in all requifite Inftances, unto the Edification of the Church in general, and all the Members of it refpectively. This Wifdom is not *notional* only, but *practical*. It confifts not in a fpeculative comprehenfion of the *fence of the Rule*, or of the Mind of Chrift therein only, though that be required in the firft place; but in an *Ability* of Mind to make Application of it, whereunto *Diligence, Care, Watchfulnefs* and *fpiritual Courage* are required. Some are to be *Admonifhed*; fome to be *Rebuked* fharply; fome to be *cut off*; in which and the like cafes, a *fpirit of Government* acting it felf in *Diligence, Boldnefs* and *Courage* is neceffary. And this is one reafon why the Lord Chrift hath appointed many Elders in each Church, and thofe of feveral forts. For it is feldom that any one Man is qualified for the whole work

work of Rule. Some may have a good understanding in the *Law* of the Churches Government; yet through a natural *Tenderness*, and an insuperable kind of Modesty, not be so ready and prompt for that part of this Discipline which consists in *Reproofs* and Severity of Censures. Some may not have so great an *Ability* for the Indagation of the sence of the Law as others have; who yet upon the *knowledge* of it being discovered unto them, have readiness and boldness in Christ to apply it as occasion doth require. All *Elders* therefore in their variety of Gifts are to be helpful to each other in the common Work, which they are called unto. But such as are utterly destitute of these Gifts, are not called unto this Work; nor any part of it.

3. THE *Power* that is exercised herein, is the *Power and Authority of Christ* committed unto the Elders. *Our Authority, which the Lord Christ hath given us for Edification, and not for Destruction*, 2 Cor. 10. 8. It is granted unto the Rulers of the Church, not *formally* to reside in them, as the *Power of a King* is in his own person; but *ministerially* and *instrumentally* only. For it must be the *Authority of Christ himself*, whereby the Consciences of Men are spiritually affected, with reference unto spiritual Ends; whereby they are bound or losed in Heaven and Earth, have their *Sins remitted* or *retained*. And the consideration hereof is that alone which gives a due regard unto the *Ministry of the Church*, in the discharge of their Office among them that desire to commend their Consciences unto the Lord Christ in what they do.

4. THE especial *Design* of the Rule of the Church in its Government is *to represent the Holiness, Love, Compassion, Care and Authority of Christ towards his Church*. This is the great end of Rule in the Church, and of all the Discipline which is to be exercised by virtue thereof. Whilst this is not attended unto, when the Officers and Rulers of the Church do not endeavour in all the actings of their Power and Office, to set forth these *Vertues of Christ*; to exemplifie that impression of them which he hath left in his Laws and Rule, with the Divine Testimonies which he gives of them in his own person,

they

they utterly deviate from the principal end of all Rule in the Church. For Men to act herein in a way of *Domination*, with a visible *Elation* of Mind and Spirit above their Brethren, with *Anger*, *Wrath* and *Passion*, by *Rules*, *Order* and *Laws* of their own devising; without the least consideration of what the Lord Christ requires, and what is the frame of his Heart towards all his Disciples, is to reflect the highest Dishonour imaginable upon Christ himself. He who comes into the *Courts of the King in* Westminster-*Hall*, when filled with Judges, Grave, Learned and Righteous, most ordinarily be allowed to judge of the *King himself*, his Wisdom, Justice, Moderation and Clemency, by the *Law* which they proceed upon, and their manner of the Administration of it. But God forbid that Christians should make a Judgment concerning the *Holiness*, *Wisdom*, *Love* and *Compassion* of Christ, by the Representation which (as is pretended) is made of him and them in some Courts, wherein Church-Rule and Discipline is Admistred. When any had offended of old, their Censure by the Church was called the *Bewailing of them*, 2 *Cor.* 12. 24. and that because of the *Sorrow*, Pity and Compassion whereby in that Censure they evidenced the compassion of the Lord Christ towards the Souls of Sinners. This is scarce answered by those *pecuniary mulcts* and other *penalties*, which, with indignation and contempt, are inflicted on such as are made Offenders, *whether they will or no*. Certainly, those who love the Lord Jesus Christ in sincerity, and have a due honour for the Gospel, will at one time or another begin to think meet, that this stain of our Religion should be washed away.

2*dly*. THE *Rule* and Law of the exercise of Power in the Elders of the Church, is the *Holy Scripture only*. The Lord Christ is the only Law-giver of the Church; all his Laws unto this end are recorded in the Scripture; no *other Law* is effectual, can oblige or operate upon the *object* or unto the *ends* of Church-Rule. If the Church make a Thousand Rules or *Canons*, or Laws for Government, neither any of them, nor all of them in general, have any the least power to oblige Men unto

unto *obedience* or compliance with them, but only so far, as *virtually* and *materially* they contain what is of the Law of Christ, and derives force from thence. As the *Judges* in our Courts of Justice, are bound to judge and determine in all cases, out of and according to the *Law of the Land*; and when they do not, their Sentence is of no validity, but may and ought to be reversed. But if wilfully or of choice, they should introduce Laws or Rules not *legally established* in this Nation, judging according unto them, it would render them highly criminal and punishable. It is no otherwise in the *Kingdom of Christ*, and the *Rule* thereof. It is by *his Law* alone that Rule is to be exercised in it. There is nothing left unto the *Elders of the Church*, but the *Application* of his Laws, and the General Rules of them unto particular cases and occasions. To make, to bring, to execute any other Rules, Laws or *Canons* in the Government of his Church, is to usurp on his Kingly Dominion, whereunto all Legislative Power in the Church is appropriate. Nor is it possible that any thing can fall out in the Church, that any thing can be required in the Rule of it, nor can *any instance be given* of any such thing, wherein, for the ends of Church-Rule, there is or can be any more left unto the Rulers of it, but only the *Application* and *Execution* of the Laws of Christ. Unto this *Application* to be made in a due manner, the *Wisdom and Skill* before described is requisite, and that alone. Where there are other *Laws, Rules* or *Canons* of the Government of the Church; and where the Administration of them is directed by *Laws Civil* or *Political*, there is a *skill in them* required unto that Administration, as all will confess. So is the *Wisdom* we before described, and that alone, necessary unto that *Rule* of the Church which the Lord Christ hath ordained; the Instrument and means whereof, is his Word and Law alone.

3dly. THE *matter of this Rule* about which it is conversant, and so the *Acts and Duties* of it may be reduced unto Three Heads.

1. THE *Admission and Exclusion of Members*. Both these are Acts of Church-Power and Authority, which are to be exercised by the Elders only in a Church that is *Organical* and
compleat

compleat in its Officers. There is that in them both, which is founded in and warranted from the Light and Law of Nature and Rules of Equity. Every Righteous *voluntary Society* coalefcing therein rightfully, upon known Laws, and Rules for the Regulation of it unto certain ends, hath naturally a *power inherent in it* and infeparable from it, to *receive* into its *incorporation*, fuch as being meet for it, do voluntarily offer themfelves thereunto ; as alfo to *reject*, or withhold the Privileges of the Society, from fuch as refufe to be Regulated by the Laws of the Society. This power is inherent in the Church *effentially* confidered *antecedently* unto the enftating of Officers in it : By virtue of their *mutual confederation* they may receive into the privileges of the Society thofe that are meet, and withdraw the fame privileges from thofe that are unworthy. But in thefe actings of the Church, effentially confidered, there is no exercife of the *Power of the Keys*, as unto Authoritative Rule, but what is meerly Doctrinal. There is in what it doth a declaration of the Mind of Chrift, as unto the State of the Perfons whom they do receive or reject. But unto the Church as *Organical*, as there are *Elders* or *Rulers* inftated in it according unto the Mind of Chrift, there is a *peculiar Authority* committed for thofe Acts of the Admiffion and Exclufion of Members. Unto this end is the *Key of Rule* committed unto the Elders of the Church, to be applied with the confent of the whole Society, as we fhall fee afterwards.

2*dly.* THE *Direction* of the Church in all the Members of it, unto the obfervance of the Rule and Law of Chrift in all things, unto his Glory and their own Edification. And all thefe things may be reduced unto thefe Four Heads. (1.) *Mutual,* Intenfe, peculiar *Love* among themfelves, to be exercifed continually in all the Duties of it. (2.) *Perfonal Holinefs* in Gracious Moral Obedience. (3.) *Ufefulnefs* towards the Members of the fame Church, towards other Churches, and all Men abfolutely, as occafion and opportunity do require. (4.) The *due performance* of all thofe Duties, which all the Members of the Church owe mutually unto each other, by virtue of that Place and Order which they hold and poffefs in the Body. About thefe these things is Church-Rule to be exercised; for they all belong unto the preservation of its *Being*, and the attainment of its *Ends*.

3*dly.* HEREUNTO also belongs the *disposal of the outward concernments of the Church in its Assemblies*, and in the management of all that is performed in them, *that all things may be done Decently and in Order*. The disposal of Times, Seasons, Places, the way and manner of managing all things in Church-Assemblies, the Regulation of Speeches and Actions, the appointment of Seasons for extraordinary Duties, according unto the *General Rules of the Word*, and the Reason of things from present Circumstances, are Acts of *Rule*, whose Right resides in the *Elders* of the Church.

THESE things being premised, we may consider what is the Work and Duty of *that sort of Elders*, which we have proved to be *placed* by Christ for Rule in the Church. For, considering that which hath been spoken before concerning the *Pastoral Office*, or the Duty of *Teaching-Elders* of the Church, and what hath now been added concerning its *Rule* in general; I cannot but admire that any one Man should have such a confidence in his own Abilities, as to suppose himself *meet and able* for the Discharge of the Duties of both sorts in the least Church of Christ that can well be supposed. Yea, supposing more *Teaching-Elders* in every Church than one, yet if they are all and every one of them equally bound to *give themselves unto the Word and Prayer*, so as not to be diverted from that Work by any inferior Duties, if they are obliged to *labour in the Word and Doctrine* to the utmost of their strength continually, it will appear at length to be necessary, that there should be some whose peculiar Office and Duty is to attend unto *Rule* with *Diligence*. And the Work of these Elders consists in the things ensuing.

1. THEY are joined unto the *Teaching Elders* in all Acts and Duties of Church-Power, for the Rule and Government of the Church. Such are those before declared. This is plain in the Text, 1 *Tim.* 5. 17. Both sorts of Elders are *joined* and do concurr in the *same Rule* and all the Acts of it; one sort of them

them labouring alfo in the Word and Doctrine. Of both forts is the *Presbytery* or *Elderſhip* compoſed, wherein reſides all Church-Authority. And in this conjunction, thoſe of both forts are every way *equal*, determining all Acts of Rule by their common ſuffrage. This gives Order, with a neceſſary repreſentation of Authority, unto the Church in its Government.

2. THEY are in particular to attend unto all things wherein the *Rule or Diſcipline* of the Church is concerned, with a due care that the Commands of Chriſt be duly obſerved by and among all the Members of the Church. This is the ſubſtance of the *Rule* which Chriſt hath appointed, whatever be pretended unto the contrary. Whatever is ſet up in the World, in oppoſition unto it or inconſiſtent with it, under the Name of the *Government of the Church*, is foreign unto the Goſpel. *Church-Rule* is a due care and proviſion, that the Inſtitutions, Laws, Commands and Appointments of Jeſus Chriſt be duly obſerved, and nothing elſe. And hereof, as unto the Duty of the Elders, we may give ſome inſtances: As,

1. TO *watch diligently* over the ways, walking and converſation of all the Members of the Church, to ſee that it be *blameleſs*, without offence, uſeful, exemplary and in all things anſwering the holineſs of the Commands of Chriſt, the honour of the Goſpel, and profeſſion which in the World they make thereof. And upon the obſervation which they ſo make, in the *watch* wherein they are placed, to inſtruct, admoniſh, charge, exhort, encourage, comfort, as they ſee cauſe. And this are they to attend unto, with *Courage* and *Diligence*.

2. TO watch againſt all riſings or appearances of ſuch *differences* and diviſions on the account of things Eccleſiaſtical or Civil, as unto their Names, Rights and Proprieties in the World, that are contrary unto that *Love* which the Lord Chriſt requireth in a peculiar and eminent manner to be found amongſt his Diſciples. This he calls *his own new Command*, with reſpect unto his *Authority* requiring it, his *Example* firſt illuſtrating it in the World, and the peculiar *fruits* and effects of it which he revealed and taught. Wherefore, the due obſervance of this *Law of Love* in it ſelf and all its fruits, with the Prevention, Removal,

Removal or Condemnation of all that is contrary unto it, is that in which the *Rule of the Church* doth principally confift. And confidering the Weaknefs, the Paffions, the Temptations of Men, the mutual Provocations and Exafperations that are apt to fall out even among the beft, the influence that Earthly occafions are apt to have upon their Minds, the *frowardnefs* fometimes of Mens natural Tempers; the attendance unto this one Duty or part of Rule, requires the utmoft diligence of them that are called unto it. And it is meerly either the want of Acquaintance with the nature of that Law and its Fruits, which the Lord Chrift requires among his Difciples, or an undervaluation of the Worth and Glory of it in the Church, or inadvertency unto the caufes of its decays, and of breaches made in it; or ignorance of the Care and Duties that are neceffary unto its prefervation, that induce Men to judge that the Work of an efpecial Office is not required hereunto.

3. THEIR Duty is to *warn all the Members of the Church* of their efpecial Church-Duties, that they be not found negligent or wanting in them. There are *efpecial Duties* required refpectively of all Church-Members, according unto the diftinct *Talents*, whether in things Spiritual or Temporal, which they have received. Some are *Rich*, and fome are *Poor*; fome are *Old*, and fome are *Young*; fome in *Peace*, fome in *Trouble*; fome have received more *fpiritual Gifts* than others, and have more *opportunities* for their Exercife. It belongs unto the *Rule of the Church*, that all be Admonifhed, Inftructed, and Exhorted to attend unto their refpective Duties; not only publickly in the *preaching of the Word*, but *perfonally* as occafion doth require, according to the obfervation which thofe in Rule do make of their Forwardnefs or Remiffnefs in them. In particular, and in the way of inftance, Men are to be warned that they contribute unto the Neceffities of the Poor, and other occafions of the Church according unto the *Ability* that God in his Providence hath intrufted them withal; and to admonifh them that are *defective* herein, in order to their Recovery unto the difcharge of this Duty, in fuch a meafure as there may be an *Equality* in the Church, 2 *Cor.* 8. 14. And all
other

other Duties of an a-like nature are they to attend unto.

4. THEY are to watch against the beginnings of any *Church-Disorders*, such as those that infested the Church of *Corinth*, or any of the like sort; with remissness as unto the Assemblies of the Church and the Duties of them, which some are subject unto, as the Apostle intimates, *Heb.* 10. 25. On the Constancy and Diligence of the Elders in this part of their Work and Duty, the very Being and Order of the Church do greatly depend. The want hereof hath opened a door unto all the Troubles, Divisions and Schisms, that in all Ages have invaded and perplexed the Churches of Christ from within themselves. And from thence also have *Decays* in Faith, Love and Order insensibly prevailed in many, to the dishonour of Christ, and the danger of their own Souls. First one grows remiss in attending unto the Assemblies of the Church, and then another; first to one degree, then to another, until the whole *Lump* be infected. A diligent watch over these things as to the *beginnings* of them in all the members of the Church will either heal and recover them that offend, or it will *warn others*, and keep the Church from being either corrupted or defiled, *Heb.* 3. Chap. 12.

5. IT belongs unto them also to *visit the Sick*, especially such as whose inward or outward conditions do expose them unto more than ordinary *trials* in their Sickness; that is the Poor, the *Afflicted*, the *Tempted* in any kind. This in general is a *moral Duty*, a Work of Mercy; but it is moreover a peculiar Church-Duty by virtue of *Institution*. And one end of the *Institution* of Churches, is, that the Disciples of Christ may have all that Spiritual and Temporal Relief which is needful for them, and useful to them in their Troubles and Distresses. And if this Duty were diligently attended unto by the Officers of the Church, it would add much unto the Glory and Beauty of our Order, and be an abiding reserve with Relief in the Minds of them whose outward condition exposeth them to straits and Sorrows in such a season.

6. ADD hereunto as a Duty of the same nature, the *visitation if those who suffer unto Restraint and Imprisonment* upon

the

the account of their Profeſſion, adherence unto Church-Aſſemblies, or the Diſcharge of any Paſtoral or Office-Duties in them. This is a caſe wherewith we are not unacquainted, nor are like ſo to be. Some look on this as the Duty of all the Members of the Church, who yet enjoy their Liberty; and ſo it is, as their Opportunities and Abilities will allow them, provided their diſcharge of it be uſeful unto thoſe whom they viſit, and inoffenſive unto others. But this Duty diligently attended unto by the *Elders*, repreſenting therein the care and love of the whole Church, yea, of Chriſt himſelf unto his *Priſoners*, is a great Spring of Relief and Comfort unto them. And by the *Elders* may the Church be acquainted what yet is required of them in a way of Duty on their account. The care of the *Primitive Churches* herein was moſt eminent.

6. IT belongs unto them and their Office, to *adviſe* with and give *direction* unto the *Deacons* of the Church, as unto the making Proviſion and Diſtribution of the Charity of the Church for the Relief of the Poor. The Office of the *Deacons* is principally *Executive*, as we ſhall ſee afterwards. Inquiſition into the ſtate of the Poor, with all their circumſtances, with the warning of all the Members of the Church unto Liberality for their Supply, belongs unto the *Elders*.

7. WHEN the State of the Church is ſuch, through Suffering, Perſecution and Affliction, that the *Poor be multiplied among them*, ſo as that the Church it ſelf is not able to provide for their Relief in a due manner, if any *Supply* be ſent unto them from the love and bounty of other Churches, it is to be depoſited with *theſe Elders*, and diſpoſed according to their advice, with that of the Teachers of the Church, *Act*. 11. 30.

8. IT is alſo their Duty, according to the advantage which they have by their peculiar inſpection of all the Members of the Church, their ways and their walking, to acquaint the *Paſtors* or *Teaching-Elders* of the Church, with the *State of the Flock*, which may be of ſingular uſe unto them for their Direction in the preſent Work of the Miniſtry. He who makes it not his buſineſs to *know the State of the Church* which he miniſters unto in the *Word and Doctrine*, as to their Knowledge, their judgment

ment and Understanding, their Temptations and Occasions, and applies not himself in his Ministry to search out what is necessary and useful unto their *Edification*; he fights *uncertainly* in his whole Work, as a Man *beating the Air*. But, whereas their obligation to attend unto the *Word and Prayer*, confines them much unto a retirement for the greatest part of their time, they cannot by themselves obtain that Acquaintance with the whole Flock, but that others may greatly assist therein from their daily Inspection, Converse and Observation.

9. AND it is their Duty to *meet and consult with the Teaching-Elders*, about such things of importance, as are to be proposed in and unto the Church, for its consent and compliance. Hence, nothing crude or indigested, nothing unsuited to the sence and Duty of the Church, will at any time be proposed therein, so to give occasion unto contests or janglings, disputes contrary unto Order or Decency; but all things may be preserved in a due regard unto the *Gravity* and *Authority* of the Rulers.

10. TO take care of the due *Liberties* of the Church, that they be not imposed on by any *Diotrephes* in Office, or without it.

11. IT is incumbent on them in times of Difficulties and Persecution, to *consult together with the other Elders* concerning all those things which concern the present Duty of the Church, from time to time, and their preservation from violence, according unto the will of Christ.

12. WHEREAS, there may be, and oft-times is but One *Teaching-Elder*, *Pastor* or *Teacher* in a Church, upon his Death or Removal, it is the Work and Duty of *these Elders*, to preserve the Church in Peace and Unity; to take care of the continuation of its Assemblies; to prevent Irregularities in any Persons or Parties among them; to go before, to direct and guide the Church in the *Call* and *Choice* of some other meet Person or Persons in the room of the deceased or removed.

THESE *few instances* have I given of the Work and Duty of Ruling Elders. They are all of them such as deserve a greater enlargement in their Declaration and Confirmation, than

than I can here afford unto them. And sundry things of the like nature, especially with respect unto *Communion* with other Churches and *Synods*: But what hath been spoken is sufficient unto my present purpose. And to manifest that it is so, I shall add the ensuing Observations.

1. ALL the things insisted on, do undoubtedly and unquestionably belong unto the *Rule* and Order appointed by Christ in his Church. There is no one of them, that is liable unto any just Exception from them by whom all Church Order is not despised. Wherefore where there is a Defect in them or any of them, the *Church* it self is defective as unto its own Edification. And where this Defect is great, in many of them, there can be no *Beauty*, no *Glory*, no Order in any Church, but only an outward shew and appearance of them. And that all these things do belong unto the Duty of these Elders, there needs no other Proof nor Confirmation, but that they all undoubtedly and unquestionably belong unto that Rule and Order, which the Lord Christ hath appointed in his Church, and which the Scripture testifieth unto, both in general and particular. For all the things which belong unto the Rule of the Church, are committed to the care of the Rulers of the Church.

2. IT is a vain Apprehension to suppose that *one or two Teaching Officers* in a Church, who are obliged *to give themselves unto the Word and Prayer, to labour with all their might in the Word and Doctrine, to preach in and out of season*; that is, at all times, on all opportunities as they are able, to *Convince Gain-sayers* by Word and Writing, pleading for the Truth; to assist and guide the Consciences of all, under their Temptations and Desertions, with sundry other Duties, in part spoken to before, should be able to *take Care of*, and *attend with Diligence unto* all these things, that do evidently belong unto the Rule of the Church. And hence it is, that Churches at this day *do live on the Preaching of the Word*, the proper work of their Pastor, which they greatly value, and are very little sensible of the Wisdom, Goodness, Love and Care of Christ in the Institution of this Rule in the Church, nor are

partakers of the Benefits of it unto their Edification. And the supply which many have made hitherto herein, by persons either unacquainted with their Duty, or insensible of their own Authority, or cold if not negligent in their Work, doth not answer the end of their Institution. And hence it is that the *Authority of Government* and the Benefit of it, are ready to be lost in most Churches. And it is both vainly and presumptuously pleaded, to give countenance unto a neglect of their Order, that some *Churches* do walk in Love and Peace, and are Edified without it; supplying some defects by the *prudent Aid* of some Members of them. For it is nothing but a preference of our own Wisdom unto the Wisdom and Authority of Christ; or at best an unwillingness to make a venture on the warranty of his *Rule*, for fear of some disadvantages that may ensue thereon.

3. WHEREAS sundry of the Duties before-mentioned, are, as unto the substance of them, required of the *Members of the Church*, in their several stations, without any especial Obligation to attend unto them *with Diligence, to look after them*, or *power* to Exercise any Authority in the discharge of them, to leave them from under the *Office-Care* of the Elders, is to let in Confusion and Disorder into the Church, and gradually to remove the whole advantage of the *Discipline of Christ*, as it is come to pass in many Churches already.

IT is therefore Evident, that neither the *Purity*, nor the *Order*, nor the *Beauty* or *Glory* of the Churches of *Christ*, nor the Representation of his own *Majesty* and *Authority* in the Government of them, can be long preserved without a *Multiplication of Elders* in them, according to the proportion of their respective Members, for their Rule and Guidance. And for want hereof have Churches of old and of late, either degenerated into *Anarchy* and Confusion, their *self Rule* being managed with vain Disputes and Janglings, unto their Division and Ruine; or else given up themselves unto the *Domination* of some *Prelatical Teachers*, to Rule them at their pleasure, which proved the bane and poison of all the *Primitive* Churches; and they will and must do so in the neglect of this Order for the Future.

CHAP. IX.

Of DEACONS.

THE *Original Institution, Nature* and *Use* of the Office of *Deacons* in the Church, are so well known, as that we need not much insist upon them. Nor shall I treat of the *Name* which is common unto any kind of Ministry Civil or Sacred; but speak of it as it is appropriated unto that especial Work for which this Office was ordained.

The remote foundation of it lieth in that of our Saviour, *The poor you have always with you*, Joh. 12. 8. He doth not only *foretel*, That such there should be in the Church, but *recommends* the care of *them who should be so*, unto the Church. For he maketh use of the words of the Law, *Deut.* 15. 11. *For the poor shall never cease out of the Land; therefore I command thee, saying, Thou shalt open thy hand wide unto thy Brother, to thy poor, and to thy needy.* This Legal Institution, founded in the Law of Nature, doth the Lord Christ by his Authority transferr and translate unto the use of Gospel Churches among his Disciples.

AND it may be observed, that at the same instant Hypocrisie and Avarice began to attempt their Advantage on the consideration of this Provision for the Poor, which they afterwards effected unto their safety. For on the pretence hereof, *Judas* immediately condemned an *eminent Duty* towards the *person of Christ*, as containing a *cost* in it, which might have been better laid out in Provision for the Poor: The *Ointment* poured on our Saviour he thought might have been sold for *Three hundred pence* (it may be about Forty or Fifty Pound) and given to the Poor, *But this he said, not that he cared for the*

A a 2 *Poor,*

Poor but because he was a Thief, and had the Bag; out of which he could have made a good prey unto himself, *Joh.* 12. 6. And it may be observed, that although *Judas* malitiously began this murmuring; yet at last some of the *other Disciples* were too credulous of his insinuation, seeing the other *Evangelists*, ascribe it to them also. But the same pretence, on the same grounds, in following Ages was turned unto the greatest advantage of *Hypocrisy and Covetousness* that ever was in the World. For under this pretence of *providing for the Poor*, the *Thieves who had got the Bag*, that is the Ruling part of the Clergy, with the *Priests, Friars* and *Monks* who served them, allowed Men in the neglect of the greatest and most important Duties of Religion towards Christ himself, so as that they would *give all that they had to the Poor*; not that they cared for the Poor, but because *they were Thieves, and had the Bag*; by which means they possessed themselves of the greatest part of the Wealth of the Nations professing Christian Religion. This was their compliance with the Command of Christ; which they equally made use of in other things.

THIS Foundation of their Office was farther raised by the Preaching of the Gospel *among the Poor*. Many of them who first received it, were of that state and condition as the Scripture every where testifieth. *The Poor are Evangelized, Matth.* 11. 5. God hath chosen the Poor, *Jam.* 2. 5. And so it was in the *First Ages of the Church*; where the Provision for them was one of the most eminent Graces and Duties of the Church in those days. And this way *became* the *Original Propagation* of the Gospel. For it was made manifest thereby, that the *Doctrine* and Profession of it was not a matter of Worldly Design or Advantage; God also declared therein of how little esteem with him the Riches of this World are; and also Provision was made for the exercise of the Grace of the Rich in their Supply, the only way whereby they may Glorify God with their Substance. And it were well if all Churches, and all the Members of them would wisely consider how eminent is this Grace, how excellent is this Duty, of *making Provision for the Poor*, how much the Glory of Christ and Honour of

Of Deacons.

of the Gospel are concerned herein. For, whereas for the most part it is looked on as an *ordinary Work* to be performed transiently and curiously, scarce deserving any of the time which is allotted unto the Churches publick Service and Duties, it is indeed one of the most eminent Duties of Christian Societies, wherein the principal exercise of the *Second Evangelical Grace,* namely *Love,* doth consist.

THE care of making Provision for the Poor being made in the Church an Institution of Christ, was naturally incumbent on them who were the *First only Officers of the Church,* that is, the *Apostles.* This is plain from the occasion of the Institution of the Office of the *Deacons, Act.* 6. The whole Work and Care of the Church being in their hands, it was impossible that they should attend unto the whole and all the parts of it in any manner. Whereas therefore they gave themselves, according to their Duty, mostly unto those parts of their Work, which were incomparably more excellent and necessary than the other, namely *Preaching of the Word and Prayer;* there was such a *defect* in this other part of ministration unto the Poor, as must unavoidably accompany the actings of humane nature, not able to apply it self constantly unto things of diverse natures at the same time. And hereon those who were concerned quickly, as the manner of all is, expressed their resentment of a *neglect* in somewhat an undue Order; there was *a murmuring about it,* Ver. 1. The Apostles hereon declared that the principal part of the Work of the Ministry in the Church, namely the *Word and Prayer,* was sufficient for them constantly to attend unto. Afterwards indeed Men began to think that they could do *all* in the Church themselves, but it was when they began to do *nothing* in a due manner. And whereas the Apostles chose, as their Duty, the Work of Prayer and Preaching, as that which they would and ought entirely give up themselves unto, and for the sake of that Work would deposite the care of other things on other hands; they are a strange kind of Successors unto them, who lay aside that Work which they determined to belong unto them principally and in the first place, to apply themselves unto any thing else whatever.

YET

Of Deacons.

YET did not the *Apostles* hereon utterly forgo the care of *providing for the Poor* which being originally committed unto them by Jesus Christ, they would not *divest themselves* wholly of it. But by the Direction of the Holy Ghost they provided such assistance in the Work, as that for the future it might require no more of their time or pains but what they should spare from their principal Employment. And the same care is still incumbent on the *ordinary Pastors and Elders* of the Churches, so far as the execution of it doth not interfere with their principal Work and Duty, from which those who understand it aright, can spare but little of their time and strength.

HEREON the Apostles, by the Authority of Christ and direction of the Holy Spirit, under whose Infallible Guidance they were in all the general concernments of the Church, Instituted the *Office of Deacons*, for the discharge of this necessary and important Duty in the Church, which they could not attend unto themselves. And whereas the Lord Christ had in an especial manner committed the *care of the Poor unto the Disciples*, there was now a declaration of his Mind and Will, in *what way* and by what means he would have them provided for.

AND it was the *Institution of a new Office*, and not a present supply in a *Work or Business* which they designed. For the limitation of an especial Ecclesiastical Work, with the Designation of Persons unto that Work, with Authority for the discharge of it, (*set over this business*) with a separation unto it, do compleatly constitute *an Office*, nor is there any thing more required thereunto.

BUT whereas there are three things that concurr and are required unto the *ministration unto the Poor of the Church*. (1.) The *Love*, Charity, Bounty and Benevolence of the Members of the Church, in contribution unto that ministration. (2.) The *care* and oversight of the discharge of it. And, (3.) The *actual Exercise* and Application of it; the last only belongs unto the Office of the *Deacons*, and neither of the first are discharged by the *Institution* of it. For the first is both a Duty of the Light and Law of Nature, and in its moral part enforced

Of Deacons.

enforced by many especial Commands of Christ; so as that nothing can absolve Men from their obligation thereunto. The Office and Work of the Deacons is to excite, direct and help them in the exercise of that Grace, and discharge of the Duty therein incumbent on them. Nor is any Man, by the entrusting a due proportion of his good things in the hands of the *Deacons* for its distribution, absolved thereby from his own *personal discharge* of it also. For it being a moral Duty required in the Law of Nature, it receiveth peculiar obligations unto a present exercise by such Circumstances as Nature and Providence do suggest: The care also of the whole Work is as was said, still incumbent on the *Pastors* and *Elders* of the Church; only the ordinary Execution is committed unto the *Deacons*.

NOR was this a *Temporary Institution* for that season, and so the Officers appointed *Extraordinary*; but was to abide in the Church throughout all Generations. For, (1.) The *Work it self*, as a distinct work of Ministry in the Church, was never to cease, it was to abide for ever; *The Poor you shall have always with you*. (2.) The *Reason of its Institution* is perpetual; namely, that the Pastors of the Churches are not sufficient in themselves to attend unto the whole work of *Praying*, *Preaching*, and *this Ministration*. (3.) They are afterwards not only in this Church at *Jerusalem*, but in all the Churches of the *Gentiles* reckoned among the *fixed Officers* of the Church, *Phil.* 1. 1. And, (4.) *Direction* is given for their *Continuation* in all Churches, with a prescription of the Qualifications of the person to be Chosen and called into this Office, 1 *Tim*. 3. 8, 10, 11. (5.) The way of their Call is directed, and an *Office* committed unto them, *Let them be first proved, then let them use the Office of a Deacon*. (6.) A Promise of Acceptance is annexed unto the diligent discharge of this Office, *Vers.* 13.

HENCE those who afterward utterly perverted all Church Order, taking out of the hands and care of the *Deacons*, that work which was committed to them by the Holy Ghost in the Apostles, and for which End alone, their Office was Instituted

stituted in the Church, assigning other Work unto them; whereunto they are not called nor appointed; yet thought meet to continue the Name and the pretence of such an Office, because of the evident Institution of it, unto a Continuation. And whereas when all things were swelling with Pride and Ambition in the Church, no sort of its Officers contenting themselves with their Primitive Institution; but striving by various degrees to some-what in Name and Thing, that was high and a-loft, there arose from the Name of this Office the *Meteor* of an *Archdeacon,* with strange Power and Authority, never heard of in the Church for many Ages: But this belongs unto the Mystery of Iniquity; whereunto neither the Scripture nor the Practice of the Primitive Churches do give the least countenance. But some think it not inconvenient even to *sport themselves* in matter of Church Order and Constitutions.

THIS Office of *Deacons,* is an Office of service, which gives not any Authority or Power in the Rule of the Church. But being an Office, it gives Authority with respect unto the special Work of it under a general notion of Authority; that is, a Right to attend unto it in a peculiar manner, and to perform the things that belong thereunto. But this Right is confined unto the particular Church whereunto they do belong. Of the Members of that Church are they to make their Collections, and unto the Members of that Church are they to Administer. *Extraordinary Collections* from, or for other Churches, are to be made and disposed by the *Elders, Acts* 11. 30.

WHEREAS, the Reason of the Institution of this Office was in general to *free* the Pastors of the Churches who labour in the Word and Doctrine from Avocations by outward things, such as wherein the Church is concerned; it belongs unto the *Deacons* not only to take care of and provide for the Poor, but to manage all other Affairs of the Church of the same kind; such as are providing for the *place* of the Church-Assemblies, of the *Elements* for the Sacraments, of Keeping, Collecting and Disposing of the *Stock of the Church,* for the maintenance of its Officers, and incidencies, especially in the time of Trouble or Persecution.

Of Deacons.

Persecution. Hereon are they obliged to attend the *Elders* on all occasions, to perform the Duty of the Church towards them, and receive directions from them. This was the constant practice of the Church in the Primitive Times, until the Avarice and Ambition of the Superior Clergy enclosed all *Alms and Donations* unto themselves; the Beginning and Progress whereof is excellently described and traced by *Paulus Sharpius*, in his Treatise of *matters Beneficiary*.

THAT maintenance of the Poor which they are to distribute, is to be collected by the *voluntary Contributions* of the Church, to be made ordinarily every *first Day of the Week*, and as occasion shall require in an extraordinary manner, 1 Cor. 16. 1, 2. And this Contribution of the Church ought to be, (1.) In a way of *Bounty*, not sparingly, 2 Cor. 9. 5, 6, 7. (2.) In a way of *Equality*, as unto Mens Abilities, 2 Cor. 8. 13, 14. (3.) With respect unto present Successes and Thriving in Affairs, whereof a Portion is due to God ; *as God hath prospered him*, 1 Cor. 16. 2. (4.) With *willingness* and freedom, 2 Cor. 8. 12. Chap. 7. Wherefore it belongs unto the *Deacons* in the Discharge of their Office, (1.) To acquaint the Church with the present necessity of the Poor. (2.) To stir up the particular Members of it unto a free Contribution according unto their Ability. (3.) To admonish those that are negligent herein, who give not according to their proportion; and to acquaint the Elders of the Church with those who persist in a neglect of their Duty.

THE consideration of the State of the Poor unto whom the Contributions of the Church are to be ministred, belongs unto the discharge of this Office. As, (1.) That they are *Poor indeed*, and do not pretend themselves so to be, for advantage. (2.) What are the *Degrees* of their Poverty, with respect unto their Relations and Circumstances, that they may have suitable Supplies. (3.) That in other things they walk according unto Rule. (4.) In particular that they *Work and Labour* according to their Ability ; for he that will not labour must not eat at the publick Charge. (5.) To Comfort, Counsel and Exhort them unto *Patience*, Submission, Contentment with
their

B b

Of Deacons.

their Condition, and Thankfulness; all which might be enlarged and confirmed, but that they are obvious.

THE Qualifications of Persons to be called unto this Office, are distinctly laid down by the Apostle, 1 *Tim.* 3. 8, 9, 10, 11, 12, 13. Upon the Trial, Knowledge and Approbation of them, with respect unto these Qualifications, their Call to this Office consists. (1.) In the *choice of the* Church. (2.) In a *separation* unto it by Prayer and Imposition of Hands, *Act.* 6. 3, 5, 6. And the Adjuncts of their ministration are, (1.) *Mercy* to represent the tenderness of Christ towards the Poor of the Flock, *Rom.* 12. 8. (2.) *Cheerfulness* to relieve the Spirits of them that receive against thoughts of being troublesome and burdensome to others. (3.) *Diligence* and Faithfulness by which they *purchase to themselves a good Degree, and great boldness in the Faith which is in Christ Jesus.*

IT remains only that we enquire into some few things relating unto this Office, and those that are called unto it. As,

1. WHAT is the meaning of the Apostle, where he affirms, that the Deacons in the Discharge of their Office, βαθμὸν ἑαυτοῖς καλὸν περιποιοῦνται, 1 *Tim.* 3. 13. *Do purchase* or procure *unto themselves a good Degree.* Βαθμὸς is a Step, a Degree, a Seat a little Exalted, and Metaphorically it is applied to denote Dignity and Authority. This *good Degree,* which Deacons may obtain, is in the judgment of most the Office of *Presbytery.* This they shall be promoted unto in the Church. From *Deacons* they shall be made *Presbyters.* I cannot comply with this Interpretation of the Words. For, (1.) The Office of *Presbytery* is called καλὸν ἔργον, a *good Work,* no where καλὸς βαθμὸς, a *good Degree.* (2.) The difference between a *Deacon* and a *Presbyter* is not in *Degree,* but in *Order.* A *Deacon* made a *Presbyter* is not advanced unto a further *Degree* in his *own* Order; but leaves it for *another.* (3.) The diligent discharge of the Work of a *Deacon,* is not a due preparation for the Office of the *Presbytery,* but an hinderance of it; for it lies wholly in the providing and disposal of Earthly things, in a serving of the Tables of the Church, and those private of the Poor: But *preparation for the Ministry* consists in a Mans giving himself unto Study, Prayer and Meditation. I SHALL

I SHALL only give my conjecture on the Words, the Apoſtle ſeems to me to have reſpect unto Church-Order, with Decency therein, in both theſe Expreſſions, *ſhall purchaſe to themſelves a good Degree, and great confidence in the Faith:* Βαθμὸς is of the ſame ſignification with Βαθμὶς, which is a Seat raiſed in an Aſſembly to hear or ſpeak. So ſaith the *Schol.* on *Sophoc. Oed.* ὁ τόπος ἔνθα ἡ ἐκκλησία ἐγίνετο, βαθμίσιν ἦν κύκλῳ διειλημμένος, ἄλλαις ἐπ᾽ ἄλλαις· ἔνθα οἱ συνελθόντες πάντες καθήμενοι ἀνεμποδίσως ἠκροῶντο τοῦ ἱσταμένου ἐν μέσῳ. *The place where the Aſſembly* (or Church) *met, was divided round about with Seats in Degrees, ſome above others, where all that met might without trouble hear him that ſtood in the midſt as they ſate.* And countenance is given hereunto by what is obſerved concerning the cuſtom of *ſitting in the Jewiſh Synagogues.* So *Ambroſe*; *Traditio eſt Synagoga, ut ſedentes diſputarent, Siniores dignitate in Cathedris, ſubſequentes in ſubſelliis, noviſſimi in pavimento;* *It is the Tradition or Order of the Synogogue, that the Elders in Dignity* (or Office) *ſhould diſcourſe ſitting in Chairs;* *the next Order on Forms or Benches, and the laſt on the Floor.* So ſpeaks *Philo* before him; εἰς ἱεροὺς ἀφικνούμενοι τόπους καθ᾽ ἡλικίας ἐν τάξεσιν ὑπὸ πρεσβυτέροις νεοὶ καθίζουσι), *when we meet in ſacred places,* places of Divine Worſhip, *the younger ſort according to their Quality ſit in Orders under the Elders.* And this *James* the Apoſtle hath reſpect unto in the Primitive Aſſemblies of the *Chriſtian Jews.* For reproving their partiality in accepting of Mens Perſons, preferring the Rich immoderately before the Poor, he inſtanceth in their diſpoſing of them unto Seats in their Aſſemblies. *They ſaid unto the Rich Man,* σὺ κάθου ὧδε καλῶς, *ſit thou here in a good place*; that is in βάθμῳ καλῷ, in the *beſt degree*; and to the Poor, *ſtand thou there* on the floor, *or ſit at my foot-ſtool,* without reſpect unto thoſe other Qualifications whereby they were to be diſtinguiſhed. Wherefore, the Apoſtle having reſpect unto Church-Aſſemblies, and the Order to be obſerved in them, the καλὸς βαθμὸς here intended, may ſignifie no more but a *place of ſome eminency in the Church-Aſſemblies,* which is due unto ſuch *Deacons,* where with boldneſs and confidence they may aſſiſt in the management of the Affairs of the Church, which belongs unto the Profeſſion of the Faith which is in Chriſt Jeſus.

Of Deacons.

IF any shall rather think that both of the Expressions do signify an *encrease in Gifts and Grace*, which is a certain consequence of Mens faithful discharge of their Office in the Church, wherein many Deacons of old were eminent unto Martyrdom, I shall not contend against it.

2. WHEREAS there are Qualifications expresly required in the *Wives of Deacons*, as that they should be *grave, not slanderers, sober, faithful in all things,* 1 *Tim.* 3. 12. which is to be considered before their call to Office; supposing that any of them do fall from the Faith as becoming *Papists, Socinians,* or *Quakers,* whether their Husbands may be continued in their Office?

Ans. 1. HE who in his own Person faithfully dischargeth his Office, may be continued therein, yea, though his Wife should be actually Excommunicated out of the *Church*. *Every One of us must give an account of himself unto the Lord.* He rejects us not for what we cannot remedy. The sinning Person shall bear his own judgment. (2.) Such an one ought to take care, by virtue of his *Authority* as an Husband, that as little offence as possible may be given to the Church by his Wife, when she loseth the qualification of *not being a slanderer,* which is inseparable from such *Apostates*.

3. *MAY a Deacon be dismissed from his Office wholly, after he hath been solemnly set apart unto it by Prayer?*

Ans. 1. THE very end of the Office being only the *convenience of the Church* and its accommodation, the continuation of Men in this Office is to be regulated by them. And if the Church at any time stand not in need of the Ministry of this or that Person, they may, upon his desire, discharge him of his Office. (2.) Things may so fall out with Men, as unto their outward circumstances, with respect unto either their Persons in Bodily Distempers and Infirmities, or their Condition in the World, as that they are not able any longer to attend unto the due discharge of this Office; in which case they ought to be released. (3.) A Man may be solemnly set apart unto a Work and Duty by Prayer *for a limited Season*, suppose for a year only; wherefore this doth not hinder but that a Man on just Reasons may be dimissed

at

at any time from his Office, though he be so set apart unto it. *(4.)* A *Deacon* by unfaithfulness and other offences, may forfeit his Office, and be justly excluded from it, losing all his Right unto it and Interest in it, and therefore on just Reasons may be dismissed wholly from it. *(5.)* For any one to *desert his Office* through forwardness, covetousness, sloth or negligence, is an offence and scandal which the Church ought to take notice of. *(6.)* He who desires a dismission from his Office, ought to give an account of his desires and the Reasons of them unto the Church, that the Ministry which he held may be duly supplied, and love continued between him and the Church.

4. *HOW many Deacons may there be in one Congregation?*

Ans. AS many as they stand in need of, for the ends of that Ministry; and they may be at all times *encreased*, as the State of the Church doth require; and it is meet that there should always be so many, as that none of the Poor be neglected in the daily Ministration, nor the Work be made burdensome unto themselves.

5. *WHAT is the Duty of the Deacons towards the Elders of the Church?*

Ans. WHEREAS the care of the whole Church in all its concernments is principally committed unto the Pastors, Teachers, and Elders, it is the Duty of the Deacons in the discharge of their Office, (1.) To *acquaint them* from time to time with the state of the Church, and especially of the Poor, so far as it falls under their Inspection. *(2.)* To seek and take their Advice in matters of greater importance relating unto their Office. *(3.)* To be assisting unto them in all the outward concerns of the Church.

6. *MAY Deacons Preach the Word and Baptize authoritatively by virtue of their Office?*

Ans. (1.) THE Deacons, whose Office is instituted, *Act.* 6. and whose Qualifications are fixed, 1 *Tim.* 3. have no call unto, or *Ministerial Power* in these things. The limitation of their Office, Work and Power, is so express, as will not admit of any debate. *(2.)* Persons once called unto this Office, might of old in an extraordinary manner, may at present in an ordinary way,

be

be called unto the preaching of the Word; but they were not then, they cannot be now authorized thereunto by vrtue of this Office. (3.) If a *new Office* be erected under the name of *Deacons*, it is in the will of them by whom it is erected, to Assign what Power unto it they please.

CHAP. X.

Of EXCOMMUNICATION.

THE *Power* of the Church towards its Members (for it hath nothing to do *with them that are without*) may be referred unto Three Heads, (1.) The *Admission* of Members into its Society. (2.) The *Rule* and Edification of them that belong unto it. (3.) The *Exclusion* out of its Society of such as *obstinately* refuse to live and walk according unto the Laws and Rules of it. And these things belong essentially and inseparably unto every free Society, and are comprehensive of all Church-Power whatever.

THE *Second* of these hath been treated of in the Discourse concerning *Church Offices and Rule*. And all that belongs unto the *first* of them, is fully declared in the Chapters of the *Essential Constituent parts of Gospel Churches*, namely their Matter and *Form*. The *Third* must be now spoken, unto which is *the Power of Excommunication*.

THERE is nothing in Christian Religion, about which the contest of Opinions hath been more fierce than this of *Excommunication*, most of them proceeding evidently from false Presumptions and secular Interests. And no greater instance can be given of what the *Serpentine* wits of Men ingaged by the desire of Domination and Wealth, and assisted by opportunities may attain unto. For whereas, as we shall see immediately, there is nothing more plain, simple, and more exposed unto the common understanding of all *Christians*, yea of all

Man-

Mankind, than is this Institution of Christ; both as unto its Nature, Form and Manner of Administration, nothing more *wholsome* nor useful unto the Souls of Men; nothing more remote from giving the least disturbance or prejudice to Civil Society, to Magistrates or Rulers, unto the *Personal* or *Political Rights* or Concernments of any one individual in the World: It hath been *Metamorphosed* into an hideous Monster; an Engine of *Priestly Domination and Tyranny*, for the *Deposition* or Assassination of Kings and Princes, the *Wasting of Nations* with bloody Wars, the *Terror* of the Souls of Men, and the destruction of their Lives, with all their Earthly Concerns, unto the Erection of a *Tyrannical Empire*, no less pernicious unto the Christian World, than those of the *Saracens* or the *Turks*. He is a stranger unto all that hath passed in the World for near a *Thousand Years*, who knows not the Truth of these things. And to this very day the greatest part of them that are *called Christians* are so supinely Ignorant and Doating, or so infatuated and blinded by their Prejudices and Corrupt Interests, as to suppose, or to say, That if the *Pope of Rome* do Excommunicate *Kings or Princes*, they may be lawfully *deposed* from their Rule, and in some cases killed; and that other persons being rightly Excommunicated according unto certain Laws, Rules, and Processes, that some have framed, ought to be *Fined, Punished, Imprisoned*, and so *Destroyed*. And about these things there are many Disputes and Contests; when if Men were awakned out of their Lethargy they would be laughed at, as the most ridiculous and contemptible *Mormo's* that ever appeared in the World; though they are no *laughing matter* at present, unto them that are concerned in them.

SUPPOSING then, *Ecclesiastical Excommunication* (as I at present suppose, and shall immediately prove it) to be an appointment of our Lord Jesus Christ; these things are plain and evident concerning it, not capable of any modest Contradiction, (1.) That there is no *Divine Evangelical Institution*, that is more suited unto the Light of Nature, the Rules of common Equity, and Principles of *unseared Consciences*, as unto the Nature,

ture, Efficacy and Rule of it, than this is. *(2.)* That the *way* of the Administration and Exercise of the Power and Acts of it, is so determined, described and limited in the Scripture, and the Light of Nature, as that there can be no *gross error* or mistake about it, but what proceeds from *Secular Interests, Pride, Ambition, Covetousness,* or other vitious Habits and Inclinations of the minds of Men. *(3.)* That the whole *Authority* of it, its Sentence, Power and Efficacy, are *meerly Spiritual,* with respect unto the Souls and Consciences of Men only; and that to extend it *directly* or *indirectly, immediately* or by *consequences,* unto the temporal hurt, evil or damage of any in their Lives, Liberties, Estates, Natural or Legal Privileges, is opposite unto, and destructive of the whole Government of Christ in and over his Church. All these things wilfully appear in the account which we shall give of it.

IT is therefore evident, as was intimated, that nothing in Christian Practice hath been, or is more *abused*, corrupted or perverted, than this of *Excommunication* hath been and is. The Residence of the Supream Power of it to be exercised towards and over all Christians, Rulers and Subjects, in the *Pope of Rome,* or in other *single Persons* absolutely; over less or greater Distributions of them; the Administration of it by *Citations, Processes, Pleadings* and *Contentions* in wrangling Law Courts according unto *Arbitrary Canons* and Constitutions, whose Original is either *known,* or *unknown* ; the Application of it unto the *Hurt, Damage, Evil* or Loss of Men in their Temporal Concerns, are utterly and openly foreign unto the Gospel, and expresly contrary unto what the Lord Christ hath appointed therein. It would require a *whole Volume* to declare the *horrible abuses* that both in point of Right, and in *matter of Fact,* with the pernicious consequences that have ensued thereon, which the corruption of this Divine Institution hath produced : But to make a Declaration hereof, doth not belong to my present design ; besides, it hath in some good measure been done by others. In brief, it is so come to pass that it is made a *meer Political Engine,* of an *external forcible Government,* of the *Persons* of Men, unto the ends of the *Interests* of some, who have got a pretence a pretence of its Power, adminiſtred by *ſuch ways* and means, as wherein the *Conſciences* of Men, neither of thoſe by whom it is Adminiſtred, nor of thoſe unto whom it is Applied, are any way concerned, with reſpect unto the Authority, or any Inſtitution of Jeſus Chriſt.

FROM an obſervation hereof, and a deſire to vindicate as well Chriſtian Religion from ſuch a *ſcandalous Abuſe* as *Mankind* from Bondage, to ſuch a monſtrous fiction as is the preſent power and exerciſe of it, ſome have fallen into *another extream*, denying that there is any ſuch thing as *Excommunication*, appointed or approved by the Goſpel. But this neither is, nor ever will be a way to reduce Religion nor any thing in it, unto its Primitive Order and Purity. To deny the *Being* of any thing becauſe it hath *been abuſed*, when there could have been *no abuſe* of it, but upon a ſuppoſition of its *Being*, is not a rational way to reprove and convince that abuſe. And when thoſe who have *corrupted this Inſtitution*, find the inſufficiency of the Arguments produced to prove that there *never was any ſuch Inſtitution*, it makes them ſecure in the practice of their own Abuſes of it. For they imagine that there is nothing incumbent on them to juſtify their preſent poſſeſſion and exerciſe of the Power of Excommunication; but that *Excommunication* it ſelf is appointed in the Church by Chriſt, whereas the true conſideration of this *Appointment*, is the only means to diveſt them of their power and practice. For the moſt effectual courſe to diſcharge and diſprove all corruptions in the *Agenda* or *Practicals* of Religion, as the *Sacraments, publick Worſhip, Rule* and the like, is to propoſe and declare the things themſelves in their Original ſimplicity, and purity, as appointed by Chriſt, and recorded in the Scriptures. A real view of them in ſuch a *Propoſal*, will diveſt the minds of Men, not corrupted and hardened by Prejudice and Intereſt, of thoſe erroneous conceptions of them, that from ſome kind of Tradition they have been prepoſſeſſed withal. And this I ſhall now attempt in this particular of *Excommunication*.

THERE hath been great enquiry about the nature and exerciſe of this Ordinance, under the *Old Teſtament*, with the Account

Of Excommunication.

count given of it by the latter *Jews*. For the Right and Power of it in general, belongs unto a *Church as such, every Church*, and not that which is purely *Evangelical* only. This I shall not enquire into; it hath been sifted to the bran already, and intermixed with many *Rabbinical* conjectures and mistakes. In general, there is nothing more certain, than that there was a *double Removal* of Persons by Church-Authority, from the communion of the whole Congregation in Divine Worship. The one *for a Season*, the other *for Ever*; whereof I have given Instances elsewhere. But I intend only the consideration of what belongs unto Churches under the New Testament. And to this end we may observe,

1. THAT all *lawful Societies*, constituted such by *voluntary confederation*, according unto peculiar Laws and Rules of their own choice, unto especial Duties and Ends, have a *Right* and *Power* by the Light of Nature, to receive into their Society those that are *willing* and meet, ingaging themselves to observe the Rules, Laws and Ends of the Society; and to *Expel* them out of it who wilfully deviate from those Rules. This is the life and form of every *lawful Society* or Community of Men in the World, without which they can neither coalesce nor subsist. But it is required hereunto,

1. THAT those who so enter into such a Society, have *Right or Power so to do.* And many things are required unto this end: As, (1.) That those who enter into such a Society be *sui Juris*; have a *lawful Right to dispose of themselves*, as unto all the Duties and Ends of such a Society. Hence *Children, Servants, Subjects,* have no power in themselves to enter into such Societies, without the interposition of and obligation from a power Superior unto that of Parents, Masters, or Princes, namely, that of God himself. (2.) That the Rules, Laws, and ends of the Society be *lawful*, good and useful unto themselves and others. For there may be a *confederation* in and for evil; which is a combination that gives no Right nor Power, over one another, or towards others that enter into it. (3.) That it contains nothing that is *prejudicial* unto others in things Divine or Humane. (4.) Nor oblige unto the *omission*

or

Of Excommunication.

or neglect of any Duty, that Men by virtue of any Relations, Natural, Moral or Political, do owe unto others: Nor, *(5.)* Is *hurtful* unto themselves in their Lives, Liberties, Names, Reputation, usefulness in the World, or any thing else, unto whose preservation they are obliged by the Law of Nature. Nor, *(6.)* Can be, or are such Persons obliged to forsake the *conduct of themselves* in things Divine and Humane, by the Light of their own Consciences, by an Ingagement of blind obedience unto others, which would render every *Society unlawful* by the Law of God and Light of Nature. *(7.)* Least of all, have any Persons Right or Power to oblige themselves in such Societies, unto things *Evil, Sinful, Superstitious* or *Idolatrous*.

THESE things are plain, and evident in themselves, and every way sufficient to divest all the *Religious Societies* and *Fraternities* that are erected in the *Church of Rome*, of all that Right and Power which belongs unto *lawful Societies*, constituted by voluntary confederation. And if any thing inconsistent with these principles of *Natural Light* be pretended in Churches, it divests them of *all Power*, as to the exercise of it, by virtue of any compact or confederation whatever.

2. IT is required that a *Society, by voluntary consent* vested with the Right and Power mentioned, do neither give nor take away any Right, Privilege or Advantage, to, or from any Members of the Society which belong unto them *Naturally* or *Politically*; but their Power is confined unto those things alone, wherein Men may be benefited and advantaged by the Society. And this is the foundation of all *political Societies*. Men, for the sake and benefit of them, may and ought to forego many particular Advantages, which, without them, they might make unto themselves. But they cannot forego any of those Rights, which in their several Relations are inseparably annexed unto them by the Law of Nature, nor give power over themselves in such things unto the Society. So is it with Churches; the power of *expulsion* out of their Society, extends only unto the *Benefits* and *Advantages* which the Society, as such, doth afford and communicate. Now these are only things *Spiritual*, if Churches be an institution of him, whose

Kingdom is not of this World. The power then that is in Churches, by virtue of their being what they are, extends not it self unto any *outward concernments of Men*, as unto their Lives, Liberties, Natural or Political Privileges, Estates or Possessions; unless we shall say, that Men hold and possess these things by virtue of their Relation unto the Church, which is to overthrow all Natural and Humane Right in the World. *De facto*, Men are now compelled whether they will or no, to be esteemed to be of this or that Church, and to be dealt withal accordingly. But if they had not been divested of their natural Liberty, they know not how, without their own consent, and should be taught, that by entering into a Church, they must come under a new *Tenure of their Lives, Liberties* and Estates, at the Will of the Lords of the Society according to the *Customs of their Courts*, there would not be so many Wise Men in Churches, as now there are thought to be.

BUT this is the true State of things in the Church of *Rome*, and *among others* also. Christians are esteemed to be of them, and belong unto them, whether they will or no. Immediately hereon all the *Rights, Liberties, Privileges,* Possessions which they enjoy by the Law of God and Nature, and by the just Laws and Constitutions of Men in Civil Governments, under which they live, come to depend upon, and be subject unto the especial *Laws and Rules of the Society* which they are adjudged to belong unto. For upon expulsion out of that Society by *Excommunication*, according unto the Laws and Rules which it hath framed unto it self, all their *Rights* and *Titles*, and *Liberties* and *Enjoyments* are forfeited and exposed to Ruine. Some indeed do earnestly and learnedly contend that the *Pope of Rome* hath not Power to Excommunicate Sovereign *Kings and Princes*; and that if he do, they make no forfeiture of Life or Dignity thereby. And there are good Reasons why they do so. But in the mean time, they deal with other poor Men after the same manner. For if a poor *Man* be Excommunicated, immediately he loseth the free Tenure of his Life, Liberty and Goods, by the Law of the Church and the Land, and is Committed to the Gaol without Bail or Mainprize. So that

Of Excommunication.

that by this *Artifice*, all Men hold their Natural and Civil Rights, by the Rules *of the Church Society* whereto they are supposed to belong. And as this utterly overthrows the foundation of all that *Property* according to the Laws of the Land, which is so much talked of and valued; so indeed it would be destructive of all Order and Liberty, but that the Church is *wise enough* not to employ this Engine unto *Great Men* and Men in Power, who may yet deserve *Extommunication* as well as some of their poor Neighbours, if the Gospel be thought to give the Rule of it. But those that are poor, helpless and friendless, shall in the pursuit of this Excommunication be driven from their *Houses, cast into Prisons*, and kept there until they and their Families starve and perish. And it is apparent that we are beholding unto the *Greatness, Authority,* and *Wealth of many,* whom the *Ecclesiastical Courts* care not to conflict withal, that the whole Nation is not actually brought under this *new Tenure* of their *Lives, Liberties and Estates,* which on this presumption they are obnoxious unto.

AND all this evil ariseth from the neglect and contempt of this *fundamental Rule of all Societies,* apparent unto all in the Light of Nature it self; namely, that *they have no Power in or over any Thing, Right, Privilege or Advantage, but what Men are made Partakers of by virtue of such Societies, their Rule and Laws whereunto they are obliged.* But of this sort are not the Lives, the Liberties, the Houses and Possessions of Men, with respect unto the Church. They receive them not from the Church, and a Man would certainly think, that the Church could not take them away.

YEA, we live and subsist in Order, upon the good Nature and Wisdom of Men, who judge it best neither to exert their Power, nor act their Principles in this matter. For, whereas they esteem all the *Inhabitants of the Land* to belong unto their Church; if they should in the first place *Excommunicate* all that ought to be Excommunicated by the *Rule and Law of the Gospel,* and then all that ought to be so, according to their *own Laws and Canons,* both which a Man would think they were obliged in point of Conscience unto; and in pursuit of their
Sentence,

Sentence, send out the *Capias* for them all, I very much question whether any of them would *go to Prison or no*; and then in what a fine case would this Government be; and if they should all go to *Gaol*, I am perswaded the King would be in an ill State to defend his *Realms* against his Enemies.

3. EVERY Society hath this Power towards those who are *incorporated in it by their own consent*, and not towards others. For whence should they have such a Power, or who should commit it unto them? Nor can any be cast out from those Privileges which they never had an Interest in, nor a Right unto. The Apostles Rule holds in this case, especially with respect unto Churches; *What have we to do to judge them that are without*. And as unto the exercise of this Power, they are all to be esteemed *to be without*, who are not rightly incorporated into that particular Church, by which they may be ejected out of it. A Power of Excommunication at *Random* towards all that those who exercise it can extend force unto, hath *no foundation* either in the Light of Nature or Authority of the Scripture. And it would be ridiculous in any Corporation to *disfranchise* such as never belonged unto it, who were never Members of it.

4. THE only Reason or Cause for the expulsion of any Person out of such a Society, is a *wilful deviation from the Rules and Laws of the Society*, whose observance he had engaged unto upon his entrance into it. Nothing else can be required unto the *Preservation* of a Mans Interest in any Right or Privilege, but what he took upon himself to perform in his Admittance into it. And if the great Rule of every Church-Society, be, That *Men observe and do whatsoever the Lord Christ hath commanded*, none can be justly ejected out of that Society, but upon a *wilful disobedience* unto his Commands. And therefore the casting of Men out of Church-Communion on light and trivial occasions, or for any Reasons or Causes whatever, but such as *essentially* belong unto the Rules and Laws whereon the Church doth originally coalesce into a Society, is contrary unto Natural Light, and the Reason of the Things themselves.

THUS

Of Excommunication.

THUS far I say is every lawful confederate Society enabled and warranted by the Light of Nature, to remove from its Communion, and from a participation in its Rights and Privileges any of its number who will not walk according to the Rules and Principles of its Coalescency and Constitution. Whereas therefore the Rule of the Constitution of the Church is, That Men walk together in holy Obedience unto the Commands of Christ, and the observance of all his Institutions, without giving Offence unto one another, or those that are without, by any sinful miscarriage, and do abide in the Profession of the Truth; if any one shall wilfully and obstinately transgress in any of these things, it is the Right and Duty, and in the Power of the Church to remove him from its Society.

BUT this is not the entire nor the next immediate Ground, Reason, or Warranty of Ecclesiastical Excommunication. For this natural Equity will not extend it self unto cases that are in things Spiritual and Supernatural; nor will the actings of the Church thereon reach unto the Consciences of Men, for the proper ends of Excommunication. Wherefore it was necessary that it should have a peculiar Institution in the Church by the Authority of Jesus Christ. For,

1. THE Church is such a Society as no Men have Right or Power either to enter into themselves, or to exclude others from, but by virtue of the Authority of Christ. No warranty from the Light of nature, or from the Laws of Men, or their own voluntary confederation, can enable any to constitute a Church-Society, unless they do all things expresly in obedience unto the Authority of Christ. For his Church is his Kingdom, his House; which none can constitute or build but himself. Wherefore it is necessary, that the power of Admission into, and Exclusion from the Church, do arise from his Grant and Institution. Nor is it in the power of any Men in the World, to admit into, or exclude from this Society but by virtue thereof.

2. EXCOMMUNICATION is an act of Authority, as we shall see afterwards. But no Authority can be exercised in
the

the Church, towards any perſon whatever, but by virtue of the Inſtitution of Chriſt. For the Authority it ſelf however miniſterially exerciſed by others, is his alone; and he exerts it not, but in the ways of his own appointment. So in particular the Apoſtle directs, that Excommunication be exerted in *the Name of our Lord Jeſus Chriſt*; that is, in and by his Authority, 1 *Cor.* 5. 4.

3. THE *Privileges* from which Men are excluded by Excommunication are not ſuch, as they have any Natural or Civil Right unto (as hath been proved) but meerly ſuch as are granted unto the Church by Jeſus Chriſt; and Men cannot by virtue of any Agreement among themſelves, without a Warranty from him by his Inſtitution, *Expel others* from the Privileges which are meerly of his Grant and Donation. He alone therefore hath given and granted this Power unto the Church, namely of Excluding any by the Rules and Ways of his Appointment from the Privileges of his Grant, which is the peculiar Power of Excommunication inquired after.

4. THERE is ſuch an *Efficacy* aſſigned unto Excommunication in *binding* the Conſciences of Men, in *retaining* their Sins, in the *Deſtruction* or Mortification of the Fleſh, in the Healing and Recovery of Sinners; as nothing but the Authority of a Divine Inſtitution can give unto it. By virtue of natural Light and mutual Conſent, Men may free themſelves from the Company and Society of thoſe who will not walk with them according to Rules of Communion agreed upon among them; but they cannot reach the Minds and Conſciences of others with any of theſe Effects.

5. THAT Excommunication is an expreſs Ordinance of our Lord Jeſus Chriſt in his Churches is fully declared in the Scripture. For, (1.) The power of it is contained in the Authority given by Chriſt unto the Church, under the Name of *the Keys of the Kingdom of Heaven*. For the Power expreſſed therein is not meerly *Doctrinal* and Declarative as is the *preaching of the Goſpel*, the conſequent whereof upon the Faith or Unbelief of them that hear it, is the *Remitting* or *Retaining* of their Sin in Heaven and Earth; but it is *Diſciplinary* alſo,

as

as it is appropriated unto the House whose *Keys* are committed unto the Stewards of it. And seeing the design of Christ was to have his Church *Holy, Unblamable* and *without offence* in the World, that therein he might make a Representation of his own Holiness, and the Holiness of his Rule; and whereas those of whom it is constituted, are liable and subject unto Sins *scandalous* and offensive, reflecting dishonour on himself and the Church, in being the occasion of sinning unto others; that design would not have been accomplished, had he not given this *Authority* unto his Church to cast out and separate from it self all that do by their Sins so give offence. And the neglect of the exercise of this Authority in a due manner, was the principal means whereby the Glory, Honour, and usefulness of the Churches in the World, were at length utterly lost. (2.) It hath a direct Institution, *Matth.* 18. 15, 16, 17, 18, 19, 20. *If thy Brother shall Trespass,* &c. *tell it unto the Church; but if he neglect to hear the Church, let him be unto thee as an Heathen Man and a Publican. Verily I say unto you, whatsoever ye shall bind on Earth shall be bound in Heaven, and whatsoever ye shall loose on Earth, shall be loosed in Heaven,* &c. After all the Learned and Unlearned Contests that have been about this place, the sence of it is plain and obvious, unto such as whose Minds are not clouded with prejudices about such Churches and such Excommunications as are utterly foreign unto the Scripture. But that by *Trespasses* in this place, Sins against God giving scandal or offence, are intended, hath been proved before; as also, that by a Church, a particular Christian Congregation is intended. This Church hath the cognizance of the *scandalous offences* of its Members committed unto it, when brought before it in the due Order described. Hereon it makes a *Determination,* designing in the first place the Recovery of the Person offending, from his Sin, by his hearing of its Counsel and Advice. But in case of *Obstinacy,* it is to remove him from its Communion, leaving him in the outward condition of an Heathen and a Publican. So is he to be esteemed by them that were offended with his Sin, and that because of the Authority of the Church binding him in Heaven and Earth unto the puniſhment due unto his Sin, unleſs he doth Repent. The *Rejection* of an offending Brother out of the Society of the Church, leaving him as unto *all the Privileges of the Church*, in the State of an Heathen, declaring him liable unto the Diſpleaſure of Chriſt, and Everlaſting Puniſhment without Repentance, is the Excommunication we plead for; and the Power of it, with its Exerciſe, is plainly here granted by Chriſt and Ordained in the Church. (3.) According unto this Inſtitution was the practice of the Apoſtles, whereof we have ſeveral Inſtances. I might inſiſt upon the Excommunication of *Simon* the Magician, a baptized profeſſor, by *Peter*, who declared him *to have neither part or lot in the Church* upon the diſcovery of his wickedneſs, *Act.* 8. 13, 20, 21, 22, 23. Yet becauſe it was the ſingle Act *of one Apoſtle*, and ſo may be eſteemed extraordinary, I ſhall omit it. However, that fact of the Apoſtle is ſufficiently declarative of what is to be done in the Church in like caſes, and which if it be not done, it cannot be preſerved in its purity according unto the mind of Chriſt. But that which was directed by the Apoſtle *Paul* in the Church of *Corinth* towards the *inceſtuous Perſon*, is expreſs, 1 *Cor.* 5. 1, 2, 5, 6, 7. (1.) He *declares the Sin* whereof the Perſon charged was guilty, with the Ignominy and Scandal of it, *Ver.* 1. (2.) He *blames the Church* that they had not been affected with the Guilt and Scandal of it, ſo as to have proceeded to his Removal or Expulſion out of the Church, that he might be taken away or cut off from them, *Ver.* 2. (3.) He declares his *own judgment* in the caſe, that he ought to be ſo taken away or removed, which yet was not actually effected by that Judgment and Sentence of his, *Ver.* 3. (4.) He declares the *cauſes* of this Exciſion. (1.) The Supream efficient cauſe of it, is the *Power or Authority of the Lord Jeſus Chriſt* inſtituting this Ordinance in his Church, giving Right and Power unto it for its adminiſtration, *In the Name of our Lord Jeſus Chriſt*, and with his Power. (2.) The *declarative cauſe* of the Equity of this Sentence, which was the Spirit of the Apoſtle, or the Authoritative Declaration of his judgment in the caſe, *with my Spirit*. (3.) The *Inſtrumental Miniſterial*

sterial cause of it, which is the Church; do it in the Name of the Lord Jesus Christ, *when you are gathered together*, Ver. 4. and thereby *purge out the old Leaven, that you may be a new Lump*, Ver. 7. whence the *punishment* of this Sentence is said to be *inflicted by many*, 2 Cor. 2. 6. that is, all those who on his Repentance were obliged to forgive and comfort him, that is the whole Church, *Ver.* 7. (5.) The nature of the Sentence is the *delivering of such an one to Satan for the destruction of the Flesh, that the Spirit may be saved in the day of the Lord Jesus*, Ver. 5. Not the destruction of his Body by Death, but the through *mortification of the Flesh*, whereby he was shortly afterwards recovered and restored into his former condition. The whole of what we plead for, is here exemplified; as, (1.) The *cause* of *Excommunication*, which is a scandalous Sin unrepented of. (2.) The preparation for its execution, which is the Churches sense of the Sin and Scandal, with Humiliation for it. (3.) The *warranty* of it, which is the Institution of Christ, wherein his Authority is engaged. (4.) The *manner* and form of it, by an Act of Authority with the consent of the whole Church. (5.) The *effect* of it in a total separation from the Privileges of the Church. (6.) *The end* of it. (1.) With respect unto the Church, its purging and vindication. (2.) With respect unto the Person Excommunicated; his Repentance, Reformation and Salvation.

IT is usually replied hereunto, that this was an *extraordinary act of Apostolical Power*, and so not to be drawn by us into Example. For he himself both determines the case, and asserteth his presence in Spirit, that is by his Authority to be necessary unto what was done. Besides, it was a *delivery of the Man to Satan*, that is, into his power to be afflicted and cruciated by him, to be terrified in his Mind, and punished in his Body to the destruction of the Flesh, that is unto Death. Such was the *Delivery of a Man to Satan* by the Apostle mentioned here, and 1 *Tim.* 1. 9, 20. in the judgment of many of the Ancients. But there is no such Power in any Church at present to *deliver an offender unto Satan*, nor any appearing effects of such a pretence. Wherefore, this

this is a matter which belongs not unto Churches at present.

I ANSWER, (1.) What the Apostles did in any Church, whether present or absent, by their own Authority, did not prejudice the Right of the Churches themselves, nor their Power acted in *Subordination* unto them and their guidance. So it is evident in this place, that notwithstanding the exerting of any *Apostolical Power* intimated, the Church it self is charged with its Duty, and directed to exercise its Authority in the Rejection of the Offender. (2.) There is nothing *extraordinary* in the case. (1.) It is not so that a Member of a Church should fall into a *scandalous* Sin, unto the dishonour of Christ and the Church, giving offence unto Persons of all sorts. (2.) It is an ordinary Rule, founded in the Light of Nature, confirmed here and elsewhere by express Divine Commands, that such an one be rejected from the Society and Communion of the Church, until he give satisfaction by Repentance and Reformation. (3.) It is that without which the Church cannot be preserved in its *purity*, nor its being be continued, as both Reason and Experience do manifest. (4.) The *judgment* both of the *Fact* and *Right* was left unto the Church it self, whence it was afterwards highly commended by the Apostle for the diligent discharge of its Duty herein, 2 *Cor.* 2. In brief, it is such a Divine Order that is here prescribed, as without the observance whereof, no Church can long subsist. (5.) There is no difficulty in the other part of the Objection, about the *Delivery unto Satan*. For, (1.) It cannot be proved, that hereon the Offender was delivered *so into the power of Satan* to be cruciated, agitated, and at length killed, as some imagine; nor can any instance of any such thing, be given in the Scripture or Antiquity; though there be many of them, who upon their rejection out of the Church, were enraged unto an opposition against it, as it was with *Simon Magus, Marcian,* and others. (2.) Yea, it is evident that there was no such thing included in their delivery unto *Satan*, as is pretended. For the design and end of it was the *Man's Humiliation, Recovery and Salvation*, as is expressly presly affirmed in the Text; and this effect it actually had, for the Man was *healed* and restored. Wherefore, this *Delivery unto Satan*, is an Ordinance of Christ for the exciting of Saving Grace in the Souls of Men, adapted unto the case of falling by scandalous Sins, peculiarly effectual above any other Gospel Ordinance. Now this cannot be *such a Delivery unto Satan*, as that pretended, which can have no other end but Destruction and Death. (3.) This *Delivery unto Satan* is no more but the casting of a Man out of the visible Kingdom of Christ, so giving him up as unto his outward condition into the state of Heathens and Publicans which belonged unto the Kingdom of *Satan*. For he, who by the Authority of Christ himself, according unto his Law and Institution, is not only debarred from a participation of all the privileges of the Gospel, but also *visibly* and regularly devested of all present Right to them and Interest in them, he belongs unto the visible Kingdom of *Satan*. The gathering of Men by Conversion into the Church, is the *turning of them from the Power of Satan unto God*, *Act.* 26. 18. a *delivery from the Power of Darkness*, that is, the Kingdom of *Satan*, and a translation unto the Kingdom of Christ, *Col.* 1. 13. Wherefore, after a Man hath by Faith, and his conjunction unto a visible Church, been translated into the Kingdom of Christ, his just rejection out of it, is the *Redelivery* of him into the visible Kingdom of *Satan*, which is all that is here intended. And this is an act suited unto the end whereunto it is designed. For a Man hereby is not taken out of his own Power and the conduct of his own Mind, not acted or agitated by the Devil, but is left unto the sedate consideration of his present state and condition. And this, if there be any spark of ingenuous Grace left in him, will be effectually operative, by shame, grief and fear, unto his Humiliation, especially understanding that the design of Christ and his Church herein, is only his Repentance and Restauration.

HERE is therefore, in his instance, an *Everlasting Rule* given unto the Church in all Ages, the ordinary Occurrences of the like cases requiring an ordinary Power for Relief in
them,

Of Excommunication.

them, without which the Church cannot be preserved. That it is the Duty of the Church enjoined unto it by the Lord Jesus Christ, and that necessary unto its Glory, its own Honour and Edification to reject scandalous Offenders out of its Communion, is evidently declared in this place: And to suppose that to be the Duty of the Church, which it hath no Power or Authority to discharge, (seeing without them it cannot be discharged) is a wild imagination.

4. THE *Duty of the Church* herein, with such other particular Duties as suppose the Institution hereof, are in many places directed and enjoined. It is so in that insisted on, 1 *Cor.* 5. The foundation of the whole Discourse and practice of the Apostle there Recorded lies in this, That *Churches ought to cut off from among them scandalous Offenders*; and that to the End they may preserve themselves pure; and that this they ought to do in the Name of Christ, and by virtue of his Authority, *Vers.* 2, 4, 7. And this is the whole of that *Excommunication* which we plead for. The manner of its Administration we shall consider afterwards, 2 *Cor.* Chap. 2. 6, 7, 8. The Apostle commends the Church for what they had done in the *Excommunication* of the *Incestuous person*, calling it a *Punishment, inflicted on him by them,* Vers. 6. He gives also an account of the Effect of this Sentence against him, which was his *Humiliation and Repentance,* Vers. 7. And hereon gives direction for his *Restauration,* by an Act of the Church *forgiving him,* and *confirming their Love unto him.* Men may fansie to themselves strange Notions of *Excommunication*, with reference unto its Power, the Residence of that Power, its Effects, Extent and Ends; and so either on the one hand erect it into an Engine of Arbitrary Domination over the Church and all the Members of it; or deny on the other, that there is any such Institution of Christ in force in his Churches. But we can be taught nothing more plainly of the Mind of Christ, than that he hath given Power unto his Church to cast out of their Communion obstinate *scandalous* Offenders, and to restore them again upon their *Repentance,* enjoining it unto them as their Duty. And it is an Evidence of a woful degeneracy in Churches,
from

from their Primitive Institution, when this sentence is so administred, as that it hath an effect, by virtue of *Humane Laws*, or the outward concerns of Men, but *no influence* on their Consciences unto Humiliation and Repentance, which is the principal End of its appointment. The Apostle treats of the same matter, *Gal.* 5. 7, 8, 9, 10, 11, 12. He speaks of those false Teachers who opposed and overthrew what lay in them, *the Fundamental Doctrine of the Gospel*. These at that time were in great Power and Reputation in the Churches of the *Galatians* whom they had corrupted with their false Opinions; so as that the Apostle doth not directly enjoin their *immediate Excision*; yet he declares what they did deserve, and what was the Duty of the Church towards them, when freed from their Delusions, *Verf.* 12. *I would they were even cut off that trouble you.* Men have exercised their Minds in curious conjectures about the sence of these Words, altogether in vain and needlesly. The curiosity of some of the best of the Ancients, applying it unto a forcible *Ennuchism* is extreamly fond. No other *Excision* is intended, but that which was *from the Church*, and to be done by the Church in obedience unto the Truth. Neither the Subject Matter treated of, the nature of the Crime condemned, nor the state of the Church, or design of the Apostle, will admit of any other Exposition, 2 *Theffal.* 3. 7. The Apostle gives command unto the Brethren of the Church, and that in the Name of our Lord Jesus Christ, *to withdraw from every Brother that walketh disorderly*. What it is to *walk disorderly* he declares immediately, namely, to live in an open disobedience unto any of the commands of Christ, *not after the Tradition which he received of us*, that is, the Doctrine of the Gospel which he had *delivered* unto them. This *withdrawing* is as unto Church-Communion, which cannot be done but upon some act of the Church, depriving them of the Rights of it. For if every Member of the Church should be left unto his own judgment and practice herein, it would bring all things into confusion. And therefore, *Verf.* 14. he requires that a *note be set* on such a Person by the Church, that is, a Sentence be denounced against him, before the Duty of withdrawing

drawing from him by the Brethren be incumbent on them. See to the same purpose *Tit.* 3. 10, 11. 1 *Tim.* 5. 20, *Revel.* 2. 2, 14, 15, 20, 21.

IT is therefore evident that this *Cenſure, Judgment, Spiritual puniſhment,* is an Inſtitution of Chriſt, for whoſe Adminiſtration he hath given *Authority* unto his Church, as that which is neceſſary unto its Edification, with its preſervation in Honour, Purity and Order.

THERE have been many Diſputes about it, as unto its *Order and Kinds.* Some ſuppoſe that there are *two ſorts* of Excommunication; the one they call the *leſſer*, and the other the greater: Some *three ſorts*, as it is ſuppoſed there were among the *Jews.* There is no mention in the Scripture of any more ſorts, but *one*, or of any *Degrees* therein. A *ſegregation from all participation in Church-Order, Worſhip and Privileges,* is the only Excommunication ſpoken of in the Scripture. But, whereas an offending Perſon may cauſe great diſorder in a Church, and give great ſcandal unto the Members of it, before he can be regularly cut off or expelled the Society; ſome do judge that there ſhould a *Suſpenſion of him from the Lords Table at leaſt*, precede total or compleat Excommunication in caſe of Impenitency. And it ought in ſome caſes ſo to be. But this Suſpenſion is not properly an eſpecial Inſtitution; but only an act of *prudence* in Church-Rule to avoid offence and ſcandal. And no Men queſtion but that this is lawful unto, yea, the Duty of the Rulers of the Church, to require any one to forbear for a ſeaſon from the uſe of their *Privilege* in the participation of the Supper of the Lord, in caſe of *ſcandal* and offence which would be taken at it, and enſue thereon. And if any Perſon ſhall refuſe a Submiſſion unto them in this *Act of Rule*, the Church hath no way for its Relief, but to proceed unto *the total Removal* of ſuch a Perſon from their whole Communion. For the Edification of the whole Church muſt not be obſtructed by the Refractorineſs of any one among them.

THIS *Excommunication*, as we have proved before, is an *act of Church-Authority*, exerted in the Name of our Lord
Jeſus

Of Excommunication.

Jesus Christ. And if so, then it is an act of the Officers of the Church, namely, so far as it is *Authoritative*; for there is no Authority in the Church properly so called, but what resides in the Officers of it. There is an Office in the Church, which is meerly *Ministerial* without any formal Authority, that is of the *Deacons*. But there is no *Authority* in exercise, but what is in the *Elders* and *Rulers* of the Church. And there are two *Reasons*, which prove that the power of Excommunication, as to the *Authoritative Exercise* of it, is in the Elders of the Church. (1.) Because the Apostles, by virtue of their Office-Power in every Church, did join in the *Authoritative Excommunication*, as is plain in the case insisted on, 1 *Cor.* 5. And there is no Office-Power now remaining, but what is in the *Elders* of the Church. (2.) It is an *Act of Rule*. But all *Rule*, properly so called, is in the hands of *Rulers* only. We may add hereunto, that the *care* of the preservation of the Church in its purity, of the Vindication of its Honour, of the Edification of all its Members, of the Correction and Salvation of Offenders, is principally incumbent on them, or committed unto them as we have declared; as also, that they are *best able to judge* when and for what this Sentence ought to be denounced against any, which requires their best skill in the Wisdom of Spiritual Rule. And therefore the omission of the exercise of it, when it was necessary, is charged as a neglect on *the Angels or Rulers of the Churches*, as the due execution of it is commended in them. And therefore unto them it doth belong with respect unto their Office, and is thereon an Office-Act, or an Act of Authority.

HOWBEIT, it cannot be denied, but that the Interest, yea, the power of the whole Church in the *Fraternity* of it, is greatly to be considered herein. For indeed, where-ever the Apostle Treats of it, he doth not any where recommend it unto the *Officers of the Church* in a peculiar manner, but unto the *whole Church* and the Brethren therein. This is evident in the places before quoted. Wherefore the *whole Church* is concerned herein, both in point of Duty, Interest, and Power. (1.) In point of Duty; for by virtue of the *mutual watch* of all the

Members of the Church over each other, and of the care incumbent on every one of them, for the Good, the Honour, the Reputation and Edification of the whole, it is their *Duty* jointly and severally to endeavour the *purging out from among them* of every thing that is contrary unto those ends. And they who are not concerned in these things, are dead and useless Members of the Church. (2.) In *Interest*, they have also a concernment therein. They are to look that no *root of bitterness spring up among them, lest themselves are at length defiled thereby.* It is usually said, that the good are not defiled by holding Communion with them that are wicked in a participation of holy Ordinances. And there is some Truth in what is said, with reference unto wicked undiscovered Hypocrites; or such as are not scandalously flagitious: But to promote this *Perswasion*, so as to beget an opinion in Church-Members, that they are *no way* concerned in the *scandalous Sins and Lives* of those with whom they walk in all Duties of Spiritual Communion, openly avowing themselves Members of the same Body with them, is a *Diabolical Engine* invented to countenance Churches in horrible security unto their ruine. But yet besides that defilement, which may be contracted in a joint participation of the same Ordinances with such Persons; there are other ways almost innumerable, whereby their *Example*, if passed by without Animadversion, may be pernicious unto their Faith, Love and Obedience. Wherefore they are obliged in point of *Spiritual Interest*, as they take care of their own Souls, to concurr in the ejection out of the Church, of obstinate Offenders. (3.) In point of *Power*. For the *Execution* of this Sentence is committed unto and rests in the Body of the Church. According as they concurr and practise, so it is put in Execution or Suspended; for it is they who must withdraw Communion from them, or the Sentence is of no use or validity; this punishment must be inflicted by the many; who also are to restore him who is so rebuked. Wherefore, Excommunication, without the consent of the Church, is a meer nullity.

BUT if any one shall say, that Excommunication is not an Act of

Of Excommunication.

of *Authority* nor of Office, but of Power residing in the *community* resulting from their common suffrage, guided and directed by the Officers or Elders of the Church, I shall again take up this Enquiry immediately, and speak unto it more distinctly; lest what is here spoken should not be sufficient unto the satisfaction of any.

OUR next Enquiry is concerning *the object* of this Church *Censure*; or who they are that ought to be Excommunicated. And,

1. THEY must be *Members of that Church*, by which the Sentence is to be denounced against them. And this, as we have proved before, they cannot be without their *own consent*. One Church cannot Excommunicate the Members of another. They are unto them as unto this matter *without*, and they have no power to judge them. The foundation of the Right to proceed against any herein, is in their own *voluntary engagement* to observe and keep the Rules and Laws of the Society whereunto they are admitted. The offence is given unto that Church in the *first place*, if not *only*. And it is an Act of the Church for its own Edification. And there is a *nullity* in the Sentence which is ordained, decreed or denounced by any who are not *Officers* of that Church in particular, wherein the Sin is committed.

2. THESE Church-Members that may be justly Excommunicated, are of Two sorts.

1. SUCH as continue *obstinate* in the practice of any *scandalous Sin*, after private and publick admonition. The process from the first Offence in *Admonition*, is so stated in ordinary cases, *Matth.* 18. that there is no need farther to declare it. The *Time* that is to be allotted unto the several Degrees of it, shall be spoken unto afterwards. And unto a right judgment of *obstinacy* in any scandalous Sin, it is required, (1.) That the Sin considered in it self be such, as is *owned to be such, by all*, without doubting, dispute or hæsitation. It must be some Sin that is judged and condemned in the Light of Nature, or in the express Testimony of Scripture; yea, such as the Holy Ghost witnesseth, that *continued in without Repentance*, it is inconsistent with Salvation. If the thing it self, to be Animadverted

Ee 2   on,

on, be dubious or disputable whether it be a Sin or no, especially such a Sin, either from the Nature of the Fact, or the Qualifications of the Person offending, or from other Circumstances, so as that the guilty Person is not *self-condemned*, nor are others fully satisfied in their Minds about the nature of it, there is no room for Excommunication in such cases. And if it be once allowed to be applied towards *any Sins*, but such as are evident to be so (as the Apostle says, the *Works of the Flesh are manifest*) in the Light of Nature, and Express Testimony of Scripture, not only will the Administration of it be made difficult, a matter of *dispute*, unfit for the Determination of the *Body of the Church*, but it will leave it unto the wills of Men to prostitute unto litigious brawls, quarrels and differences, wherein Interest and Partiality may take place; which is to profane this Divine Institution. But confine it as it ought to be, unto such Sins as are condemned in the Light of Nature, or by Express Testimony of Scripture, as inconsistent with Salvation by Jesus Christ, if persisted in, and all things that belong unto the Administration of it, will be plain and easie.

FROM the neglect of this Rule proceeded that horrible confusion and disorder in Excommunication and the Administration of it, which for sundry Ages prevailed in the World. For as it was mostly applied unto things *holy*, *just*, and *good*, or the performance of *such Gospel Duties* as Men owed to Christ, and their own Souls; so being exercised with respect unto *irregularities*, that are made such meerly by the *Arbitrary* Constitutions and Laws of Men, and that in cases frivolous, trifling, and of no importance, it was found necessary to be managed in and by such *Courts*, such *Processes*, such *forms of Law*, such *Pleadings* and intricacies of Craft, such a burden of Cost and Charge, as is uncertain whether it ought to be more bewailed, or derided.

2. IT is required hereunto, that the *matter of Fact*, as unto the Relation of the Sin unto the particular Offender, be *confessed*, or not *denied*, or *clearly proved*. How far this is to extend, and what ground of procedure there may be in Reports

or

Of Excommunication.

or *Fame* concurring with leading Circumstances, we shall enquire afterwards. And although in such cases of *publick Fame*, a good Testimony from those of Credit and Repute in the Church given unto the supposed guilty Person, is of *use* and sufficient in some cases, singly to oppose unto publick **Reports**; yet to require a Man to *purge himself* by others, from any feigned scandalous imputation, is an unwarrantable Tyranny.

3. IT is also required, that the previous process in and by private and publick Admonition, and that repeated with *patient waiting* for the success of each of them, be duly premised. Whether this extend it self unto all *causes* of Excommunication, shall be afterwards enquired into. Ordinarily it is so necessary unto the Conviction of the Mind and Conscience of the *Offender*, and to leave him without either provocation from the Church, or excuse in himself, so suited to be expressive of the Grace and Patience of Christ toward Sinners, so requisite unto the satisfaction of the Church it self in their proceedure, as that the *omission of it* will probably render the Sentence useless and ineffectual. A crying out, *I admonish a First, a Second, a Third time*, and so to Excommunication, is a very absurd observation of a Divine Institution.

4. IT is required, that the *case* of the Person to be censured as unto his profession of Repentance on the one hand, or obstinacy on the other, be judged and determined by the whole Church in love and compassion. There are *few* who are so profligately wicked, but that, when the Sin wherewith they are charged, is evidently such in the Light of Nature and Scripture, and when it is *justly proved against them*, they will make some profession of *Sorrow* and Repentance. Whether this be sufficient, as in most cases it is, to suspend the present proceeding of the Church, or quite to lay it aside, is left unto the judgment of the Church it self, upon consideration of present Circumstances, and what is necessary unto its own Edification. Only this Rule must be continually observed, that the least appearance of *haste* or undue precipitation herein, is to be avoided in all these cases, as the bane of Church-Rule and Order.

AGAIN,

Of Excommunication.

AGAIN, The manner of its *Administration*, according to the mind of Christ, may be considered. And hereunto are required, (1.) *Prayer*, without which it can no way be administred in the Name of our Lord Jesus Christ. The Administration of any solemn Ordinance of the Gospel, without Prayer, is an horrible profanation of it. And the neglect or contempt hereof, in any who take upon them to Excommunicate others, is an open Proclamation of the *nullity* of their Act and Sentence. And the observation of the Administration of it without any due Reverence of God, without solemn invocation of the Name of Christ, thereby ingaging his Presence and Authority in what they do, is that principally which hath set the Consciences of all mankind at liberty from any concernment in this Ecclesiastical Censure; and whence those that Administer it expect no other success of what they do, but what they can give it by outward force. And where this fails, Excommunication is quickly laid aside. As it was when the *Pope* threatned the *Cantons of the Swissers*, that if they complied not with some of his Impositions, he would Excommunicate them; whereon they sent him word *they would not be Excommunicated*, which ended the matter. Wherefore, when our Lord Jesus Christ gives unto his Church the power of binding and loosing, directing them in the exercise of that power, he directs them to ask assistance by *Prayer, when they are gathered together*, Matth. 18. 18, 19, 20. And the Apostle directs the Church of *Corinth*, that they should proceed unto this Sentence when they were *gathered together in the Name of the Lord Jesus Christ*, 1 Cor. 5. 4. which could not be without calling on his Name. In brief, without *Prayer*, neither is the Ordinance it self sanctified unto the Church, nor are any meet to Administer it, nor is the Authority of Christ either owned or engaged, nor Divine Assistance attained; neither is what is done any more *Excommunication* than any rash *Curse* is, so that many proceed inordinately out of the Mouths of Men.

AND the Prayer required herein is of three sorts. (1.) That which is *previous* for guidance and direction in a matter of so great

great weight and importance. It is no small thing to fall into mistakes, when Men act *in the Name of Christ*, and so engage his Authority in what he will not own. And the best of Men, the best of Churches, are liable unto such mistakes, where they are not under the guidance of the holy Spirit, which is to be obtained by Prayer only. (2.) *In, or together with the Administration* of it; that what is done on Earth may be ratified in Heaven, by the approbation of Christ, and be made effectual unto its proper End. (3.) It must be *followed* with the *Prayer of the Church* unto the same purpose; all with respect unto the Humiliation, Repentance, Healing and Recovery of the Offender.

2*ly*, IT is to be accompanied with *Lamentation* or Mourning. So the Apostle reproving the Church of *Corinth* for the omission of it when it was necessary, tells them, That *they had not mourned; that the offender might be taken away from among them,* 1 Cor. 5. 2. It is not to be done without *mourning*: And himself calls the Execution of this Sentence from this Adjunct, his *bewailing* of them. *I shall bewail many that have sinned already,* 2 Cor. 12. 2. *Compassion* for the person offending, with respect unto that dangerous condition whereinto he hath cast himself; the Excision of a Member of the same Body with whom they have had Communion in the most holy Mysteries of Divine Worship, and sate down at the Table of the Lord, with a due sense of the Dishonour of the Gospel by his fall, ought to ingenerate this *Mourning* or *Lamentation* in the Minds of them who are concern'd in the Execution of the Sentence. Nor is it advisable for any Church to proceed thereunto, before they are so affected.

3*ly*, IT is to be accompanied with a *due sence of the future Judgment of Christ*. For we herein Judge for Christ, in the matters of his House and Kingdom. And woe to them who dare pronounce this Sentence without a perswasion on good grounds, that it is the *Sentence of Christ himself*. And there is a Representation also in it of the *future Judgment*, when Christ will Eternally cut off and separate from himself all Hypocrites and impenitent Sinners. This is well expressed by
Tertullian,

Tertullian, Ibidem etiam Exhortationes, Castigationes & Censura Divina (speaking of the Assemblies of the Church) *nam & judicatur magno cum pondere, ut apud certos de Dei conspectu; summumque futuri judicii præjudicium est, si quis ita deliquerit ut à Communicatione Orationis & Conventus, & omnis sancti commercii relegetur,* Apol. cap. 39. Were this Duty observed, it would be a preservative against that inter-mixture of corrupt Affections, and corrupt Ends, which often impose themselves on the Minds of Men, in the exercise of this Power.

Lastly, THE *Nature and End* of this Judgment or Sentence being *Corrective,* not *Vindicative;* for Healing, not Destruction, what is the Duty of the Church, and those principally concerned in the pursuit of it to render it effectual, is plainly evident. Of what use a *Significavit* and *Capias* may be in this case I know not; they belong not unto Christian Religion; much less do *Fire and Faggot* do so. *Prayer* for the person cut off; *Admonition* as occasion is offered; *Compassion* in his distressed Estate, which is so much the more deplorable, if he know it not; *forbearance* from common Converse, with *readiness* for the Restauration of Love, in all the fruits of it, contain the principal Duties of the Church, and all the Members of it towards them that are justly Excommunicate.

WHAT farther belongeth unto this Head of *Church-Rule or Order* shall be spoken unto in the Resolution of some *Cases or Enquiries,* wherein also some Things only mentioned already, shall be more fully explained.

I HAVE made some enquiry before, whether Excommunication be an act of *Authority* and *Jurisdiction* in the *Officers* of the Church, or an act of *Power* in the *Fraternity* of the Church. But for the sake of some by whom it is desired, I shall a little more distinctly enquire after the Truth herein; though I shall alter nothing of what was before laid down. And,

1. IT is certain, it hath been proved, and I now take it for granted, That the Lord Christ hath given *this Power unto the Church.* Wherefore in the exercise of this Power, both the Officers and Members of the Church are to act according unto

Of Excommunication.

to their *respective* Interests. For that Exercise of Power in the Church towards any, which is not an act of Obedience unto Christ, in them that exercise it, it is in it self *null*. There is therefore no Distinction or Distribution of Power in the Church, but by the interposition of especial Duty.

2. THE Institution of Christ, with respect unto a Church as it is a *peculiar Society* for its *especial Ends*, do not deprive it of its natural Right, as it is *a Society*. There is in every *Community*, by voluntary Confederation, a natural Right and Power to *expel* those from its Society, who will not be ruled by the Laws of its Constitution. And if the Church should, by the Institution of a Power, new as unto the way, manner and ends of its Exercise, be deprived of its *Original*, radical Power, with respect unto the general End of its own Preservation, it would not be a gainer by that Institution. It may be easily understood, that the Lord Christ should in particular appoint the Way and Manner of the Exercise of this Power or Administration of this Sentence, committing the care thereof unto the *Officers* of the Church. But it cannot be well understood, that thereby he should deprive the Church of its *Right*, and forbid them their Duty in preserving their Society entire and pure. Neither can it be so in an especial manner committed unto any, as that upon their neglect, whereby those who by the Law and Rule of Christ, ought to be cast out of the Churches Communion, are continued in it unto its Sin and Defilement, the Church it self should be free from guilt. Wherefore the Apostle expresly chargeth the *whole Church* of *Corinth* with Sin and neglect of Duty, in that the incestuous person was not put away from among them: This could not be, if so be the Power of it were so in the Hands of a *few of the Officers*, that the Church had no Right to act in it. For none can incurr a Guilt meerly by the defect of others in the Discharge of their Duty.

3. THE Church *essentially* considered is before its ordinary Officers; for the Apostle *ordained Officers in every Church*. But the Church in that State hath Power to put away from among them and their Communion an obstinate Offender. They have

Of Excommunication.

it, as they are a Society, by voluntary confederation. Wherein this comes short of Authoritative Excommunication, will immediately appear.

4. WHERE a Church is compleat and *Organized* with its stated Rulers, as the Church of *Corinth* was, yet Rules, Instructions and Commands are given expresly unto the *Fraternity* or *Community* of the Church, for their Duty and Acting in the Administration of this Sentence, and the cutting off an Offender, 1 *Cor.* 5. 2, 4, 6, 7. 2 *Cor.* 2. 7, 8. Yea, the ἐπιτιμία, or infliction of the Sentence, is ascribed unto them, *Ver.* 5. All these things do suppose a *Right* and *Duty* thereon to Act according to their Interest in Excommunication, to reside in the whole Church: Wherefore,

5. THERE are *some Acts* belonging hereunto, that the Church it self in the Body of the Fraternity, cannot be excluded from without destroying the nature of the Sentence it self, and rendring it ineffectual. Such are the *previous cognizance of the Cause*, without which they cannot be blamed for any neglect about it; *preparatory Duties* unto its Execution, in Prayer, Mourning and Admonition, which are expresly prescribed unto them; and a Testification of their consent unto it, by their common Suffrage. Without these things, Excommunication is but a Name with a noise; it belongs not unto the Order appointed by Christ in his Church.

6. HENCE arise the *Duties* of the Church towards an Excommunicated Person, that are consequential unto his exclusion from among them. Such are *Praying* for him, as one *noted* by the Church, and under the Discipline of Christ; *avoiding Communion* with him in publick and private, that he may be ashamed, and the like; all which arise from their own voluntary actings in his exclusion; and such, as without a judgment of the cause, they cannot be obliged unto.

7. YET on the other side, unto the formal compleatness of this Sentence, an *Authoritative Act of Office-Power* is required. For, (1.) There is in it such an Act of *Rule*, as is in the hands of the Elders only. (2.) The *Executive* Power of the Keys in binding and loosing, so far as it comprizeth

Of Excommunication.

prizeth *Authority* to be acted in the Name of Christ, is entrusted with them only.

8. WHEREFORE I shall say no more in answer unto this Enquiry; but that *Excommunication* is an act of Church-Power in its Officers and Brethren, acting according unto their respective Rights, Interests, and Duties particularly prescribed unto them. The *Officers* of the Church act in it as Officers with *Authority*, the *Brethren* or the Body of the Church with Power; yet so, as that the Officers are no way excluded from their Power, Consent and Suffrage in the acting of the Church, but have the same Interest therein with all other Members of the Church; but the Community of the Church have no Interest in those Authoritative actings of the Officers which are peculiar unto them. Where either of these is wanting, the whole Duty is vitiated, and the fence of the Sentence rendred ineffectual.

I. IT is Enquired, *Whether Excommunication, justly deserved, may and ought to be omitted in case of trouble, or danger that may ensue unto the Church therein.*

IT is usually granted that so it may and ought to be; which seems in general to have been the judgment of *Austin*.

THE Troubles and Dangers intended, are three-fold. (1.) From the Thing it self. (2.) From the *Persons* to be Excommunicated. (3.) From the *Church*.

1. TROUBLE may arise from the *Thing* it self. For there being an exercise of Authority or Jurisdiction in it over the Persons of Men, not granted from the *Civil Magistrate* by the Law of the Land, those that execute it may be liable unto Penalties ordained in such cases.

2. THE *Persons to be Excommunicated* may be *Great*, and of great Interest in the World, so as that if they receive a provocation hereby, they may occasion or stir up Persecution against the Church, as it hath often fallen out.

3. THE Church it self may be *divided* on these considerations, so as that lasting differences may be occasioned
among

Of Excommunication.

among them, which the *omiſſion* of the Sentence might prevent.

FOR Anſwer hereunto, ſome things muſt be premiſed. As,

1. HERE is no ſuppoſition of any thing *ſinful* or *morally* evil in the Church, its Officers, or any of its Members, by refuſing to omit the pronouncing of this Sentence. Whether there be any Sin in giving occaſion unto the *troubles* mentioned, to be avoided by an omiſſion of Duty, is now to be enquired into.

2. WE muſt ſuppoſe, (1.) That the *cauſe* of Excommunication be clear and evident, both as unto the merit of the Fact, and the due Application of it unto the Perſon concerned; ſo as that *no Rational indifferent Man* ſhall be able to ſay, that it is meet that ſuch an one ſhould be continued a Member of ſuch a Society; as it ought to be, where-ever Excommunication is adminiſtred. (2.) That *ſufficient Time* and ſpace of Repentance, and for giving ſatisfaction unto the Church (whereof afterwards) hath been allowed unto the Perſon after Admonition. (3.) That the Church doth really ſuffer in Honour and Reputation by tolerating ſuch a ſcandalous Offender among them.

I *ANSWER*, On theſe ſuppoſitions I ſee no juſt Reaſon to countenance the *omiſſion of the Execution of this Sentence*, or to acquit the Church from the guilt of Sin in ſo doing. For,

1. THE firſt pretence of *Danger* is vain. There is not the leaſt *ſhadow of Juriſdiction* in this Act of the Church. There is nothing in it that toucheth any thing which is under the Protection and Conſervation of *Humane Laws*. It reacheth not the *Perſons* of Men in their *Lives*, or *Liberties*; nor their *Eſtates* or the leaſt *Secular Privileges* that they do enjoy; it doth not expoſe them to the *Power* or *Cenſures* of others, nor prejudge them as unto Office or Advantage of Life. There is therefore no concernment of the *Law of the Land* herein, no more than in a Parents diſenheriting a Rebellious Child.

2. AS unto *danger of Perſecution*, by the means of the Perſon provoked, I ſay, (1.) The ſame may be pleaded as unto all other Duties of obedience unto Jeſus Chriſt wherewith the World is provoked; and ſo the whole profeſſion of the Church ſhould

Of Excommunication.

should give place to the *fear of Persecution*. To *testify against Sin* in the way of Christs appointment, is a case of Confession. (2.) The Apostles were not deterred by this consideration from the Excommunication of *Simon Magus*, the *seducing Jews, Hymeneus* and *Alexander*, with others. (3.) The Lord Christ commandeth and reproveth his Churches, according as they were *strict* in the observation of this Duty, or neglective of it, notwithstanding the fear of Persecution thereon, *Revel.* 2. 3. And, (4.) He will take that care of his Church in all their obedience unto him, as shall turn all the consequents thereof unto their advantage.

3. AS unto danger of *Differences in the Church*, there is nothing to be said; but that if Rule, Order, Love and Duty will not prevent such Differences, there is no way appointed of Christ for that end: And if they are sufficient for it, (as they are abundantly) they must bear their own blame who occasion such Differences.

II. BUT it may be said, *What if such an Offender as justly deserves to be Excommunicated, and is under admonition in order thereunto in case of Impenitency, should voluntarily withdraw himself from, and leave the Communion of the Church, is there any necessity to proceed against him by Excommunication?*

Answ. 1. SOME say it is enough, if it be declared in the Church that such an one hath *cut off himself* from the Church, and is therefore no longer under their watch or care, but is left unto himself and the World. And this is sufficient with them who own no Act *of Office-Power* or Authority in Excommunication, but esteem it only a noted cessation of Communion, which destroys a principal Branch of the Power of the Keys. Wherefore,

2. WHERE the offence is plain, open, scandalous, persisted in; where Admonition is despised or not complied with, it is the Duty of the Church to denounce the Sentence of Excommunication against such a Person, notwithstanding his voluntary departure: For,

1. NO

Of Excommunication.

1. NO Man is to make an *Advantage* unto himself, or to be freed from any *Disadvantage*, Censure or Spiritual Penalty, by his own Sin; such as is the *voluntary Relinquishment* of the Church, by a Person under Admonition for scandalous Offences.

2. IT is necessary unto the Church, both as unto the Discharge of its Duty, and the *vindication of its Honour*; as also from the Benefit and Edification it will receive by those Duties of Humiliation, Mourning and Prayer, which are necessary unto the Execution of this Sentence.

3. IT is necessary for the *good and benefit* of him who so deserves to be Excommunicated. For, (1.) The end of the *Institution* of the Ordinance, is his *Correction*, not his *Destruction*, and may be effectual unto his Repentance and Recovery. (2.) It is to be followed with *sharp Admonition* and *Prayer*, which in due time, may reach the most profligate Sinner.

4. IT becomes not the *Wisdom* and *Order* of any Society entrusted with Authority for its own preservation, as the Church is by Christ himself; to suffer Persons obnoxious unto Censure by the fundamental Rules of that Society, to cast off all respect unto it, to break their Order and Relation, without Animadverting thereon; according to the Authority wherewith they are intrusted. To do otherwise is to expose their Order unto contempt, and Proclaim a Diffidence in their own Authority, for the Spiritual punishment of Offenders.

5. ONE end of the Appointment of the Power and Sentence of Excommunication in the Church, is to give Testimony unto the *future final judgment* of Christ against impenitent Sinners, which none of them can run away from, nor escape.

III. A THIRD Enquiry may be, *Whether in case of any great and scandalous Sin, the Church may proceed unto Excommunication, without any previous Admonition.*

Answ. 1. PERSONS may be *falsly accused of*, and charged with great Sins, the greatest of Sins, as well as those of a lesser Degree, and that both by particular Testimonies and
publick

Of Excommunication. 223

publick Reports, as it was with the *Lord Christ* himself; which daily Experience confirms. Wherefore, all haste and precipitation like that of *David* in judging the Case of *Mephibosheth*, is carefully to be avoided, though they are pressed under the pretences of the greatness and notoriety of the Sin.

2. THERE is no *individual actual Sin*, but it is capable of great Aggravation or Alleviation from its *Circumstances*: These the Church is to *enquire into*, and to obtain a full knowledge of them, that all things being duly weighed, they may be affected with the Sin in a due manner, or *after a goodly sort;* which is essential unto the right administration of this Ordinance.

3. THIS cannot be done, without *Personal Conference* with the Offender, who is to be allowed to speak for himself: This Conference, in case guilt be discovered, cannot but have in it the nature of an *Admonition*, whereon the Church is to proceed, as in case of previous solemn admonition, in the Order, and according to the Rule which shall be immediately declared.

IV. FOURTHLY, *Whether on the first knowledge of an Offence or scandalous Sin, if it be known unto the Church, that the offending Party is penitent, and willing to declare his Humiliation and Repentance for the satisfaction of the Church, may the Church proceed unto his Excommunication, in case the Sin be great and notorious?*

Answ. 1. IT is certain, that in an orderly Progress, as unto more private Sins, a compliance by Repentance with the First or Second Admonition, doth put a stop unto all further *Ecclesiastical* proceedure.

2. BUT whereas the Enquiry is made concerning Sins, either in their own Nature or in their Circumstances, *great and of disreputation* unto the Church: I Answer,

IF Repentance be evidenced unto the Consciences of the Rulers of the Church to be *sincere*, and proportionable unto the Offence in its outward Demonstration, according unto the

Rule

Of Excommunication.

Rule of the Gospel, so as that they are obliged to judge in Charity, that the Person sinning is pardoned and accepted with Christ, as all *sincerely penitent Sinners are undoubtedly*; the Church cannot proceed unto the Excommunication of such an Offender. For,

1. IT would be publickly to *reject* them whom they acknowledge that *Christ doth receive*. This nothing can warrant them to do; yea, so to do is to set up themselves against Christ, or at least to make use of his Authority against his Mind and Will. Yea, such a *Sentence* would destroy it self; for it is a Declaration that Christ doth disapprove them, whom he doth approve.

2. THEIR *so doing* would make a *misrepresentation of the Gospel*, and of the Lord Christ therein. For, whereas the principal design of the Gospel, and of the Representation that is made therein of Christ Jesus, is to evidence that *all sincerely Penitent Sinners*, that *Repent according unto the Rule of it*, are and shall be *Pardoned* and Accepted; by the Rejection of such a Person in the face of his *sincere Repentance*, there is an open contradiction thereunto. Especially it would give an undue sence of the *Heart, Mind*, and *Will* of Christ towards Repenting Sinners; such as may be dangerous unto the Faith of Believers, so far as the Execution of this Sentence is Doctrinal: For such it is, and declarative of the Mind of Christ according unto the judgment of the Church. The Image therefore of this Excommunication, which is set up in some Churches, wherein the Sentence of it is denounced without any regard unto the Mind of Christ, as unto his Acceptance or Disapprobation of those whom they Excommunicate, is a *Teacher of Lyes*.

3. SUCH a proceedure is *contrary unto the nature and end of this Sentence*. For it is *Corrective* and *Instructive*, not properly punishing and vindictive. The sole end of it, with respect whereunto it hath its Efficacy from Divine Institution, is the *Humiliation, Repentance* and Recovery of the Sinner. And if this be attained before, the *infliction of this Sentence* is contrary to the nature and end of it.

IT

Of Excommunication.

IT will be said, that it hath another end also; namely, the *preservation of the purity of the Church, and the vindication of its Honour and Reputation, wherein it suffers by the scandalous offences of any of its Members.* Whereunto, I say, (1.) No Church is or can be made *impure* by them whom Christ hath *purged*; as he doth all those who are truly penitent. (2.) It is no *Dishonour* unto any Church to have Sinners in it, who have evidenced *sincere Repentance*. (3.) The present offence and scandal may be provided against by an Act of *Rectoral Prudence*, in causing the offending Person to abstain from the Lords Table for a Season.

V. IT is Enquired, (Fifthly) *Whether such as voluntarily, causlesly and disorderly, do leave the Communion of any Church whereof they are Members, though not guilty of any scandalous immoralities, ma and ought to be Excommunicated?*

Answ. 1. WHERE Persons are esteemed Members of Churches by *external causes without their own consent*, or by *Parochial* cohabitation, they may remove from one Church unto another by the Removal of their Habitation, according unto their own Discretion. For such cohabitation being the only *formal Cause* of any Relation to such a Church in particular, upon the ceasing of that cause, the Relation ceaseth of its own accord.

2. WHERE Persons are Members of Churches by *mutual confederation*, or express personal consent, causless departure from them is an *evil* liable unto many Aggravations.

3. BUT whereas the principal end of all particular Churches is *Edification*, there may be many just and sufficient Reasons why a Person may remove himself from the *constant Communion of one Church* unto that of another. And of these Reasons he himself is judge, on whom it is incumbent to take care of his own Edification above all other things. Nor ought the Church to deny unto any such Persons their Liberty desired peaceably and according unto Order.

4. IT was declared before, that where any Persons guilty

of, and under Admonition for any *scandalous* Sin, do withdraw from the Communion of any Church, their so doing, is no impediment unto a farther procedure against them.

5. WHEREAS there are amongst us Churches, or those who are so esteemed in the Consciences of Men, so far differing in Principles and Practices, as that they have not entire Communion with one another in all parts of Divine Worship, it may be Enquired, *Whether if a Man leave a Church of one sort to join with one of another; as suppose he leave a select Congregation to join in a Parochial Church constantly and totally, he may be justly Excommunicated for so doing, without the consent of the Church whereunto he did belong.*

Answ. 1. IT is certain on the one hand, that if any Man leave the Communion of *Parochial* Assemblies to join himself unto a Select Congregation, those who have Power over those *Parishes*, will make no question whether they shall *Excommunicate* him or no in their way. But,

2. SUPPOSING Persons so departing from particular Congregations, (1.) To be free from *scandalous Sins.* (2.) That they depart *quietly* without attempting Disorder or Confusion in the Church. (3.) That they do *actually join themselves* unto the Communion of some Church, whose Constitution, Principles and Worship they do approve, whereby their visible Profession is preserved; the Church may not justly proceed unto their Excommunication: It may suffice to declare, that such Persons have on their own accord *forsaken the Communion* of the Church, are no more under its *Watch* or *Care*; neither is the Church further obliged towards them, but as unto Christian Duties in general.

6. AS for those whose departure is as *voluntary* and *causeless* so accompanied with other evils, such as are *Revilings, Reproaches* and false *Accusations*, as is usual in such Cases, they may be proceeded against as obstinate Offenders.

VI. THE Sixth Enquiry is, *What Time is to be given after solemn Admonition before actual Excommunication?*

Answ. 1.

Of Excommunication.

Anſw. 1. THE manner of ſome to run over the Words, *I Admoniſh you a Firſt, Second, and Third time*, ſo immediately to make way for the Sentence of Excommunication, is that wherein Men are greatly to be pitied for their Ignorance of the nature of thoſe things which they take on themſelves to Act, Order, and Diſpoſe of, that we aſcribe it not unto worſe and more evil Cauſes.

2. THE nature of the thing it ſelf, requires a conſiderable Seaſon or *ſpace of Time*, between ſolemn Admonition and Excommunication. For the end and deſign of the former is the Repentance and Recovery of the Offender. Nor doth its Efficacy thereunto depend on, or conſiſt in the actual giving of it; but as other moral Cauſes which may Work *gradually*, upon occaſional Advantages. Want of Light, ſome preſent Exaſperation and Temptation, may ſeem to fruſtrate a preſent *Admonition*, when they do but ſuſpend its preſent Efficacy, which it may afterwards obtain on the Conſcience of the Offender.

3. IT being a *Church Admonition* that is intended; it is the Duty of the Church to abide in Prayer and waiting for the Fruit of it according to the appointment of Chriſt. And herein the caſe may poſſibly require ſome *long time* to be ſpent.

4. NO preſent *appearance of Obſtinacy* or impenitence under Admonition, (which is uſually pleaded) ſhould cauſe an immediate proceedure unto Excommunication. For, (1.) It is contrary unto the *diſtinct Inſtitution* of the one, and the other; wherein the former is to be allowed its proper Seaſon for its Uſe and Efficacy. (2.) It doth not repreſent the *patience and forbearance of Chriſt towards his Church* and all the Members of it. (3.) It is not ſuited unto the Rule of that *Love* which *hopeth all things, beareth all things*, &c. (4.) All grounds of hope for the Recovery of Sinners by Repentance, are to be attended unto; ſo as to deferr the ultimate Sentence.

Nulla unquam de morte hominis cunctatio longa eſt.

5. IF *new Sins* are added of the ſame, or any other kind, unto former

Of Excommunication.

former *scandals*, whilst Persons are under Admonition, it is an Indication of the necessity of a proceedure.

VII. IT may be farther Enquired, *Whether a Man may be Excommunicated for Errors in matters of Faith, or false Opinions about them?*

Answ. 1. THE Case is so plainly and positively stated, *Rev.* 2. 2, 6, 15, 16, 20. 1 *Tim.* 1. 19, 20. *Tit.* 3. 10, 11. and other places, that it needs no farther Determination. Wherefore,

2. IF the Errors intended, are about or against the *Fundamental Truths* of the Gospel, so as that they that hold them, cannot *hold the Head*, but really make *Shipwrack of the Faith*, no pretended usefulness of such Persons, no peaceableness as unto outward deportment, which, Men guilty of such Abominations, will frequently cover themselves withal, can countenance the Church in forbearing after *due Admonition*, to cut them off from their Communion. The nature of the evil, the danger that is from it unto the whole Church, as from a *Gangrene* in any Member, unto the Body, the Indignation of Christ expressed against such *pernicious* Doctrines, the opposition of them to the building of the Church on the Rock, which in most of them is opposed, to render a Church altogether inexcusable, who omit their Duty herein.

3. *FALSE Opinions* in lesser things, when the foundation of Faith and Christian Practice are not immediately concerned, may be *tolerated in a Church*, and sundry Rules are given unto this end in the Scripture, as, *Rom.* 14. 1, 2, 3, &c. *Phil.* 3. 15, 16. Howbeit, in that low ebb of Grace, Love and Prudence, which we are come unto, it is best for Edification, that all Persons peaceably dispose themselves into those Societies with whom they most agree in *Principles and Opinions*; especially such as relate or lead unto practice in any Duties of Worship. But,

4. WITH respect unto such Opinions, if Men will, as is usual, *wrangle and contend* to the disturbance of the peace of the Church, or hinder it in any Duty, with respect unto its own Edification, and will neither peaceably *abide* in the Church,

nor

Of Excommunication.

nor peaceably *depart* from it, they may and ought to be proceeded against with Censures of the Church.

VIII. *WHETHER persons Excommunicated out of any Church may be admitted unto the hearing of the Word in the Assemblies of that Church?*

Answ. 1. THEY *may be so*; as also to be present at all Duties of Moral Worship; for so may *Heathens* and *Unbelievers*, 1 *Cor.* 14. 23, 24.

2. WHEN persons are under this Sentence, the Church is in a state of *expecting* of their Recovery and Return; and therefore are not to prohibit them any Means thereof, such as is preaching of the Word.

IX. *HOW far extends the Rule of the Apostle towards persons rejected of the Church*, 1 Cor. 5. 11. *With such an one do not to Eat*; as that also, *Note that Man and have no company with him, that he may be ashamed?* 2 Thess. 3. 14.

1. TO *Eat* comprizeth all *ordinary Converse* in things of this Life; *Give us our daily Bread.* (2.) To *Note*, is either the act of the Church, setting the *Mark of its Censure* and Disapprobation on him; or the *Duty of the Members* of the Church, to take notice of him, as unto the End of not keeping company with him. Wherefore,

2. HEREIN all ordinary Converse of *Choice*, not made necessary by previous occasions, is forbidden. The Rule, I say, forbids, (1.) All *ordinary Converse of Choice*; not that which is occasional. (2.) Converse about *Earthly secular Things*, not that which is Spiritual; for such an one may, and ought still to be admonished, whilst he will hear the word of Admonition. (3.) It is such Converse as is not made *previously necessary*, by Mens mutual Engagement in Trade and the like. For that is founded on such Rules of Right and Equity, with such Obligations in point of Truth, as Excommunication cannot Dissolve.

3. NO

Of Excommunication.

3. NO *suspension* of Duties antecedently necessary by virtue of *natural* or *moral Relation*, is allowed or countenanced by this Rule. Such are those of *Husband* and *Wife*, *Parents* and *Children*, *Magistrates* and *Subjects*, *Masters* and *Servants*, *Neighbours*, *Relations* in propinquity of Blood. No Duties arising from or belonging unto any of these Relations, are released, or the Obligation unto them weakned by Excommunication. *Husbands* may not hereon forsake their *Wives* if they are Excommunicated, nor *Wives* their *Husbands*; *Magistrates* may not withdraw their Protection from any of their *Subjects*; because they are Excommunicate; much less may *Subjects* withhold their Obedience on any pretence of the Excommunication of their Magistrates, as such. And the same is true as unto all other *natural* or *moral Relations*.

4. THE *Ends* of this prohibition are, (1.) To testifie our *Condemnation* of the Sin, and disapprobation of the person guilty of it, who is Excommunicated. (2.) The *Preservation* of our selves from all kinds of participation in his Sin. (3.) To make him *ashamed* of himself, that if he be not utterly profligate and given up unto total Apostasie, it may occasion in him thoughts of returning.

X. HOW ought *persons Excommunicated* to be *received into the Church upon their Repentance*?

Answ. 1. AS unto the *internal manner*; with all readiness and chearfulness; with, (1.) *Meekness*, to take from them all Discouragement and disconsolation, *Gal.* 6. 1. (2.) With *Compassion*, and all means of Relief and Consolation, 2 *Cor.* 2. 7. (3.) With *Love* in all the demonstrations of it, *Verf.* 8. (4.) With *Joy*, to represent the Heart of Christ towards Repenting Sinners.

2. THE *outward manner* of the Restauration of such a person consists, in, (1.) His *Testification* of his Repentance unto the satisfaction of the Church. (2.) The *express Consent* of the Church unto his Reception. (3.) His *renewed Ingagement* in the Covenant of the Church, whereby he is re-instated, or

jointed

jointed again in the Body, in his own proper place. In all which the Elders, by their Authority, are to go before the Church.

ALL sorts of persons do now condemn the Opinions of the *Novatians,* in refusing the *Re-admission* of lapsed Sinners into the Church upon Repentance. But there may be an Evil observed amongst some, leading that way, or unto what is worse: And this is, that they seek not after the *Recovery* of those that are Excommunicated, by Prayer, Admonition, Exhortation in a spirit of Meekness and Tenderness; but are well satisfied that they have *quitted* themselves of their Society. It is better never to *Excommunicate* any, than so to carry it towards them when they are Excommunicated. But there is a sort of Men, unto whom if a Man be *once an Offender,* he shall be so for ever.

XI. OUR last Enquiry shall be, *Whether Excommunication may be regular and valid, where the matter of Right is dubious and disputable?* As many such cases may fall out, especially with respect unto the occasions of Life, and mutual Converse; or when the matter of Fact is not duly proved by positive Witnesses, on the one hand, and is denied on the other.

Answ. 1. THE foundation of the *Efficacy* of Excommunication, next and under its Divine Institution, lies in the *Light* and Conviction of the Consciences of them that are to be Excommunicated. If these are not affected with a sense of Guilt, as in *dubious cases* they may not be, the sentence will be of no Force nor Efficacy.

2. A CASE wherein there is a difference in the judgment of *good and wise Men* about it, is to be esteemed such a *dubious* Case as is exempted from this Censure. Nothing is to be admitted here to take place, but what is reprovable by natural Light, and the concurrent Judgment of them that fear God.

3. IF the case be about such a Right or Wrong, in pretended Fraud, Over-reaching, or the like, as is determinable by
Civil-

Civil-Laws, the Church is no judge in such Cases; unless it be by way of Arbitration, 1 *Cor.* 6.

4. IF the Question be about *Doctrines* that are not in Points fundamental, so as those who dissent from the Church do carry it peaceably and orderly, there can be no proceedure unto Ecclesiastical Censures: But if Men will *do at on their own Opinions*, wrangling, contending, and breaking the Peace of the Church about them, there are other Rules given in that case.

5. IF the *matter of Fact* be to be determined and stated by Witness, it is absolutely necessary, by virtue of Divine Institution, that there be *Two or Three* concurrent Testimonies; one Witness is not to be regarded. See *Deut.* 19. 15. *Numb.* 35. 30. *Matth.* 18. 16, &c. Wherefore the ensuing Rules or Directions are to be observed in the matter of Excommunication.

1. NO Excommunication is to be allowed in *cases Dubious* and Disputable, wherein Right and Wrong are not easily determinable unto all unprejudiced persons, that know the Will of God in such things. Nor is it to be admitted when the matter of Fact stands in need of Testimony, and is not proved by *Two Witnesses* at the least.

2. ALL Prejudices, all Partiality, all Provocations, all Haste and Precipitation, are most carefully to be avoided in this Administration; for the Judgment is the Lords. Wherefore,

3. WE are continually, in all things that *tend unto this Sentence*, and eminently in the Sentence it self, to charge our Consciences with the Mind of Christ, and what he would do himself in the case; considering his Love, Grace, Mercy and Patience; with instances of his Condescension which he gave us in this World.

4. THERE is also required of us herein, a constant Remembrance, *that we also are in the Flesh*, and liable to Temptation, which may restrain and keep in awe that forwardness and confidence which some are apt to manifest in such cases. In all these things, a *watchful Eye* is to be kept over the *methods of Satan*; who by all means seeks to pervert this Ordinance unto the Destruction of Men, which is appointed for their Edification;

Edification; and too often prevails in that Design. And if by the Negligence of a Church in the management and pursuit of this Ordinance, he gets advantage to pervert it, unto the Ruine of any, it is the fault of that Church, in that they have not been careful of the Honour of Christ, therein. Wherefore,

1. AS Excommunication by a *cursed Noise and Clamor with Bell, Book and Candle* (such as we have instances of in some Papal Councils) is an horrible Anti-christian Abomination. So,

2. IT is an undue Representation of Christ and his Authority, for persons openly guilty of *profaneness in sinning*, to Excommunicate them who are *blameless* in all Christian Obedience.

3. ALL Excommunication is *Evangelically* null where there is wanting an *Evangelical frame of spirit* in those by whom it is Administred; and there is present an Anti-evangelical Order in its Administration.

4. IT is sufficiently evident, that after all the Contests and Disputes about this *Excommunication* that have been in the World, the Noise that it hath made, the horrible Abuses that it hath been put unto, the wresting of all Church-Order and Rule to give countenance unto a corrupt Administration of it, with the needless Oppositions that have been made against its Institution; there is nothing in it, nothing belongs unto it, nothing required unto its Administration, wherein Mens outward Interests are at all concerned, and which the smallest number of sincere Christians in any Church-Society, may not perform and discharge unto the Glory of Christ, and their own Edification.

IT is the *Mystery of Iniquity* that hath traversed these things into such a state and posture, as is unintelligible unto spiritual Wisdom, unpracticable in the Obedience of Faith, and ruinous unto all Evangelical Order and Discipline.

CHAP.

CHAP. XI.

Of the Communion of Churches.

CHURCHES so appointed, and established in Order, as hath been declared, ought to *hold Communion among themselves*, or with each other, as unto all the ends of their Institution and Order: For these are the same in all. Yea, the *general end* of them, is in Order of Nature considered antecedently unto their Institution in *particular*. This end is the *Edification* of the Body of Christ in general, or the *Church Catholick*. The promotion hereof is committed jointly and severally unto all *particular Churches*. Wherefore, with respect hereunto, they are obliged unto *mutual Communion* among themselves, which is their *consent, endeavour and conjunction in and for the promotion of the Edification of the Catholick Church, and therin their own, as they are Parts and Members of it.*

THIS Communion is incumbent on *every Church*, with respect unto all other Churches of Christ in the World equally. And the Duties and Acts of it in all of them, are of the same kind and nature. For there is no such *disparity* between them, or *subordination* among them, as should make a difference between the Acts of their mutual Communion; so as that the Acts of some should be Acts of *Authority*, and those of others Acts of *obedience* or subjection. Where ever there is a Church, whether it be at *Rome* or *Egubium*, in a *City* or a *Village*, the Communion of them all is *mutual*, the *Acts* of it of the same kind; however one Church may have more *Advantages* to be useful and helpful therein than another. And the abuse of those *Advantages* was that which wrought effectually in the beginning of that disorder, which at length destroyed the *Catholick Church*, with all Church-Communion whatever. For some Churches, especially that of *Rome*, having many

Advantages,

Of the Communion of Churches.

Advantages, in *Gifts, Abilities, Numbers* and *Reputation* above many, above most Churches for *usefulness* in their mutual Communion; the *Guides* of it insensibly turned and perverted the *Addresses* made unto them, the *Advises* and Assistances desired of them in way of Communion, or their pretences of such *Addresses* and *Desires*, into an Usurpation, first of a *primacy of Honour*, then of *Order*, then of *Supremacy* and Jurisdiction, unto the utter overthrow of all Church-Order and Communion, and at length of the whole nature of the *Catholick Church*, as stated and subsisting in *particular Churches*, as we shall see.

ALL Churches on their first institution, quickly found themselves indigent and wanting, though not as unto their *Being, Power* and *Order*; yet as unto their *well-being*, with their preservation in Truth and Order, upon extraordinary Occurrences, as also with respect unto their *usefulness* and *serviceableness*, unto the general end of furthering the Edification of the *Church Catholick*. The care hereof, and the making provision for this defect, was committed by our Lord Jesus Christ unto the *Apostles* during their Lives, which *Paul* calls μέριμνα πασῶν τῶν ἐκκλησιῶν, 2 Cor. 11. 28. *The care of all the Churches*. For what was only a *pressing care* and burden unto them, was afterward contended for by others, as a matter of *Dignity and Power*; the pretence of it in one especially being, turned into a *cursed Domination*, under the Stile and Title of *Servus Servorum Dei*.

BUT if a Thousand pretences should be made of supplying Churches defects after the decease of the Apostles, by any other Order, Way or Means, besides this of the equal *Communion* of Churches among themselves, they will be all found destitute of any Countenance from the Scripture, Primitive Antiquity, the nature, use, and end of Churches, yea, of Christian Religion it self. Yet the pretence hereof is the sole foundation of all that disposal of Churches into *several stories of Subordination*, with an Authority and Jurisdiction over one another, which now prevails in the World. But there is no place for such Imaginations, until it be proved, either that our Lord Jesus Christ hath not appointed the *mutual Communion of Churches among themselves* by their own consent; or that it is not sufficient for the preservation of the *Union*, and furtherance of the Edification of the *Church Catholick*, whereunto it is designed.

WHEREFORE, our Lord Jesus Christ, in his *infinite Wisdom*, hath constituted his Churches in such a State and Order, as wherein none of them are able of themselves, always and in all instances, to attain all the ends for which they are appointed, with respect unto the *Edification* of the *Church Catholick*. And he did it for this end, that whereas the whole *Catholick Church* is animated by *one spirit*, which is the bond of Union between all particular Churches, (as we shall see) every one of them may Act the Gifts and Graces of it unto the Preservation and Edification of the whole.

HEREIN then, we acknowledge, lieth the great difference which we have with others about the state of the Church of Christ in this World; we do believe that the *mutual Communion of particular Churches amongst themselves*, in an equality of Power and Order, though not of Gifts and Usefulness, is the only way appointed by our Lord Jesus Christ after the Death of the Apostles, for the attaining the general end of all particular Churches, which is the *Edification of the Church Catholick*, in Faith, Love and Peace. Other ways and means have been found out in the World for this end, which we must speak unto immediately. Wherefore, it behoveth us to use some Diligence in the consideration of the *Causes*, *Nature* and *Use* of this Communion of Churches.

BUT it must be moreover premised, that whereas this *Communion of Churches* is *Radically* and *Essentially* the same among all Churches in the World, yet, as unto the ordinary *actual exercise* of the Duties of it, it is confined and limited by Divine Providence, unto such Churches, as the natural means of the discharge of such Duties may extend unto. That is unto those which are planted within such *Lines of Communication*, such precincts or boundaries of Places and Countries, as may not render the mutual performance of such Duties insuperably

perably difficult. Yet is not the World it felf fo wide, but that all places being made pervious by Navigation, this Communion of Churches may be *visibly professed*, and in some instances practised among all Churches, *from the rising of the Sun even unto the going-down of the same, where the Name of Christ is known among the Gentiles*; wherein the true nature of the Catholick Church and its Union doth consist, which is utterly overthrown by the most vehement pretences that are made unto it, as those in the Church of *Rome*.

WHEREFORE such a *Communion of Churches* is to be enquired after, as from which no true Church of Christ is or can be excluded; in whose actual exercise they may and ought all to live, and whereby the general end of all Churches in the Edification of the Catholick Church may be attained. This is the true and only *Catholicism* of the Church, which whoever departs from, or substitutes any thing else in the room of it, under that Name, destroys its whole nature, and disturbs the whole *Ecclesiastical Harmony*, that is, of Christs Institution.

HOWEVER therefore we plead for the *Rights of particular Churches*, yet our real Controversy with most in the World, is for the Being, Union and Communion of the *Church Catholick*, which are variously perverted by many, and separating it into Parties, and confining it to Rules, Measures and *Canons* of their own finding out and Establishment. For such things as these, belong neither to the *internal* nor *external* Form of *that Catholick Church*, whose *Being* in the World we believe, and whose *Union* we are obliged to preserve. And whoever gives any Description of, or Limitation to the *Catholick Church*, besides what consist in the Communion of particular Churches intended, doth utterly overthrow it, and therein an *Article* of our Faith.

BUT this *Communion of Churches* cannot be duly apprehended, unless we enquire and determine wherein their *Union* doth consist. For *Communion* is an Act of *Union*, that receives both its Nature and Power from it, or by virtue of it. For of what Nature soever the *Union* of things distinct in themselves be, of the same is the *Communion* that they have among themselves.

IN the Church of *Rome*, the *Person of the Pope*, as he is *Pope*, is the Head and Center of all Church Union. Nor is there allowed any *Union of particular Churches* with Christ or among themselves, but in and through him. An Universal subjection unto him and his Authority, is the original spring of all *Church Union* among them. And if any one Soul fail herein, if as unto things of Faith and Divine Worship, he do not depend on the *Pope*, and live in subjection unto him, he is reputed a Stranger and Foreigner unto the *Catholick Church*. Yea, they affirm, that be a Man never so willing for, and desirous of an *Interest in Christ*, he cannot have it but by the *Pope*.

THE Communion of Churches *congenial* and suited unto this Union, proceeding from it, and exercised by virtue of it, ariseth from a various *contignation* of Order, or the erection of one story of Church Interest upon another, until we come to the Idol placed on the top of this *Babel*. So is this Communion carried on from the obedience and subjection of the lowest rubbish of Ecclesiastical Order, unto *Diocesans*, of them to *Metropolitans*, of them to *Patriarchs* or *Cardinals*, of them to the *Pope*; or an ascent is made from *Diocesan Synods*, by *Provincial* and *National*, to those that are called *Oecumenical*, whose Head is the *Pope*.

YET Two things must be farther observed to clear this *Communion of the Roman Catholick Church*; as, (1.) That there is no *ascent* of Church-Order or Power by *a vital Act of Communion* from the lower Degrees, Orders or Consociations, and by them to the *Pope*, as though he should receive any thing of Church-Power from them; but all the *plenitude* of it being originally vested in him, by these several Orders and Degrees, he communicates of it unto all Churches, as the Life of their Conjunction and Communion. (2.) That no Man is so jointed in this Order, so compacted in this Body, but that he is also personally and immediately subject to the *Pope*, and depends on him as unto his whole profession of Religion.

AND this is that which constitutes him formally to be what he is, that is *Antichrist*; and the Church-State arising from its
Union

Union unto him, *holding him as its Head,* subsisting in a Communion by virtue of power received through various Orders and Constitutions from him, to be *Anti-christian.* For he and it, are set up in the room of, and in direct opposition unto the Lord Christ, as the Head of the Catholick Church, and the Church state thereon depending. This we have described, *Ephes.* 4. 15, 16. *Speaking the Truth in Love, may grow up,* &c. As also, *Col.* 2. 19. Where there is a Rejection of them who belong not unto the *Church Catholick,* taken from its Relation unto Christ, and the nature of its dependance on him; *not holding the Head,* &c.

WHEN Men shall cease to be wilfully blind, or when the *powers of the strong Delusion* that begin to abate shall expire, they will easily see the direct Opposition that is between these two Heads and two Churches, namely *Christ* and the *Pope,* the *Catholick Church* and that of *Rome.*

I KNOW well enough all the Evasions and Distinctions that are invented to countenance this *Anti-christianism.* As that there is a double Head, one of *internal influence* of Grace which Christ is, and the Pope is not; the other of *Rule and Authority,* which the Pope is. But this also is two-fold; *Supream* and *Remote;* or *Immediate* and *Subordinate;* the first is Christ, the latter is the Pope. And there is yet farther a two-fold Head of the Church, the one *invisible* which is Christ; the other *visible* which is the Pope.

NOT to insist on these gross and horrible Figments of a *twofold Head of the Catholick Church* in any sence, which are foreign to the Scripture, foreign to Antiquity, whereof never one word was heard in the Church for Six hundred Years after Christ, deforming the beautiful Spouse of Christ into a Monster; we will allow at present, that the Pope is only the *immediate, visible, subordinate Head of all Rule and Authority to their Church,* which is what they plead for. Then I say that the Church whereof he is the *Head* is his *Body*; that it holds him *as its Head*; that it is *compacted together* by the Officers and Orders that depend on him, and receive all their influence of Church-Power and Order from him, which
though

though he communicates not by an *internal influence* of Grace and Gifts (alas poor wretch,) yet he doth it by *Officers, Offices, Orders* and *Laws*; so giving Union and Communion unto the whole Body by the effectual working of every joint and part of the *Hierarchy* under him, for its Union, Communion and Edification. This, I say, is the *Anti-christ*, and the *Antichristian Church-State*, as I shall be at any time ready to maintain.

LET any Man take a due prospect of this *Head*, and this *Body* as related and united by the Bond of their own *Rules, Constitutions* and *Laws*, acting in worldly Pomp, Splendor and Power with horrid bloody Cruelties against all that oppose it, and he will not fail of an open view of all the Scriptural Lineaments of the *Apostate Anti-christian State of the Church*.

I SAY again, This assigning of the *original* of all Church Order, Union and Communion unto the *Pope of Rome*, investing him therewith as an *Article of Faith*, constituting him thereby the *Head of the Church*; and the Church thereon his *Body*, as it must be if he be its *Head*; so as that from him all power of Order, and for all Acts of Communion, should be derived, returning all in Obedience and Subjection unto him, doth set up a visible, conspicuous *Anti-christian Church State*, in opposition unto Christ and the Catholick Church. But with this sort of Men we deal not at present.

THERE is a pretence unto an *Union of Churches* not derived from the *Papal* Headship. And this consists in the *Canonical subjection of particular Churches* unto a *Diocesan Bishop*; and of such *Bishops* to *Metropolitans*; which though *de facto* it be at present terminated and stated within the bounds of a Nation; yet *de jure* it ought to be extended unto the whole *Catholick Church*.

ACCORDING unto this Principle, the *Union of the Catholick Church* consists in that Order, whereby particular Churches are distributed into *Deanaries, Arch-Deaconries, Exempt Peculiars*, under *Officials*; *Dioceses, Provinces*, under *Metropolitans*, and so by or without *Patriarchs* to avoid the Rock of the *Papacy*, issuing in a *General Council*, as I suppose. But,

1. TO

Of the Communion of Churches.

1. TO confine the *Union and Communion of the Catholick Church* hereunto, is at present absolutely destructive both of the Church and its Communion. For all *particular Churches*, when they are by a coalescency extended unto those, which are *Provincial* or *National*, have both *Politically* and *Ecclesiastically* such bounds fixed unto them, as they cannot pass to carry on Communion unto, and with the Church *as Catholick*, by any Acts and Duties belonging unto their Order: And hereby the Union and Communion of the Church is utterly lost. For the Union of the *Catholick Church*, as such, doth always equally exist, and the Communion of it is always equally in exercise, and can consist in nothing but what doth so exist and is so exercised. Where-ever is the *Catholick Church*, there is the *Communion of Saints*. But nothing of this can be obtained by virtue of this Order.

2. WE enquire at present after such an *Union* as gives particular Churches *Communion* among themselves; which this Order doth not, but absolutely overthrows it; leaving nothing unto them but subjection to *Officers* set over them, who are not of them, according to Rules and Laws of their appointment; which is foreign to the Scripture and Antiquity.

3. THIS Order it self, the only bond of the pretended Union having no *Divine Institution*, especially as to its extent unto the whole *Catholick Church*, nor any intimation in the Scripture, and being utterly impossible to be put in execution or actual *exercise*, no Man can declare what is the *Original* or *Center* of it, whence it is deduced, and wherein it rests.

HAVING removed these pretences out of our way, we may easily discern wherein the *Union*, and consequently the *Communion* of all particular Churches doth consist, and in the due observation whereof, all that Church-Order which the Lord Christ hath appointed and doth accept, is preserved.

I SAY then, that the *true and only Union* of all particular Churches, consists in that which gives Form, Life and Being unto the *Church Catholick*, with the Addition of what belongs unto them as they are *particular*. And this is, that they have all

all *one and the same God and Father, one Lord Jesus Christ, one Faith and one Doctrine of Faith, one hope of their calling* or *the promised Inheritance, one Regeneration, one Baptism, one Bread and Wine ; united unto God and Christ in one Spirit, through the bond of Faith and Love.*

THIS Description, with what is suited thereunto, and explanatory of it, is *all the account* which is given us in the Scripture of the constituting form of the *Catholick Church,* and of the *Union* of particular Churches among themselves. What Church soever fails in the *essential parts* of this Description, or any of them, it is separated from the *Catholick Church,* nor hath either Union or Communion with any true Churches of Christ.

TWO things concurr unto the compleating of this *Union* of Churches. (1.) Their *Union* or *Relation* unto Christ. (2.) That which they have *among themselves.*

1. THE Lord Christ himself is the *Original and Spring of this Union,* and every particular Church is united unto him as its Head, besides which, with or under which, it hath none. This Relation of the Church unto Christ as its Head, the Apostle expresly affirms to be the foundation and cause of its Union, *Ephes.* 4. 15, 16. *Col.* 2. 19. the places before quoted. Hereby it is also *in God the Father,* 2 *Thes.* 1. 1. Or hath God as its Father. And unless this Union be dissolved, unless a Church be *disunited* from Christ, it cannot be so from the *Catholick Church,* nor any true Church of Christ in particular; however, it may be dealt withal by others in the World.

FROM Christ, as the Head and Spring of Union, there proceedeth unto all particular Churches, a *bond of Union,* which is his *Holy Spirit,* acting it self in them by Faith and Love, in and by the ways and means, and for the ends of his appointment.

THIS is the *Kingly, Royal, Beautiful Union* of the Church. Christ, as the only head of Influence and Rule bringing it into a Relation unto himself as his Body, communicating of his *Spirit* unto it, governing it by the *Law of his Word,* enabling it unto all the Duties of Faith, Love and Holiness.

Of the Communion of Churches.

FOR unto the *compleating of this Union* on the part of the Church, thefe things are required. (1.) Faith in him, or *holding him as the Head*, in the fincere belief of all things concerning his Perfon, Office and Doctrine in the Gofpel, with whatever belongs thereunto. (2.) *Love unto him* and all that is his. (3.) That *efpecial Holinefs*, whofe foundation is Repentance and Effectual Vocation. (4.) The *Obfervance of his Commands*, as unto all Duties of Divine Worfhip. Thefe things are effentially requifite unto this Union on the part of the Church. The Reality and Power of them, is the *internal form* of the Church; and the profeffion of them is its *external form*.

2. THERE concurreth hereunto *an Union among themfelves*, I mean all particular Churches throughout the World, in whom the *Church Catholick* doth Act its Power and Duty. And the Relation that is between thefe Churches, is that which is termed *Relatio æquiparentiæ*, wherein neither of the *Relata* is the firft foundation of it; but they are *equal*. It doth not arife from the *Subordination* of one unto another, they being all equal as unto what concerns their Effence and Power. And the bond hereof is that *efpecial Love* which Chrift requireth among all his Difciples, acting it felf unto all the ends of the Edification of the whole Body.

TAKE in the whole, and the Union of Churches confifts in *their Relation unto God as their Father, and unto Chrift as their only immediate Head of Influence and Rule, with a participation of the fame Spirit, in the fame Faith and Doctrine of Truth, the fame kind of Holinefs, the fame Duties of Divine Worfhip, efpecially the fame Myfteries of Baptifm and the Supper, the obfervance of the fame Rules or Commands of Chrift in all Church-Order, with mutual Love, effectual unto all the ends of their Being and Conftitution, or the Edification of the Church Catholick*.

THERE may be *failures* in them or fome of them, as unto fundry of thefe things; there may be *differences* among them about them, arifing from the Infirmities, Ignorance and Prejudices of them of whom they do confift, the beft knowing here but in part; but whilft the *fubftance* of them is preferved, the Union of all Churches, and so of the Catholick Church is preserved.

THIS is that blessed *oneness* which the Lord Christ prayed for so earnestly for his Disciples, that they might be *one in the Father and the Son, one among themselves,* and *made perfect in one,* Joh. 17. 20, 21, 22, 23. without any respect unto that *horrid Image* of it, which was set up in the latter days of the Church, which all Men were compelled to bow down unto, and Worship, with the fire of *Nebuchadnezzars* Furnance. Of any other Union there is not the least mention in the Scripture.

THIS Union of the Catholick Church in all particular Churches, is always the same, inviolable, unchangeable, comprehending all the Churches in the World at all times; not confinable unto any State or Party, not interruptible by any external form, nor to be prevailed against by the *Gates of Hell*; and all such Disputes about a *Catholick Church,* and its *Union,* as can be so much as *questionable* among them that profess to believe the Gospel, are in direct opposition unto the Prayers and Promises of Jesus Christ. Whilst *Evangelical Faith, Holiness, Obedience unto the Commands of Christ,* and *Mutual Love* abide in any on the Earth, there is the *Catholick Church*; and whilst they are professed, that *Catholick Church is visible*; other Catholick Church upon the Earth I believe none; nor any that needs other things unto its Constitution.

THESE things being premised, I proceed unto that which is our present Enquiry, namely, *Wherein the Communion of particular Churches among themselves doth consist*.

THE Communion of Churches, is *their joint actings in the same Gospel Duties towards God in Christ, with their mutual actings towards each other, with respect unto the end of their Institution and Being, which is the Glory of Christ in the Edification of the whole Catholick Church*.

AS unto the actings of the first sort, the ground of them is *Faith,* and therein is the *first Act* of the Communion of Churches. And this Communion in Faith among all the Churches of Christ is two-fold. (1.) *General* in the belief of the same Doctrine of Truth, which is according unto
Godliness,

Of the Communion of Churches.

Godliness, the same Articles of Faith, and the publick profession thereof; so that every one of them is the *Ground and Pillar of the same Truth*. This the Primitive Church provided for in *Creeds* and *Symbols*, or Confessions of Faith, as is known. But as never any one of them was expresly owned by all Churches; so in process of time they came to be abused, as expressing the sence of the present Church, whether true or false. Hence we have as many *Arian Creeds* yet extant, as those that are *Orthodox*. But unto the Communion of all particular Churches in the World, there is nothing required but a *belief of the Scripture to be the Word of God*, with a professed assent unto all Divine Revelations therein contained; provided that no Error be avowed that is contrary to the principal or fundamental Doctrines of it. For although any *Society of Men* should profess the Scripture to be the Word of God, and avow an Assent unto the Revelations made therein, yet by the conceptions of their Minds, and misunderstanding of the sence of the Holy Spirit therein, they may embrace and adhere unto *such Errors*, as may cut them off from all Communion with the Catholick Church in Faith. Such are the denial of the *holy Trinity*, the *Incarnation of the Son of God*, *His Divine Person or Office*, the *Redemption of the Church by his Blood*; the *necessity of Regeneration by his Spirit*, and the like. And they may also add that of their own unto their professed Belief, as shall exclude them from Communion with the Catholick Church. Such are the *Assertion of Traditions* as equal with the written Word; of *another Head of the Church* besides the Lord Christ; of *another Sacrifice* besides what he once offered for all; and the like. But where any are preserved from such *Heresies* on the one hand and the other, there is no more required unto *Communion* with the whole Church, as unto Faith in general, but only the Belief before described.

2. THIS *Communion in Faith* respects the Church it self as its *material Object*. For it is required hereunto, that we believe that the Lord Christ hath had in all Ages, and especially hath in that wherein we live, *a Church on the Earth*, confined

fined unto no *Places* nor *Parties* of Men, no *Empires* nor *Dominions*, or capable of any confinement; as also that *this Church is Redeemed, Called, Sanctified by him*; that it is his *Kingdom*, his Interest, his concernment in the World; that thereunto, and all the Members of it, all the *Promises of God* do belong and are confined; that this *Church* he will *save*, preserve and deliver from all oppositions, so as that the *Gates of Hell* shall not prevail against it; and after Death will raise it up and glorify it at the last day. This is the *Faith of the Catholick Church concerning it self*; which is an Ancient fundamental Article of our Religion. And if any one deny that there is *such a Church* called out of the World, separated from it, unto which alone, and all the Members of it, all the *Promises of God* do appertain, in contradistinction unto all others, or confines it unto a Party, unto whom these things are not appropriate, he cuts himself off from the *Communion* of the Church of Christ.

IN the Faith hereof, all the true Churches of Christ throughout the World, have a comforting refreshing *Communion*, which is the spring of many Duties in them continually.

3. THIS *Communion of Churches in Faith*, consists much in the principal Fruit of it; namely, *Prayer*. So is it stated, *Ephes.* 2. 18. *For through Christ we have an Access by one Spirit unto the Father*. And that therein the Communion of the Catholick Church doth consist, the Apostle declares in the following Verses; 19, 20, 21, 22. *Now therefore*, &c. For *Prayer* in all Churches having *one object*, which is God even the Father, God as the Father, proceeding in all from one and the *same Spirit*, given unto them as a Spirit of Grace and Supplications to make Intercession for them, and all of them continually offered unto God by the *same High-Priest*, who adds unto it the Incense of his own Intercession, and by whom they have all an access unto the same Throne of Grace, they have all a *blessed Communion* herein continually. And this *Communion* is the more express in that the *Prayers of all are for all*; so as that there is no particular Church of Christ in the World, not any one Member of any of them, but they have *the Prayers*

of

of all the Churches in the World, and of *all the Members* of them every day. And however this Communion be invisible unto the eyes of Flesh, yet is it glorious and conspicuous unto the eye of Faith; and is a part of the glory of Christ the Mediatour in Heaven. This *Prayer* proceeding from, or wrought by one and the *same Spirit* in them all, equally bestowed on them all, by virtue of the Promise of Christ; having the *same object*, even God as a Father, and offered unto him by the same *High-Priest*, together with his own Intercession, gives unto all Churches a *Communion*, far more glorious than what consists in some outward Rites and Orders of Mens devising.

BUT now if there be any other Persons or Churches, who have any *other Object of their Prayers*, but God even the Father, and as our Father in Christ; or have any other *Mediators* or *Intercessors*, by whom to convey or present their Prayers unto God, but Christ alone, the only *High-Priest* of the Church; or do renounce the *Aid and Assistance of the Holy Spirit*, as a Spirit of Grace and Supplications, they cut themselves off from all Communion with the Catholick Church herein.

4. THE *Unity of Faith* in all Churches, affecteth Communion among them, in the *Administration of the same Sacraments of Baptism and the Supper of the Lord*. These are the same in, unto, and amongst them all. Neither do some, variations in the *outward manner* of their Administration, interrupt that Communion. But, where-ever the *continuation* of these Ordinances is denied, or their nature or use is perverted, or Idolatrous Worship is annexed unto their Administration, there *Communion with the Catholick Church* is renounced.

5. THEY have also by Faith Communion herein, in that all *Churches do profess a subjection unto the Authority of Christ in all things*, and an obligation upon them to do and observe all whatsoever he hath Commanded.

OTHER instances of the like nature might be given; but these are sufficient to manifest how *unscriptural* the Notion is, That there is no proper Communion with or among Churches but what consists in a compliance with certain *Powers*, Orders

and

and *Rites*, the pressing whereof under the Name of *Uniformity*, hath cast all thoughts of real, Evangelical Church Communion into Oblivion.

SECONDLY, Churches Ordained and Constituted in the way and manner, and for the Ends declared in our former Discourse on this Subject, and by virtue of their Union unto Christ and among themselves, living constantly in all places of the World in the actual exercise of that Communion, which consists in the performance of the same Church-Duties towards God in Christ, unto their own Continuation, Encrease, and Edification, have also an *especial Union among themselves, and a mutual Communion thence arising*.

THE *Bond of this Union is Love*; not the common regulated Affection of Humane nature so called; not meerly that Power and Duty which is engraven on the Hearts of Men, by the Law of Creation, towards all of the same kind and blood with themselves; but an *especial Grace of the Holy Spirit*, acting in the Church as the Principle and Bond of its Union unto its self; whence the command of it is called a *New Commandment*; because in it self, as unto the *only Example* of it in the Person of Christ, the Causes and Motives unto it, with its peculiar Ends and proper Exercise, it was absolutely *New* and *Evangelical*. An Explanation of the Nature of it belongs not unto this place although it be a *Grace and a Duty* of so much importance, wherein so much of the Life, Power and peculiar Glory of Christian Religion doth consist, and is either so utterly lost, or hath such *vile Images* of it set up in the World, that it deserves a full Consideration; which it may receive in another place.

I SAY the *Holy Spirit of Grace and Love*, being given from Christ, the Fountain and Center of all Church-Union, to dwell in, and abide with his Church, thereby uniting it unto himself, doth work in it, and all the Members of it, that *mutual Love*, which may, and doth animate them unto all those mutual Acts which are proper unto the Relation wherein they stand, by virtue of their Union unto Christ their Head, as Members of the same Body one with another.

HEREIN

Of the Communion of Churches.

HEREIN confists the Union of every Church in it felf, of all Churches among themfelves, and fo of the whole Catholick Church; their Communion confifting in regular Acts and Duties, proceeding from this *Love,* and required by virtue of it.

THIS account of the *Union* and *Communion* of Churches may feem ftrange unto fome, who are enamoured on that *Image* which is fet up of them in the World, in *Canons, Conftitutions* of *Rites,* and *outward Order* in *various Subordinations* and *Ceremonies,* which are moft remote from making any due Reprefentation of them.

THE Church, in its dependance on Chrift its Head, being by his Inftitution difpofed unto its proper Order for its own Edification, or *fitly joined together and compacted,* this Love working effectually in every Office, Officer and Member, according as unto its difpofal in the Body, for the receiving and communicating Supplies for Edification, gives the whole both its *Union* and *Communion,* all the actings of it being regulated by Divine Rule and Prefcription.

INSTEAD hereof to erect a *Machine,* the Spring and Center of whofe motions are unknown, any other, I mean, but *external force compacted by the Iron joints and bands of humane Laws,* edifying it felf by the *power of Offices and Officers,* foreign unto the Scripture, acting with *Weapons that are not Spiritual,* but Carnal, and mighty through him whofe Work it is to caft the Members of the Church of Chrift into Prifon, as unto an outward Conformity, is to forfake the Scripture and follow our own Imagination.

THE *outward Acts of Communion* among Churches, proceeding from this love, and the obligation that is on them to promote their mutual Edification, may be referred unto the Two Heads of *Advice* and *Affiftance.*

CHURCHES have Communion unto their mutual Edification, by *Advice* in *Synods* or *Councils,* which muft in this place be confidered.

SYNODS are the Meetings of divers Churches by their Meffengers or Delegates, to confult and determine of fuch things as are of common concernment unto them all, by virtue of this Communion which is exercifed in them.

1. THE

Of the Communion of Churches.

1. THE necessity and warranty of *such Synods*, ariseth, (1.) From the *Light of Nature.* For all Societies which have the same Original, the same Rule, the same Interest, the same Ends, and which are in themselves mutually concerned in the good or evil of each other, are obliged by the power and conduct of Reason, to *advise* in common for their own good, on all *Emergencies* that stand in need thereof.

CHURCHES are such *Societies*; they have all one and the same *Authoritative Institution*, one and the same *Rule of Order* and Worship, the same ends as we have declared; and their entire Interest is one and the same. When therefore any thing occurs amongst them, that is attended with such Difficulties as cannot be removed or taken away by any one of them severally, or in whose *Determination* all of them are equally concerned, not to make use herein of common Advice and Counsel, is to forsake that natural Light which they are bound to attend unto in all Duties of Obedience unto God.

2. THE *Union of all Churches*, before described *in* one Head, *by* one Spirit, *through* one Faith and Worship, *unto* the same ends, doth so *compact them into one Body mystical*, as that none of them is or can be compleat absolutely without a joint acting with other Members of the same Body unto the common good of the whole, as occasion doth require. And this joint acting with others in any Church, can be no otherwise, but by *common Advice* and *Counsel*, which natural Circumstances render impossible by any means but their *convention in Synods*, by their Messengers and Delegates. For although there may be some use of *Letters missive*, and was so eminently in the Primitive Churches, to ask the *Advice* of one another in difficult Cases, (as the first instance we have of the *Communion* of Churches after the days of the Apostles, is in the Letter of the Church of *Corinth* unto that of *Rome*, desiring their *Advice* about the composing of a difference among them, and the Answer of the Church of *Rome* thereunto;) yet many Cases may fall out among them, which cannot be Reconciled or Determined but by *present Conference*, such as that was Recorded, *Act.* 15. No Church therefore is so *Independent*, as that it can always,

always, and in all Cases, observe the Duties it owes unto the Lord Christ and the Church Catholick, by all those Powers which it is able to act in it self distinctly, without conjunction with others. And the Church that confines its Duty unto the *Acts of its own Assemblies*, cuts it self off from the external Communion of the *Church Catholick*; nor will it be safe for any Man to commit the Conduct of his Soul to such a Church. Wherefore,

3. THIS *acting in Synods* is an Institution of Jesus Christ; not in an express Command, but in the nature of the thing it self fortified with *Apostolical* Example. For having erected such a Church-State, and disposed all his Churches into that Order and mutual Relation unto one another, as that none of them can be compleat, or discharge their whole Duty without *mutual Advice and Counsel*; he hath thereby ordained this way of their Communion in *Synods*, no other being possible unto that end. And hereby such Conventions are interested in the promise of his *presence*; namely, that *where Two or Three are gathered together in his Name, there he will be in the midst of them*. For these Assemblies being the necessary effect of his own *constitution* in the nature and use of his Churches, are or may be *in his Name*, and so enjoy his presence.

4. THE *end* of all particular Churches is the Edification of the *Church Catholick* unto the Glory of God in Christ. And it is evident, that in many Instances this cannot be *attained*, yea, that it must be *sinfully neglected*, unless this way for the preservation and carrying of it on be attended unto. Truth, Peace and Love may be lost among Churches, and so the *Union of the Catholick Church* in them be dissolved, unless this means for their Preservation and Reparation be made use of. And that particular Church which extends not its Duty beyond its own Assemblies and Members, is *fallen off* from the principal end of its Institution. And every Principle, Opinion, or Perswasion, that inclines any Church to confine its Care and Duty unto its own Edification only; yea, or of those only which agree with it in some *peculiar practice*, making it neglective of all due means of the Edification of the Church Catholick, is *Schismatical*.

5. THERE

Of the Communion of Churches.

5. THERE is direction hereunto included in the *Order and Method* of Church-Proceedings in case of offence, prescribed unto it by Christ himself. The beginning and rise of it, is between *two individual Persons*; thence is it carried unto the *cognizance* and *judgment* of two or three others before unconcerned; from them it is to be brought unto the *Church*; and there is no doubt but the Church hath *Power to determine* concerning it, as unto its own Communion, to continue the Offender in it or reject him from it. This must abide, as unto outward Order and the Preservation of Peace. But no Church is *Infallible* in their judgment absolutely in any case; and in many, their determinations may be so doubtful as not to affect the Conscience of him who is Censured. But such a Person is not only a Member of that *particular Church*, but by virtue thereof of the *Catholick Church* also. It is necessary therefore that he should be heard and judged as unto his *Interest* therein, if he do desire it. And this can no way be done, but by such *Synods* as we shall immediately describe.

6. SYNODS are Consecrated unto the use of the Church in all Ages, by the Example of the Apostles, in their guidance of the First Churches of *Jews and Gentiles*; which hath the force of a *Divine Institution*, as being given by them under the Infallible conduct of the Holy Ghost, *Act.* 15. which we shall speak farther unto immediately.

HAVING seen the *Original of Church Synods* or their *Formal Cause*, we consider also their *Material Cause*, or the subject matter to be treated of or determined in them. And this in general is every thing wherein Churches are obliged *to hold Communion* among themselves, when any thing falls out amongst them, which otherwise would *disturb* that Communion. And hereof some Instances may be given.

1. CHURCHES have mutual Communion in the *profession of the same Faith*. If any doubts or differences do arise about it, any Opinions be advanced contrary unto it, either in any particular Church, which they cannot determine among themselves or among sundry Churches, the *last outward means* for the preservation of the Rule of Faith among them, and of

their

the Church it self whereunto they do belong, is not able to rebuke and suppress them; nor to maintain its profession of the Truth, or that by suffering such things in one Church, others are in danger to be infected or defiled, this is the last *external Refuge* that is left for the preservation of the Communion of Churches in the same Faith. We have multiplied Examples hereof in the *Primitive Churches*, before the degeneracy of these Synods into Superstition and Domination. Such was eminently that gathered at *Antioch* for the condemnation of the Heresies of *Paulus Samosatenus* the Bishop of that Church.

2. IT is so, with respect unto that *Order*, *Peace* and *Unity*, wherein every particular Church ought to walk in it self, and amongst its own Members. There were *Schisms*, *Divisions*, *Strife* and *Contentions* in some of the Churches that were of *Apostolical* planting and watering: So there was at *Antioch*, and afterwards at *Corinth*, as also of some of the Churches in *Galatia*. The Duty of Remedying and Healing these Divisions and Differences from what cause soever they arise, is first incumbent on each particular Member in every such Church. Unto them it is given in charge by the Apostle in the first place; and if every one of them do perform their Duty in Love, an end will be put unto all strife. In case of failure therein, the *whole Church* is charged in the exercise of its Power, Authority and Wisdom, to rebuke and compose such Differences. But in case it is not able so to do, as it fell out in the Church at *Antioch*, then an *Assembly* of other Churches walking in actual Communion with that Church wherein the Difference is arisen, and thereon concerned in their Prosperity and Edification, by their *Messengers* and Delegates, is the last outward means for its Composure.

3. WHERE there hath been any *Male Administration* of Discipline,

ſcipline, whereby any Members of a Church have been injured, as ſuppoſe they are unduly *caſt out* of the Church by the Power and Intereſt of ſome *Diotrephes* ; or that any Members of the Church make a Party and Faction to depoſe their Elders, as it was in the *Church of Corinth,* when the *Church at Rome* gave them Advice in the caſe : It is neceſſary from the Communion of Churches and the Intereſt the Perſons injured have in the *Catholick Church,* whoſe Edification is the end of all Church-Adminiſtrations, that the proceedings of ſuch a Church be renewed by a *Synod,* and a Remedy provided in the caſe. Nor was it the mind of the Apoſtle that they ſhould be left without Relief, which were *unduly* caſt out of the Church by *Diotrephes* ; nor is there any other ordinary way hereof, but only by *Synods* ; but this caſe I ſuppoſe I ſhall ſpeak unto afterwards.

4. THE ſame is the caſe with reſpect unto *Worſhip,* as alſo of Manners and Converſation. If it be *reported* or known by *Credible Teſtimony* that any Church hath admitted into the exerciſe of Divine Worſhip any thing ſuperſtitious or vain, or if the Members of it walk like thoſe deſcribed by the Apoſtle, *Phil.* 3. 18, 19. unto the Diſhonour of the Goſpel and of the ways of Chriſt, the Church it ſelf not endeavouring its own Reformation and Repentance ; other Churches walking in Communion therewith, by virtue of their common Intereſt in the Glory of Chriſt, and Honour of the Goſpel, after more private ways for its Reduction, as Opportunity and Duty may ſuggeſt unto their Elders, ought to Aſſemble in a *Synod* for Advice, either as to the uſe of farther means for the Recovery of ſuch a Church, or to *with-hold Communion* from it in caſe of Obſtinacy in its evil ways. The want of a due attendance unto this part of the Communion of Churches, with reſpect unto *Goſpel Worſhip* in its Purity, and *Goſpel Obedience* in its Power, was a great means of the Decay and Apoſtacy of them all. By reaſon of this Negligence inſtead of being helpful one to another for their mutual Recovery, and the Revival of the things *that were ready to die,* they gradually infected one another, according as they fell into their Decays, and countenanced one another by their Examples unto a continuance in ſuch Diſorders. THE

Of the Communion of Churches.

THE *Image* which in late Ages was set up hereof in *Diocesan* and *Metropolitical Visitations*, and those of *lesser districts* under Officers of Anti-christian Names, hath been useful rather unto Destruction than Edification. But so it hath fallen out in most things concerning Church-Order, Worship and Discipline. The Power and Spirituality of Divine Institutions being lost, a *Machine* hath been framed to make an appearance and representation of them to divert the minds of Men from enquiring after the Primitive Institution of Christ, with an experience of their Efficacy.

CONSIDERING what we have learned in these later Ages, by woeful experience of what hath fallen out formerly amongst all the Churches in the World, as unto their *Degeneracy from Gospel Worship and Holiness*, with the abounding of Temptations in the days wherein we live, and the spiritual decays that all Churches are prone unto, it were not amiss if those Churches which do walk in express Communion, would *frequently meet in Synods* to enquire into the spiritual state of them all, and to give advice for the correction of what is amiss, the due preservation of the purity of Worship, the exercise of Discipline, but especially of the Power, Demonstration and Fruit of Evangelical Obedience.

2. HENCE it is evident what are the *ends* of such *Synods* among the Churches of Christ. The general end of them all, is to *promote the Edification* of the whole Body or Church Catholick. And that, (1.) To *prevent Divisions* from differences in judgment and practice which are contrary thereunto. The First Christian *Synod* was an Assembly of the *two First Churches* in the World by their Delegates. The First Church of the *Jews* was at *Jerusalem*, and the First Church of the *Gentiles* was at *Antioch*; to prevent Divisions, and to preserve Communion between them, was the *First Synod Celebrated*, Act. 15. (2.) To avoid or *cure offences* against mutual love among them. (3.) To advance the light of the Gospel by a *joint Confession* and Agreement in the Faith. (4.) To give a concurrent *Testimony* against pernicious Heresies or Errors, whereby the Faith of any is overthrown or in danger so to be. (5.) To relieve such by advice,

vice, as may be by any *Diotrephes* unduly cast out of the Church.

WHAT are the *ends* whereunto they have been used, may be seen in the *Volumes* written concerning them, and the *numberless Laws* enacted in them; whereof very little belongs unto the *Discipline of the Gospel*, or real Communion of Churches.

3. THE *measure* or extent of them ariseth from concernment and convenience. All unprejudiced Persons do now acknowledge, that the pretence of *Oecumenical Councils*, wherein the whole Church of Christ on the Earth, or all particular Churches should be represented, and so obliged to acquiesce in their Determinations, is a fond Imagination. And it were easie to demonstrate in particular, how every one of them which hath in *vulgar esteem* obtained that Title, were openly remote from so being. Such *Councils* never were, and, as it is improbable, never will nor can be, nor are any way needful unto the Edification of the Church.

THEIR due measure and bounds, as was said before, are given them by *concernment and convenience*; wherein respect also may be had unto the *Ability* of some Churches to promote Edification above others. Such Churches as are in the same instances concerned in the causes of them before declared, and may be helpful unto the ends mentioned, are to *convene* in such *Synods*. And this *concernment* may be either from some of those causes in themselves, or from that Duty which they owe unto other Churches which are immediately concerned. So it was in the Assistance given by the Church at *Jerusalem*, in that case which was peculiar to the Church of *Antioch*.

WITH this *interest* or *concernment*, there must be a *concurrence* of natural, moral and political Conveniences. Some Churches are planted at such distances from others, that it is naturally *impossible* that they should ever meet together to advise by their Messengers, and some at such as that they cannot assemble but with such difficulties and hazzards as exempt them from the Duty of it. And whereas they are placed under *different Civil Governments*, and those oft-times engaged in mutual enmities, and always jealous of the actings of their own Subjects in conjunction with them that are not so, they cannot so

convene

Of the Communion of Churches.

convene and preserve the outward peace of the Churches. Hence the largest of the *Councils* of old that are called *Oecumenical*, never pretended farther than the single *Roman Empire*; when there were innumerable Churches planted under the Civil Jurisdiction of other Sovereigns.

WHEREFORE in the Assembling of Churches in *Synods*, respect is to be had unto the convenience of their meeting, that it may be so far as is possible without trouble or danger. And this, with respect unto the causes or occasions of them will determine what Churches, which or how many may be necessary on such occasions to constitute a *Synod*. And it is useful hereunto, that the Churches which are planted within such a circumference as gives facility or convenience for such conventions, should by virtue of their mutual Communion, be in express readiness to *convene* on all occasions of common concernment.

AGAIN, in the assistance which in the way of *Advice* and *Counsel*, any one Church may stand in need of from others, respect is to be had in their desire, unto such Churches as are reputed and known to have the *best ability* to give Advice in the case; on which account the Church at *Antioch* addressed themselves in a peculiar manner unto the Church at *Jerusalem* which was far distant from them.

BUT in all these cases use is to be made of *Spiritual Prudence*, with respect unto all sorts of Circumstances; which, although some would deny as the privilege of even matters of Fact, and the Application of general Scripture Rules unto Practice, because we require Divine Institution unto all parts of Religious Worship; yet we must not decline from using the *best we have* in the service of Christ and his Church; rather than comply with any thing which in the whole substance of it, is foreign to his Institution.

IT was the *Roman Empire* under *one Monarch* in its Civil Distributions for Rule and Government, which gave the first rise and occasion unto a pretended *visibly Ruling Catholick Church* under one Spiritual Monarch, distributed into those that were *Patriarchal, Diocesan, Metropolitical*, and others of inferior kinds. For retaining the people in their Civil Distributions

L l whereinto

Of the Communion of Churches.

whereinto they were cast according to the Polity and Interest of the Empire, there were *Ecclesiastical* Officers assigned unto each distribution, answerable unto the Civil Officers which were ordained in the Polity of the Empire. So in answer unto *Deputies, Exarchs, Præfects, Governours of Provinces and Cities,* there were found out and erected *Patriarchs, Metropolitans, Diocesans,* in various Allotments of Territories and Powers, requiring unto their compleat State one *visible Monarchical Head,* as the *Empire* had, which was the *Pope.* And whereas the *Emperors* had not only a *Civil Rule* and Power, but a *Military* also, exercised under them by *Legates, Generals, Tribunes, Centurions,* and the like; so there was raised an *Ecclesiastical Militia* in various Orders of *Monks, Friars,* and *Votaries* of all sorts, who under their immediate *Generals* and *Præfects* did depend absolutely on the Sovereign Power of the New *Ecclesiastical Monarch.* So was the visible professing Church moulded and fashioned into an *Image* of the old *Roman Pagan Empire,* as it was foretold it should be, *Revel.* 13, 14, 15. And although this *Image* was first framed in compliance with it, and for a resemblance of it; yet in process of time it substituted it self entirely in the room of the *Empire,* taking all its Power unto it self, and doing all its Works.

FROM this distribution of various sorts of new-framed Churches in the *Roman Empire,* arose a constitution of Synods or Councils in subordination one unto another, until by sundry degrees of Ascent they arrived unto those which they called *general* under the conduct of the *Pope,* whose *Senate* they were.

BUT these things have no countenance given them by any Divine Institution, Apostolical Example, or practice of the First Churches, but are a meer product of Secular Interest working it self in a *Mystery of Iniquity.*

SINCE the Dissolution of the *Roman Empire,* Nations have been cast into *distinct Civil Governments* of their own, whose Sovereignty is in themselves, by the event of War and Counsels thereon emergent. Unto each of these it is supposed there is a *Church-State accommodated;* as the *Church of England,* the *Church of Scotland,* the *Church of France,* and the like; whose Original and Being depends on the First event of War in that

Dissolution.

Of the Communion of Churches.

Diſſolution. Unto theſe new Church-States whoſe Being, Bounds and Limits are given unto them abſolutely by thoſe of the Civil Government which they belong unto, it is thought meet that *Eccleſiaſtical Synods* ſhould be accommodated. But in what way this is to be done there is not yet an agreement; but it is not my preſent buſineſs to conſider the differences that are about it, which are known unto this Nation on a dear account. Yet this I ſhall ſay, that whereas it is eminently uſeful unto the Edification of the *Church Catholick*, that all the Churches profeſſing the ſame Doctrine of Faith, within the Limits of the ſame Supream Civil Government, ſhould hold conſtant actual Communion among themſelves unto the ends of it before mentioned, I ſee not how it can be any abridgment of the Liberty of *particular Churches*, or interfere with any of their Rights which they hold by Divine Inſtitution, if through more conſtant *leſſer Synods* for Advice, there be a communication of their mutual concerns unto thoſe that are greater, until, if occaſion require and it be expedient, there be a *general Aſſembly* of them all to adviſe about any thing wherein they are all concerned. But this is granted only with theſe Limitations: (1.) That the *Rights of particular Churches be preſerved* in the free Election of ſuch as are to be Members of all theſe *Synods*. (2.) That they aſſume no *Authority or Juriſdiction* over Churches or Perſons in things *Civil* or *Eccleſiaſtical*. (3.) That none are immediately concerned in this *proper Synodal* Power or Authority, (which what it is we ſhall enquire) who are not preſent in them by their own Delegates.

FOR that kind of *Synods* which ſome call a *Claſſis*, which is a convention of the Elders or Officers of ſundry *Parochial* Churches, diſtinguiſhed for *Preſential Communion*, ordinarily in ſome acts of it by virtue of their Office, and for the exerciſe of Office-Power, it is the conſtitution of a new kind of particular Churches, by a combination of them into one, whoſe Original diſtinction is only in the Civil Limits of their Cohabitation; which probably may be done ſometimes, and in ſome places, unto Edification.

4. THE Perſons of whom all ſorts of *Eccleſiaſtical Synods*

are to confift, muft be enquired into. And there is nothing of meer humane *prudential* conftitution that hath longer obtained in the Church, than that thofe fhould be *Officers of the Churches only*. And, whereas after the days of the Apoftles we have no Record of any *Synods* of more Churches than one, until after the diftinction was made between *Bifhops* and *Presbyters*, they were made up of both forts of them. But afterwards, thofe who were peculiarly called *Bifhops*, enclofed this Right unto themfelves; on what grounds God knows, there being no one Tittle in the Scripture, or the Light of Reafon to give them countenance therein.

IT muft therefore be affirmed, that no Perfons, by virtue of any Office meerly, have Right to be Members of *Ecclefiaftical Synods* as fuch. Neither is there either Example or Reafon to give colour unto any fuch pretence. Farther is no *Office-Power* to be exerted in fuch *Synods* as fuch, neither conjunctly by all the Members of them, nor fingly by any of them. Officers of the Church, *Bifhops, Paftors, Elders*, may be prefent in them, *ought* to be prefent in them, are meeteft for the moft part fo to be, but *meerly as fuch*, it belongs not unto them. The Care, Overfight and Rule of the Churches whereunto they do belong, the Flock among them diftinctly is committed unto them, and for that they are inftructed with Power and Authority by virtue of their Office. But as unto their conjunction in *Synods*, which is a meer act and effect of the *Communion of Churches* among themfelves, it is not committed unto them in a way of peculiar Right by virtue of their Office. If it be fo, without refpect unto the power of the Magiftrate in calling them, or of the Churches in choofing them, then it belongs unto them all; for that which belongs unto *any* of them, as fuch by virtue of Office, belongs equally unto *all*, and if it belongs unto *all*, then it belongs unto all of *one fort only*, as for inftance *Bifhops*; or unto *all of all forts*, as for inftance *Presbyters*. alfo. If it be ftated in the *latter* way, then *every Presbyter*, as fuch by virtue of his Office, hath Right and Power to be prefent in all *Ecclefiaftical Synods*, equal with that of the *Bifhops*. For although it be fuppofed that his Office is not equal unto theirs;

yet

Of the Communion of Churches. 261

yet it is so also that this Right doth equally belong unto his Office. If the *former* be avowed, namely, that this Right belongs unto *Bishops* only (such as are pleaded for) by virtue of their Office as such; then, (1.) I desire that any tolerable proof of the confinement of this Right unto such an Office be produced, either from the Scripture or Reason, or the Example of the First Churches; which as yet I have never seen. (2.) I fear not to say, that a false presumption hereof was one principal cause and means of introducing Tyranny into the Churches, and the utter ruine of their Liberty.

CONCERNING the composition that is made herein, that some should convene in *Ecclesiastical Synods* by their own *personal Right*, and in virtue of their Office, and others by a kind of *Delegation* from some of their own Order, it being a meer political constitution, which I shall immediately speak unto, it is not here to be taken notice of.

THERE is nothing therefore in Scripture Example, or the Light of Natural Reason, with the principles of all Societies in Union or Communion, that will lead us any farther than this; that such *Synods* are to be composed, and consist of such Persons as are chosen and delegated by those Churches respectively who do act and exert their Communion in such Assemblies. So was it in the First Example of them, *Act.* 15. The Church of *Antioch* chose and sent Messengers of their own number, to advise with the *Apostles* and *Elders* of the Church at *Jerusalem*; at which Consultation the *Members of that Church* also were present. And this is the whole of the nature and use of *Ecclesiastical Synods*. It is on other accounts that they make up so great a part of the History of the Church. For the first Three Hundred years, they were nothing but *voluntary conventions* of the *Officers* or *Elders*, *Bishops* and *Presbyters*, with some others of neighbouring Churches, on the occasion of *Differences* or *Heresies* among them. In and from the Council of *Nice*, there were Assemblies of *Bishops* and others called together by the Authority of the *Roman Emperours*, to advise about *matters of Faith*. In after Ages those which were called in the Western parts of the World, in *Italy, Germany, France* and *England*,

were

were of a *mixt nature* advising about things *Civil and Political*, as well as *Sacred and Religious*, especially with respect unto mutual contests between *Popes* and *Princes*. In them the whole nature of *Ecclesiastical Synods*, was lost and buried, and all Religion almost destroyed.

THUS this laudable practice of Churches acting their mutual Communion by meeting in *Synods* or Assemblies by their Delegates or Messengers, to advise about things of their common concernment and joint Edification, as occasion should require, founded in the Light of Nature, and countenanced by Primitive, Apostolical Example, was turned by the designing Interests and Ambition of Men, unto the enstating of all Church-Power in such *Synods*, and the Usurpation of a Power given unto no Churches, nor all of them together, as might be made evident by instances innumerable.

AND whereas they have made such a noise in Christian Religion, and have filled so many *Volumes* with their *Acts* and doings, yet some of them, who under the *Pope*, would place all Religion in them, do grant and contend that they are a meer *Humane Invention*: So *Bellarmine* affirms *Pighius* to have done in his Book *de Cœlest. Hierarch. Lib.* 6. *Cap.* 1. But for his part he judgeth that it is *more probable* that they have a Divine Original by virtue of that Word; *Where Two or Three are gathered together in my Name, there I will be in the midst of them*, Matth. 18. *De Concil. Lib.* 1. *Cap.* 3. which will not bear the least part of the superstructure pretended to be built upon it.

OF these *Delegates* and Messengers of the Church, the Elders or Officers of them, or some of them at least, ought to be the principal. For there is a peculiar care of *publick Edification* incumbent on them, which they are to exercise on all just occasions: They are presumed justly to know best the state of their own Churches, and to be best able to judge of matters under consideration. And they do better represent the Churches from whom they are sent, than any private Brethren can do; and so receive that Respect and Reverence which is due to the Churches themselves. As also they are

most

Of the Communion of Churches.

most meet to report and recommend the *Synodal Determinations* unto their Churches; and a contrary practice would quickly introduce confusion.

BUT yet it is not necessary that *they alone* should be so sent or Delegated by the Churches; but many have others joined with them, and had so until *Prelatical Usurpation* overturned their Liberties. So there were others beside *Paul* and *Barnabas* sent from *Antioch* to *Jerusalem*; and the *Brethren* of that Church, whatever is impudently pretended to the contrary, concurred in the Decree and Determination there made.

5. THAT which is termed the *calling of these Synods*, is nothing but the *voluntary consent of the Churches concerned to meet together by their Delegates and Messengers, for the ends before declared*.

I NO way deny, but that a *Christian Magistrate* may convene by his Authority the Bishops, Pastors or Ministers, with such others as he shall think meet within his own Territories; yea, and receive into his Convention meet Men out of the Territories of others by their consent, to *advise among themselves*, and to *give him Advice* about such concernments of Religion, and of the Church under his Dominion, and Regulate himself accordingly. It hath been practised with good success, and may be with bad also. And I do deny that Churches have Power, without the consent and Authority of the *Magistrate*, to convene themselves in *Synods* to exercise any Exterior Jurisdiction that should affect the Persons of his Subjects, any otherwise than by the Law of the Land is allowed.

BUT whereas the *Synods* whereof we Treat, and which are all that belong unto the Church, can take no cognizance of any *Civil Affairs* wherein the Persons of Men are outwardly concerned; have no Jurisdiction in any kind, can make no determination, but only *Doctrinal Declarations* of Divine Truth, of the same nature with the Preaching of the Word; there is no more required unto their calling beyond their own consent, but only that they may meet in external

peace

peace by the permiſſion of the *Magiſtrate* ; which when they cannot obtain, they muſt deport themſelves as in caſe of other Duties required of them by the Law of Chriſt.

6. IN the laſt place I ſhall ſpeak briefly of the *Power and Authority of theſe Synods*, in what meaſures, extent and numbers ſoever they are aſſembled. For although this may be eaſily Collected from what hath been declared concerning their Original, Nature, Cauſes, Uſe and Ends ; yet it may be neceſſary to be more particularly enquired into, becauſe of the many differences that are about it.

THERE is a *three-fold Power* aſcribed unto *Synods*. The Firſt is *declarative*, conſiſting in an Authoritative Teaching and declaring the Mind of God in the Scripture. The Second is *conſtitutive*, appointing and ordaining things to be believed, or done and obſerved by and upon its own Authority : And Thirdly *executive* in Acts of Juriſdiction towards Perſons and Churches.

THE Perſons whom the Authority pleaded, may affect, are of Two ſorts. (1.) Such as have their *proper Repreſentatives* preſent in ſuch Synods, who are directly concerned in its *conciliary* determinations. (2.) Such as have *no ſuch Repreſentatives* in them, who can be no otherwiſe concerned but in the Doctrine materially conſidered, declared in them.

WHEREFORE the *ground* of any Churches receiving, complying with, or obeying the Determinations and Decrees of *Synods* muſt be ; either, (1.) The *evidence of Truth*, given unto thoſe Determinations by the Synod from the Scripture ; or, (2.) The *Authority of the Synod it ſelf* affecting the Minds and Conſciences of thoſe concerned.

IN the *Firſt* way, wherein the Aſſent and Obedience of Churches is reſolved ultimately into the *evidence of Truth* from the Scripture, upon the judgment which they make thereof, not only the diſcovery of Truth is to be owned, but there is an *Authoritative Propoſal* of it by virtue of the promiſed preſence of Chriſt in them, if duly ſought and regarded ; whence great Reſpect and Reverence is due unto them.

Of the Communion of Churches.

THE *Power* of a Synod for the *execution* of its Decrees, respects either, (1.) The *Things* or *Doctrines* declared; and is recommendatory of them on its Authority from the presence of Christ; or, (2.) *Persons*; to Censure, Excommunicate or punish those who receive them not.

THESE things being premised, the just *Power of Synods* may be positively and negatively declared in the two following Assertions.

1. THE *Authority of a Synod* declaring the mind of God from the Scripture in Doctrine, or giving Counsel as unto practice *Synodically* unto them whose proper Representatives are present in it, whose Decrees and Determinations are to be received and submitted unto on the *evidence of their Truth* and Necessity, as recommended by the *Authority of the Synod* from the promised Presence of Christ among them, is suitable unto the Mind of Christ, and the Example given by the Apostles, *Act.* 15.

HENCE it is evident, that in and after such *Synods*, it is in the power of Churches concerned, humbly to consider and weigh, (1.) The *evidences* of the Presence of Christ in them, from the manner, causes and ends of their Assembling, and from their Deportment therein. (2.) What *regard* in their Constitutions and Determinations there hath been unto the *Word of God*, and whether in all things it hath had its due preheminence. (3.) How all their Determinations have been *educed from its Truth*, and are confirmed by its Authority.

• WITHOUT a due exercise of judgment, with respect unto these things, none can be obliged by any *Synodical Determinations*; seeing without them, and on the want of them, many Assemblies of Bishops who have had the outward Appearance and Title of *Synods* or Councils, have been *Dens of Thieves*, Robbers, Idolaters, managing their Synodical Affairs with fury, wrath, horrible craft, according to their Interests, unto the Ruine of the Church; such were the *Second Ephesine*, the *Second* at *Nice*, and that at *Trent*, and others not a few.

HENCE nothing is more to be feared, especially in a state of the Church wherein it is declining in Faith, Worship and Holiness, than *Synods*, according to the usual way of their calling and convention, where these things are absent. For they have already been the principal means of leading on and justifying all the *Apostasy* which Churches have fallen into. For never was there yet Synod of that nature, which did not confirm all the Errors and Superstitions which had in common practice entred into the Church, and opened a Door to a progress in them; nor was ever the pretence of any of them for outward Reformation of any use or signification.

2. THE *Authority of a Synod* determining *Articles of Faith? constituting Orders and Decrees* for the conscientious observance of things of their own appointment, to be *submitted unto* and obeyed on the Reason of that Authority, under the penalty of *Excommunication*, and the trouble by Custom and Tyranny thereto annexed, or acted in a way of *Jurisdiction* over Churches or Persons, is a meer *Humane Invention*, for which nothing can be pleaded but prescription from the *Fourth Century* of the Church, when the progress of the fatal Apostasy became visible.

THE proof of both these Assertions depends on what was before declared of the nature and use of these *Synods*. For if they are such as we have evinced, *no other Power or Authority* can be ascribed unto them but that here allowed. Yet the whole may be farther illustrated by some brief considerations of the *Assembly* at *Jerusalem* in the nature of a *Synod*, Recorded, *Act.* 15.

1. THE *occasion* of it was a *difference* in the Church of *Antioch*, which they could not compose among themselves, because those who caused the Difference, pretended Authority from the *Apostles*, as is evident *v.* 1. and 14.

2. THE *means* of its *convention*, was the desire and voluntary reference of the matters in debate, made by the Church at *Antioch* where the difference was, unto that at *Jerusalem*, whence, as it was pretended, the cause of the difference arose unto the hazzard of their mutual Communion, to be consulted of with their own Messengers.

3. THE

Of the Communion of Churches.

3. THE *Persons constituting the Synod*, were the *Apostles, Elders* and *Brethren* of the *Church* at *Jerusalem*, and the *Messengers* of that *Antioch*, with whom *Paul* and *Barnabas* were joined in the same Delegation.

4. THE *matter* in difference was debated as unto the mind of God concerning it in the *Scripture*, and out of the *Scripture*: On *James*'s proposal the determination was made.

5. THERE was *nothing imposed a-new* on the practice of the Churches, only direction is given in one particular instance as unto Duty, necessary on many accounts unto the *Gentile Converts*, namely to abstain from *Fornication*, and from the *use of their Liberty* in such instances of its practice as whereon *scandal* would ensue, which was the *Duty* of all Christians even *before* this determination, and is so *still* in many other instances besides those mentioned in the Decree; only it was now declared unto them.

6. THE *Grounds whereon* the Synod proposed the Reception of and compliance with its Decrees were Four, (1.) That what they had determined was the *mind of the Holy Ghost*: *It pleased the Holy Ghost.* This mind they knew either by *Inspiration*, or immediate Revelation made unto themselves, or by *what was Written* or Recorded in the Scripture, which on all other occasions they alledged as what was the *Word*, and *spoken* by the Holy Ghost. And it is evident, that it was this *latter way*, namely, a *discovery of the mind of the Holy Ghost in the Scripture* that is intended. However, it is concluded that nothing be proposed or confirmed in *Synods*, but what is well known to be the *mind of the Holy Ghost* in the Scripture, either by immediate *Inspiration*, or by *Scripture Revelation*. (2.) The Authority of the Assembly as convened in the Name of Christ, and by virtue of his Presence, whereof we have spoken before: *It pleased the Holy Ghost and us.* (3.) That the things which they had determined were *necessary*, that is *antecedently* so unto that determination; namely, the *abstaining* from the use of their Liberty in things indifferent in case of scandal. (4.) From the *Duty*, with respect unto the Peace and mutual Communion

munion of the *Jewish* and *Gentile* Churches: *Doing thus*, say they, *ye shall do well*, which is all the *Sanction* of their Decree; manifesting that it was *Doctrinal*, not *Authoritative* in way of Jurisdiction.

7. THE *Doctrinal Abridgement of the Liberty of the Gentile Christians in case of scandal*, they call the *imposing of no other Burden*, in opposition unto what they rejected, namely, the *imposing a yoke of Ceremonies* upon them, v. 10. So as that the meaning of these Words is, That they would lay *no Burden on them at all*, but only advise them unto things *necessary* for the avoidance of scandal. For it is impious to imagine that the Apostles would *impose any yoke*, or lay any burden on the Disciples, but only the *yoke and burden of Christ*, as being contrary to their Commission, Matth. 28. 19, 20.

HENCE it will follow, That a *Synod convened in the Name of Christ, by the voluntary consent of several Churches concerned in mutual Communion, may declare and determine of the mind of the Holy Ghost in the Scripture, and Decree the observation of things true and necessary, because revealed and appointed in the Scripture, which are to be received, owned and observed, on the evidence of the mind of the Holy Ghost in them, and the Ministerial Authority of the Synod it self.*

FINIS.

ERRATA.

Page 16. line 31. for to read do. p. 23. l. 34. r. state. p. 27 l. 2. r. believers be. p. 31, l. 11. r. Mat. 20. p. 40. l. 23. r. if so, be. p. 41. l. 25. r. we enquire not. p. 47. l. ult. r. these. p. 53. l. 6. Ephes. 4. 7. p. 71. l. 33. r. Light. p. 72. l. 8. r. mere. p. 103 l. 33. r. Auricular. p. 112. l. 29. r. Conc. p. 117. l. 9. after publickly add Read. p. 119. l. 22. r. their mixed. p. 129. l. 5. for 18 r. 28. p. 132. l. 9. for 9. r. 3. p. 141. l. 30. read over you p. 147. l. 25. for 39. r. 38. p. 168. l. 20 for 24. r. 21. p. 186. l. 20. r. μετιπίεντοι. p 192. l. 14. r. will fully. p 205. l. 35 r. this. p. 228. l. 21 r. do. p. 244. l. 9. r. furnace. p 256. l. 15. r. probable.

www.ingramcontent.com/pod-product-compliance
Lightning Source LLC
Chambersburg PA
CBHW032104230426
43672CB00009B/1634